THE PROPHECIES OF MERLIN

"This fine work, with its perceptive analysis of the state of the Merlin tradition in the fourteenth and fifteenth centuries, provides an important addendum to the seer's influence throughout the Middle Ages and beyond. Among many other things, it illustrates just how influential a figure Merlin remained well into the Renaissance. Public fascination with his legend continues seemingly unabated today, and this handsomely produced edition will undoubtedly add to that fascination."

NIKOLAI TOLSTOY, HISTORIAN, BIOGRAPHER,
AND AUTHOR OF *THE QUEST FOR MERLIN*

"John Matthews and Maarten Haverkamp have accomplished a historic feat in translating and elucidating a little-known Old French version of the prophecies of Merlin, the magician of ancient Celtic lore and legend. A large part of the book consists of a wealth of valuable elucidatory and background material. In the prophecies themselves, skillfully presented by the two scholars, the spirit of Merlin comes alive and speaks to us loud and clear across the centuries."

CHRISTOPHER MCINTOSH, AUTHOR OF *THE CALL OF THE OLD GODS*, *OCCULT RUSSIA*, AND *OCCULT GERMANY*

"John Matthews's and Maarten Haverkamp's *The Prophecies of Merlin* is a gem for esotericists and historians alike. Not only is Haverkamp's translation splendidly accessible, but Matthews's commentary illuminates and provides extra substance—and some sparkle!—without the slightest stodginess or obscurity. This is a serious and highly recommended addition to the whole field of Arthurian studies."

LYNN PICKNETT AND CLIVE PRINCE, AUTHORS OF
WHEN GOD HAD A WIFE AND *THE TEMPLAR REVELATION*

"A valuable and fascinating addition to the Merlin corpus that, like the voice of Merlin himself, emerges from the mist when needed most. Here is mystery and poetry, prophecy and power, insight and inspiration, breathing new life into the ancient tales. A must-have for every Arthurian library."

ARI BERK, PH.D., PROFESSOR OF FOLKLORE AND MYTH AT CENTRAL MICHIGAN UNIVERSITY

"John Matthews and Maarten Haverkamp take us on an incredible 500-year journey from 1498 when *The Prophecies of Merlin* was first written in Old French, based on stories from a few hundred years earlier. For those of us who love the stories of King Arthur and Merlin, this awesome resource of 89 prophecies binds together these ancient and beloved stories while adding new stories from antiquity in a most fascinating manner. A most valuable resource."

NICHOLAS E. BRINK, PH.D., AUTHOR OF *THE POWER OF ECSTATIC TRANCE*, *ECSTATIC SOUL RETRIEVAL*, AND *BEOWULF'S ECSTATIC TRANCE MAGIC*

"A new Arthurian chronicle coming to light is rare and exciting. We are witnessing the emergence of something extraordinary. John Matthews's commentary gives us clear context and connects the original writing to the wider tradition, giving us both a helpful summary of the tradition and a way of locating the translation by Haverkamp within it. It is an essential text for those of us interested in the subject of Britain. Thoroughly recommended!"

IAN REES, AUTHOR OF *THE TREE OF LIFE AND DEATH* AND *THE WAY OF DEEP MAGICK*

"Merlin, in his various manifestations in literature and lore, has long been the voice of wisdom and vision, the open door between the struggling world of humanity and the Otherworld of spirit. In this rare and wondrous book, the authors have opened that door widely and given Merlin's voice a new clarity. This is a treasure!"

DAVID SPANGLER, FINDHORN FELLOW, AUTHOR OF *PARTNERING WITH SPIRIT* AND *DIARY OF AN AVATAR*

THE PROPHECIES OF MERLIN

THE FIRST ENGLISH TRANSLATION OF THE 15TH-CENTURY TEXT

JOHN MATTHEWS AND
MAARTEN HAVERKAMP

Inner Traditions
Rochester, Vermont

Inner Traditions
One Park Street
Rochester, Vermont 05767
www.InnerTraditions.com

Copyright © 2025 by John Matthews and Maarten Haverkamp
Translation of selections from poems attributed to Myrddin Wyllt © 2025 by
  John Matthews and Caitlín Matthews
Foreword © 2025 by R. J. Stewart

All rights reserved. No part of this book may be reproduced or utilized in any form or by any means, electronic or mechanical, including photocopying, recording, or any information storage and retrieval system, without permission in writing from the publisher. No part of this book may be used or reproduced to train artificial intelligence technologies or systems.

Cataloging-in-Publication Data for this title is available from the Library of Congress

ISBN 979-8-88850-219-8 (print)
ISBN 979-8-88850-220-4 (ebook)

Printed and bound in India at Replika Press Pvt. Ltd.

10 9 8 7 6 5 4 3 2 1

Text design by Priscilla Harris Baker and layout by Debbie Glogover
This book was typeset in Garamond Premier Pro with Friz Quadrata Std, Gill Sans MT Pro, and Montecatini Pro used as display typefaces

To send correspondence to the author of this book, mail a first-class letter to the author c/o Inner Traditions • Bear & Company, One Park Street, Rochester, VT 05767, and we will forward the communication, or contact John Matthews directly at **hallowquest.org.uk**.

Scan the QR code and save 25% at InnerTraditions.com. Browse over 2,000 titles on spirituality, the occult, ancient mysteries, new science, holistic health, and natural medicine.

. . . the dreamer Merlin and his prophecies . . .
　　　SHAKESPEARE, HENRY IV, PART 1

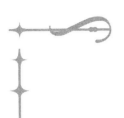

CONTENTS

Foreword by R. J. Stewart   ix

Preface   xi

PART ONE

THE HISTORY OF THE PROPHECIES AND THE MAKING OF THE TRANSLATION   1

The Origins of Merlin and the Prophecies   3

Written Records of the Prophecies   13

Timeline of Source Texts   28

Merlin's Scribes   29

Central Characters in the Prophecies   37

PART TWO

THE PROPHECIES OF MERLIN, 1498   53

PART THREE

COMMENTARY ON THE
PROPHECIES OF MERLIN, 1485   137

Appendix 1. Early Welsh Poems Containing
Prophecies Attributed to Myrddin Wyllt   235

Appendix 2. Selections from Book VII of Geoffrey
of Monmouth's *Historia Regum Britanniae*   250

Appendix 3. The Tale of Prester John   263

Appendix 4. The Letter of Prester John   266

Sources and Further Reading   275

Acknowledgments   279

Index   281

FOREWORD

R. J. Stewart

The popularity of Merlin as a fantasy figure within entertainment, be it cartoon, stage, film, or New Age product, inevitably clouds the deeper sources and the originative voice, which is a prophetic spiritual voice. A new book on Merlin themes, with genuine source material, is of considerable value to the tradition. John Matthews and Maarten Haverkamp have undertaken a huge and worthy task that will provide scholars, enthusiasts, and dreamers with material and inspiration for a long time to come.

Of considerable interest is the very lively connection between the Merlin text translated here and many themes in collected folklore throughout Britain and Europe, from oral tradition up to the early twentieth century. Indeed, the content is more European than early British, yet collected folklore and faery tales are surprisingly consistent from what was once called the Near East to the Far North. This certainly implies, as the authors propose, that the Merlin tradition, while arising from British Celtic mythical history, became something far greater that flourished out of the common ground of medieval consciousness, while still rooted in more ancient ancestral earth.

Some of the potent prophetic themes found herein, such as the Great

Dragon, are at the core of early traditions regarding Merlin, and have, of course, been subject to centuries of Christian influence. Yet they are also found in Jewish kabbalistic sources such as the *Bahir* or the *Book of Formation*, which have no Christian influence whatsoever and have no connection to themes of the Antichrist. The relationship of the Dragon, which features strongly in the Merlin text found here, to the *Theli*, found in a number of Jewish and Arabic early sources, has a well-defined cosmological model. This is explored in detail in *Hamlet's Mill: An Essay on Myth and the Frame of Time* (Giorgio Santillana and Hertha von Dechend, Gambit, 1969).

One further aspect of this book made a strong impression upon me. While strongly associated with widespread oral traditions, the loosely interlaced stories in this Merlin source were, of course, for literate people. Over time, the various themes, at first available in handwritten manuscripts to a relatively small readership, became very popular indeed, as the many printed editions and complex branches of iteration will attest. Merlin is immensely popular today, but John Matthews and Maarten Haverkamp make it clear to us, in the twenty-first century, that Merlin was vastly popular as soon as he could get into print—which is to say, as soon as printing arose in European culture. Long may he remain so!

R. J. STEWART is a Scottish author and musician. Among other books, he is the author of *Merlin: The Prophetic Vision and the Mystic Life* (first published by Arkana in 1995), a detailed exploration of the esoteric lore in twelfth-century Merlin texts written by Geoffrey of Monmouth.

PREFACE

Imagine the scene. Merlin, however you see him—as a grey-bearded but ageless man or as a youth with more knowledge in his eyes than he should have—sits in a room somewhere in Wales. He is speaking to a second man, a cleric or possibly a monk, who writes as fast as he can with a sharpened quill on parchment, by the light of a rush lamp or wavering candle, the words of the great prophet. Almost in what we now would call stream of consciousness, Merlin, perhaps with eyes closed, watches events unfold on the screen of his eyelids, describing things only he can see: the coming of the Great Dragon, the Antichrist; the crowning of Arthur, the greatest king of the Western world; the fall of kingdoms, the loss of crowns—all this and more. And in between these prophetic utterances, he tells fragments of stories from the vast panoply of Arthurian romance, some familiar—the quest for the Grail, the adventures of Lancelot and Percival—others never heard before—the dream of Guinevere and the bringing of letters to King Arthur from the mighty Prester John, whose fabled kingdom in the Far East became a beacon of hope for the beleaguered West in this long-ago time.

All this and more the scribe writes. Later, the scene darkens. Merlin falls in love with the Lady of the Lake and is imprisoned by her in a tomb beneath the earth. From there his voice continues to be heard, and a succession of other scribes and seekers hear and copy down his words. These are the prophecies of Merlin. Some so mysterious that even now we do not fully understand them. This is the voice of Merlin—hear him now!

◆

Discovering a hitherto lost or forgotten book about Merlin and King Arthur is a rare event these days. Yet here we present a virtually forgotten and, to date, untranslated book, which includes much that is new—and exciting—about the legendary king and his magical adviser.

Throughout the Middle Ages, a number of volumes were produced purporting to contain the prophecies of Merlin. Most of these were written retrospectively, after the events they predicted, and as actual prophecies are of little interest. However, within several of these volumes were hidden a series of clues that led to the heart of the Arthurian mysteries—secrets long hidden behind the obscure language of the prophetic utterances.

In 1498, Antoine Vérard—a French publisher, bookmaker, and bookseller—published *Romans de Merlin* in three folio volumes. The third volume, *Les Prophecies de Merlin*, was compiled and translated from Latin into Old French in the thirteenth century (c. 1279) by an unknown author, who wrote under the pseudonym Maistre Richart d'Irlande (Master Richard of Ireland). The book is a compilation of several older documents and purports to be actual prophecies given by Merlin, the great Arthurian magician. It is from this text, augmented by several other sources, that the anonymous scribe created the present volume in the fifteenth century, which we present here.

In 2017, Maarten Haverkamp, who is a collector of ancient texts, acquired an original copy of the fifteenth-century incunabulum, or early printed book, from a bookseller in present day Paris. Having gone in search of a book about Charlemagne, he was told this had already sold but was offered *Les Prophecies de Merlin*. He has never regretted that the book about Charlemagne had already been sold.

Heretofore, this book had received scant attention from scholars because the text was considered confused and unreadable and no one had attempted to translate the Old French into English. Maarten likes to translate the books in his collection and decided to undertake the challenge of translating the *Prophecies*. After he started, it became an addiction. He could not stop. He wanted to share the beauty of the story.

Despite its title, the book contains very much more than the prophecies—most of which, as noted, refer to events that had already occurred and, as with most such collections, were written with hindsight. The compiler took the opportunity to criticise corruption within the Catholic Church and various political events that took place during his lifetime. But in collecting the prophecies, he included a large body of Arthurian material, much of which adds to existing versions or is completely unfamiliar. Clearly, he must have had access to a large library, most likely that of the Franciscan monastery on the island of San Francesco del Deserto in the Venetian Lagoon, and was thus able to bring into his collection a number of currently unknown or unfamiliar works. For students and lovers of Arthurian literature, this is a uniquely important manuscript, which adds significantly to our knowledge of the myths and legends of Europe's most popular subject matter. Then, as now, stories of Arthur were in great demand, and the author was himself clearly interested in the subject matter, filling several holes in existing traditions.

In 2018 Maarten contacted Arthurian scholar John Matthews, coauthor of *The Lost Book of the Grail* with Caitlín Matthews and Gareth Knight, which uncovered another overlooked text known as the *Elucidation*. John's enthusiasm prompted Maarten to continue with the translation. Now, five years on, he has completed the first English translation of the book, which both authors have studied for context and significance. The result is this book—*The Prophecies of Merlin*—which contains most of the original text, translated by Maarten Haverkamp and edited by John Matthews, with commentary from both Maarten and John.

Essentially, this is the first modern look into a book that was published in the fifteenth century but which has lain mostly forgotten for over five hundred years. Now it sees the light of day and exists for the first time in English. In this book, we have unravelled these lost stories and laid them out for all to see and understand. Here you will find the story of Merlin's birth, his first adventures, his love affair with the Lady of the Lake, and much more. All those interested in the Arthurian legends, Merlin, and magic will be excited, as we were, by this unique volume, which adds to our understanding of Arthurian literature almost at the end of its initial period of development.

JOHN MATTHEWS, OXFORD, ENGLAND
MAARTEN HAVERKAMP, RIJSWIJK, NETHERLANDS

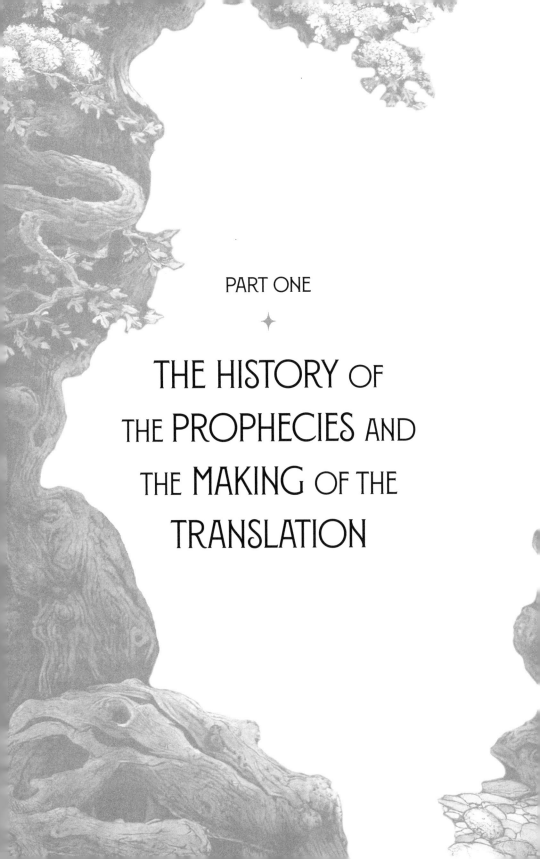

PART ONE

✦

THE HISTORY OF THE PROPHECIES AND THE MAKING OF THE TRANSLATION

The book you are about to read contains most of the surviving text of a fifteenth-century incunabulum, produced in Paris in 1498, by the publisher Antoine Vérard, possibly copying from an even older text written in circa 1270–1278, which now exists only in fragments. It has been largely ignored by interpreters of the Arthurian myths due to the often confused nature of the text.

Much of the material is indeed, at first glance, wildly confused, but repeated reading and checking of details has resulted in a surprisingly rational text, which both the authors felt was more than worthy of sharing.

Here you will read detailed accounts of the famous liaison between Merlin and the Lady of the Lake as well as an early glance at the Grail quest; a deep review of the imminent coming, at the time the manuscript was written, of the Antichrist; several interesting and mysterious adventures, hitherto unknown; a list of the various scribes responsible for writing down Merlin's prophetic utterances— and much more. We will also demonstrate an extraordinary connection between King Arthur and Prester John, the semi-mythical ruler of a forgotten kingdom in the Far East and possibly the last recorded guardian of the Grail after the ending of Arthur's reign.

Much of this was difficult to uncover and required a considerable amount of research, based upon an already detailed understanding of the Arthurian mythos. We will explain how we arrived at the text you are about to read more fully below. For the moment, we need to look more closely at the figure of Merlin himself and how his prophecies survived for so long and were so often copied and recopied, and at the way in which these writings attracted so much additional material, which was only tangentially connected with the prophecies themselves.

THE ORIGINS OF MERLIN AND THE PROPHECIES

Really, there are several Merlins. To begin with, we have Welsh and Irish analogues, who bear all the characteristics of the seer, and then we have versions in the romances of the Middle Ages that range from the heroic to the demonic—depending on which version you follow. However, one aspect is largely unvarying: the seership and wisdom that permeates the stories that feature Merlin either as central or subsidiary figure.

The Welsh analogue is Taliesin the bard, reborn from the womb of the Goddess Cerridwen, cast adrift on the sea—much like Meliadus, who appears in our text and who, as an infant, was cast adrift on a boat. Taliesin speaks his first poem to the man who finds him while still an infant. The birth of Aí (the name means "poetry"), a less well known Irish divinity, is announced by a gust of wind, which brings with it a prophecy that the baby will come to equal his uncle Fiachu, a king of the magical race of the Tuatha Dé Danann. Fiachu at once demands the child to be killed, but Aí speaks a poem from his cradle, demanding his recognition as a bard, who under Irish law was a sacred personage.

Neither Taliesin nor Aí are Merlin exactly, though in the twelfth-century *Vita Merlini* (Life of Merlin) Taliesin visits him in the forest to which he has escaped in his madness, and the two have a discussion of the cosmos every bit as erudite as anything in the *Prophecies*.

Both are bards, both are prophets, and both spoke wisdom as infants.

The earliest written references to Merlin come from the bardic literature of the Celts and from the life of the seventh-century Celtic saint Kentigern. Both refer to the figure of a wild man living alone in the woods, driven mad by his witnessing a battle in which his friends and kinfolk were slain. In the *Vita Sancti Kentigerni* (Life of Saint Kentigern), a hagiography of Kentigern written by Joceyln of Furness (c. 1200), we hear of the madman Lailoken who is brought back to sanity through the actions of the saint. In a handful of poems attributed to Merlin himself (here called Myrddin Wyllt; for a translation of these poems see appendix 1), there appears a fragmentary story in which the seer appears to be living alone in the woods, half mad and half inspired, occasionally attended by his half-sister Gwenddydd.

Because none of this material was written down before the Middle Ages, it is difficult to say with any certainly how old the stories are. It was the pseudo-historian Geoffrey of Monmouth (c. 1095–1155) who, circa 1134, made the Latinised name Merlinus into a household name by compiling his version of the *Prophecies*. When, in 1138, Geoffrey published his *Historia Regum Britanniae* (History of the Kings of Britain), he included the prophecies again and added a version of the story of the wondrous child Merlin, probably taken from the earlier writings of a ninth-century monk named Nennius. Geoffrey's work rapidly became one of the most famous and popular books of its time, something, indeed, of a medieval "bestseller," and the name and character of Merlin were forever after inseparably connected with those of Arthur, whose deeds Geoffrey also chronicled.

The earlier figure of Myrddin Wyllt (Merlin the Wild) was soon further immortalised by Geoffrey in his *Vita Merlini* in which the story of the king driven mad by the sight of the death of his friends and family is repeated and elaborated. His sources for this story were almost certainly founded on earlier Welsh legends and traditions relating to the figure of the Wild Man of the Woods or, as he is termed in Irish tradition, the Gelt. A description of this character, from the thirteenth-century Norse *Speculum regale* (The King's Mirror) describes him thus:

It happens that when two hosts meet and are arrayed in battle-array, and when the battle-cry is raised on both sides, that . . . men run wild and lose their wits. . . . And then they run into a wood away from other men and live there like wild beasts, and shun the meeting of men like wild beasts. And it is said of these men that when they have lived in the woods in that condition for twenty years then feathers grow on their bodies as on birds, whereby their bodies are protected against frost and cold.[1]

In fact, Merlin and Taliesin have much in common. Both are the product of mysterious births, both possess prophetic abilities, and both are connected to the Arthurian court, Merlin as Arthur's adviser, Taliesin as court poet. Their prophecies also have many points of similarity. They appear to be largely made up of compilations based on much earlier, genuine prophetic material, mostly anonymous, to which later generations have added stanzas in the style of the original bards. Myrddin's prophecies are contained chiefly in dialogues either between himself and Taliesin, or himself and his sister, Gwenddydd, who was herself recognised as a prophet. These prophecies are, for the most part, of a general kind, referring to battles, political events, other known events, and people. They are identifiable as separate from the underlying matter of the poems, which deal with the story of Myrddin's madness and of the period he spent in the wilderness attended by a pig (a creature sacred to the Celts) and remembering the terrible battle in which he lost his reason. He thinks also of his sister, Gwenddydd, who has deserted him because he (apparently) killed her son, and of his enemies, who seek his destruction. Interspersed with this are prophecies of events that took place long after—probably in the eighth or ninth centuries, when heroes like Cynan and Cadwallader had replaced Arthur as the expected deliverer of the Cymry.

That some of the material relating to Myrddin has been suppressed is beyond question, so we have little or no chance of establishing

---

1. Trans. by Laurence Marcellus Larson.

a full text of the remaining Myrddin poems. At one time these may have formed verse interludes of a longer prose account of Myrddin's life—such as that one that evidently formed the basis of Geoffrey of Monmouth's Latin *Vita Merlini*, which tells the story in full and makes use of the poems attributed to Myrddin Wylt (see appendix 1) as well as others that belonged to the ancient saga of Myrddin.

THE LOSS OF MERLIN

According to the thirteenth-century French Arthurian text *Suite du Merlin*, the last person to hear the voice of the great seer was Sir Gawain, who carried home to Arthur the last words of the mage: "Never shall no man speak with me after you, therefore it is for nothing that any man should try to seek me out."[2]

But this last call, the *Cri de Merlin* as it is called in some texts, still echoes in our ears, just as the figure of Merlin himself continues to exert a profound fascination on the Western world. The dozens of books, plays, and films that have appeared in recent years about Merlin have kept attention focussed on this remarkable being, who combines the roles of sage, seer, prophet, and shaman and whose story is one of the great native epics of Britain.

That Merlin is a British or at least Celtic figure is important. While the Arthurian legends of which he is such an important part betray the extensive influence of French and Germanic storytellers, the story of Merlin, in its purest form, draws almost entirely upon native British traditions and beliefs.

Merlin also represents a very ancient strand of wildness within human nature. He grows out of the tradition of the wild man who was seen, by medieval writers, as akin to "natural man," a being somehow poised between the states of wildness and civilisation, belonging perhaps to a lost golden age. This is especially poignant when we consider that, in the mythology, Merlin himself strove to re-create that golden

---

[2]. Gaston and Ulrich, *Suite du Merlin*.

time, a perfect earthly kingdom over which Arthur, his protégé, would rule, guided by the mage's wisdom, protected by his magic, steered through the shoals of life on his way to winning the greatest of goals—the Holy Grail.

But these things were not to be, given the nature of humanity. The kingdom fell because the vessels—including Arthur himself—were too weak to contain the glories of the Grail. The great vision of the Round Table, built by Merlin himself—"Round, in the likeness of the world"—where all men would meet as equals, fell away, broken by the internecine quarrels of the knights, the illicit love of Lancelot and Guinevere (strength and beauty personified), wracked by the bitterness of Arthur's son Mordred, begotten upon the king's own half sister. Small wonder if Merlin chose to flee from this failure of his dream—chose to withdraw into his *esplumoir* (moulting cage), or else into an observatory built for him by his sister, there to live out his days studying the patterns of the heavens: a far more productive study than that of human frailty. Alternately still, as in the present text, he is murdered by the Lady of the Lake and installed in a tomb in a state of living death from which his spirit could speak.

It is this atmosphere of potential glory, crossed by impending doom, that provides the Arthurian cycle with its peculiar power to enthral us to this day. We know the torments and sufferings of these people as well as we know ourselves. Merlin, a principal mover in all of this, is bound to capture our attention, concentrating as he does so many of the themes of the great story of King Arthur in his person. In our own time, archetypes of Merlin have continued to reemerge in a variety of disguises. He can be recognised in the character of Obi-Wan Kenobi in George Lucas's *Star Wars* films, in the figure of Dr. Who in the popular British TV series, and in the powerful character of Gandalf from J. R. R. Tolkien's *The Lord of the Rings*.

The most interesting thing about all these appearances—as in the character of Merlin summoned up in so many modern versions of the story—is the underlying consistency of the characterisation. Despite all the years that have elapsed since Merlin first walked the stage of literature and tradition, his personality has changed very little. He is still, to this day, a wise and generally beneficent being, whose actions and purpose, while seldom wholly revealed, suggest an ongoing influence in the affairs of humanity. An element of the trickster also exists, and Merlin can be at times as cunning as he is wise.

Nowhere is this more obvious than in his collected prophecies, though these were not initially written down until the twelfth century. Collected from earlier sources by Geoffrey of Monmouth, they can be seen to date from a much earlier period and to be part of the great tradition of prophetic literature, which begins in the Roman Empire with the Sibylline Oracles and continues into the time of the great eighteenth-century poet and prophet William Blake.

It is interesting that Merlin is almost always presented with two aspects: the nonhuman, supernatural being and the somehow very human man who longs for love and human experience, even as he uses his otherworldly skills to advise and shape King Arthur and his father, Uther Pendragon (spelled Uterpendragon in the manuscript translation). In the text edited here, we find one of the clearest accounts of this dual nature. It follows the idea, first proposed in Latin and then the French romances, that presented Merlin as the son of a demon—an inevitable characterisation in a medieval Christian world—while at the same time giving him the needs and ideas of a human male. This Merlin is, on the one hand, able to prophesy events, not only from the time of Arthur but also of later times, while at the same time falling for the wiles of the Lady of the Lake, whose teacher he becomes, ending up caught between the two worlds as a spirit that may, or may not, be subject to death. In this form he gives forth a series of prophecies concerning events happening from the thirteenth to fifteenth centuries, overheard by passing seekers or those employed to relay his words. The Cri de Merlin thus gave the present manuscript's author an opportunity to criticise the establishment, in the form of the church and the rulers of the time, while at the same time offering a unique perspective on the Arthurian epic.

Less well known than the central Arthurian theme of Merlin as the son of a demon, the circa fourteenth-century Middle English romance

Sir Gowther[3] deals with a second child begotten by the same demon (or more simply the devil) with a noble lady. Gowther, the offspring, described as Merlin's half brother, grows to manhood and leaves a trail of violence and terror, including the burning of a monastery and the rape of its nuns. Finally, the truth of his fatherhood emerges, and Gowther heads to Rome to ask forgiveness. This is granted by the Pope, but with the prohibition that he will not speak to anyone and only eat food intended for dogs. With this penance, Gowther then undergoes a series of adventures, ending when he saves an unnamed emperor from a Saracen invasion and marries the emperor's daughter, finally inheriting the throne. The romance falls into the category of penitential literature and was a powerful propaganda vehicle for the church. It demonstrated the idea that demons were able to beget children, who are more generally inclined to evil than good—Merlin clearly being an exception.

THE PROPHECIES AS STORY DEVICES

The history of Merlin's prophecies has always been intimately tied to his own story and character. Sage, visionary, enchanter, magician—these are the words used to describe him. Yet it is significant that in the stories told of him throughout the Middle Ages, he is seldom given any title but that of his name. Merlin is thus synonymous both with his own story and the role he plays in events—while the dream of the Round Table and ultimately of Camelot itself is specific to him rather than to Arthur himself. Merlin is thus the true architect of the Arthurian epic.

In the *Prophecies*, we find this spelled out for us. The order of Merlin's visions—not infrequently muddled—serves as a key to the underlying narrative of the book. Merlin is thus shown to be a master storyteller who offers us the keys to his true place within the Arthurian epic—and beyond this in the medieval world, where he was seen as a real (if ancient) figure whose wisdom was undeniable, even though his origins were as mysterious as any other character in the stories themselves.

---

3. In Mills, *Six Middle English Romances.*

There are, essentially, three types of prophecy within the various collections attributed to Merlin—both in our book and the many others, dating from the twelfth to sixteenth centuries, which preceded and followed the 1498 edition. These are:

1. Political
2. Religious
3. Arthurian

The first two are closely linked and very typical of all prophetic literature, where the pre-Christian, biblical, or fabulous are treated with equal seriousness. Their purpose is to offer a means of criticising and attacking established foundations such as the church, political organisations, and the ruling classes. Attributing the prophecies to Merlin, a source that by its nature was difficult to impugn, gave the authors a freedom they would not have under ordinary circumstances. The prophecies contained in this book include references to the teachings of the polemicist Joachim of Fiore, to the followers of James the brother of Jesus, and to the prophecies attributed to the biblical Jonah, all of which were, at one time or another, pronounced at worst heretical and at best suspicious by the Roman Church. Merlin's voice is thus heard though a series of filters. His persona can be seen as a kind of puppet, delivering the polemic of others.

We should be in no way surprised at the connection between magical and occult beliefs and ideas and politics. As Francis Young has outlined in his groundbreaking book *Magic in Merlin's Realm*, this link has existed for a considerable time. Nor are we talking of more ancient civilizations such as Greek, Roman, and Hebrew, each of which incorporated magical beliefs into both daily life and politics. Looking back to the early medieval period—when the *Prophecies of Merlin* were first produced—we can see that in the years that followed up to the end of the seventeenth century, many of the same precepts were followed. Merlin's name, whether believed in or not, counted for something and was literally used by politicians throughout this whole period. The prophecies we find here were based on the idea that Merlin knew of the patterns of history and prophesied of them. The resulting texts began in the twelfth century and continued until the sixteenth and were regarded as serious knowledge. Here, in the 1498 edition, traces of this can still be seen in the many references to contemporary political events and figures. But it is to the stories included by the scribes who continued to compile new editions that we owe so much in the context of our theory and law and literature.

In fact, the tradition of what we may call political prophecy existed over many generations during the Middle Ages. These prophetic utterances were usually ascribed to figures such as Merlin or Thomas the Rhymer and were often written in deliberately obscure language, thus giving the writer the freedom to say whatever they wished about an important person or organisation, very often of royal birth or hallowed establishment.

The language often included references to animals of various kinds, including the mythological. Geoffrey of Monmouth's huge collection of prophecies, attributed to Merlin and dating from the eleventh century, were quite clearly made to be both acceptable to his Norman audience and to augment the adventures of Arthur.

Geoffrey used the prophecy about the battle between the red and white dragons, in which the red dragon represented the British and the white represented the Saxons, to fit his own agenda—or at least that of his masters. In its original form the British dragon was triumphant, but Geoffrey implied that the British had requested help from the Norman invaders as a fulfilment of the prophecy. The earliest version of this story survived in Wales and along the borders, where it was frequently borrowed by would-be leaders and used to suggest their own triumph. The most obvious and well known of these is that of the Owain Glyndwr, who sought to overcome the Norman occupation of Wales territory—and who vanished under mysterious circumstances in a manner similar to that of Arthur's passage to Avalon.

In this way stories of Arthur and Merlin were interpreted and reinterpreted by various writers during the medieval and even

Renaissance periods to support their own theories, ideas, or beliefs. The *Prophecies of Merlin* can thus be seen to remain a very important underlay for so much of the history of Britain from the twelfth to the sixteenth century.

The third category—with which we are principally concerned in this book—consists of references to stories from the Arthurian tradition: many from existing works but some apparently devised for the first time. The figure of Merlin himself, therefore, becomes a character whose prophecies frequently open the way for the authors or compilers to retell or create their own additions to existing literature.

Thus, in our collection, we have for example the link provided by Meliadus, as the brother of the famed knight Sir Tristan, which becomes the jumping-off point for a lengthy retelling of episodes borrowed from the literature concerning this hero. And, of course, there is Merlin's own, often-told story of his passion for the Lady of the Lake (or one of her handmaids), which resulted in his death or interment. The punishment meted out by she whom he loved enabled him to prophesy into the future and also made him a safe source for Christian compilers seeking to record the visions of a Pagan seer. In this way, the scribes responsible for compiling Merlin's prophetic visions could demonstrate the doom that came upon unbelievers and sinners, while at the same time enabling Merlin to offer several kinds of wisdom, which could be seen to benefit all. Merlin's antiquity authorises religious propaganda while still delivering extensions to the Arthurian canon.

The *Prophecies* thus become a storytelling device. Merlin prophesies an event or episode, which is then described in a varying degree of detail—ranging from two or three lines to two or three pages. Merlin opens the door to the Arthurian story in all its detail, prophesying not only the later events of Arthur's life, up to his final battle and departure for Avalon, but also the Quest for the Grail and much more.

WRITTEN RECORDS OF THE PROPHECIES

To understand and appreciate the nature and content of the collection of the *Prophecies* presented here, it is necessary to understand how the book came to be written. Collections of prophecies attributed to Merlin began as long ago as the sixth century, where poems relating the sage's prophetic visions were composed by Celtic bards in Wales. (A selection of these can be found in appendix 1.) Later, Geoffrey of Monmouth compiled a large collection of prophecies, which initiated so much interest that he later included them, in a revised form, in his widely disseminated bestseller *Historia Regum Britanniae* (History of the Kings of Britain), which as well as dealing with early and semi-mythical kings, such as Brutus, Lear, and Cymbeline, also introduced the figure of King Arthur, who was already famous in the folklore and traditions of Britain but, thanks to Geoffrey, became a phenomenon. Since Geoffrey's time, the fascination with all things Arthurian has not really ceased, despite something of a lapse during the seventeenth and eighteenth centuries, until the present.

Among other things, Geoffrey was responding to political pressures, which by his time had seen a consolidation of British and Norman traditions following the invasion led by William of Normandy in 1066. In response to this, Geoffrey made Arthur into a Norman warlord and even took him to the walls of Rome as a conqueror, thus reframing the traditional stories for all time.

Building upon this, Geoffrey next composed *Vita Merlini* (Life of Merlin), drawing on older Welsh myths and painting a very different character than the one who has since become familiar to us from the Arthurian canon, which began to develop in the twelfth and thirteenth centuries and continued to supply a vast outpouring of literature from Europe until the fifteenth century. After this it lost some of its glamour, which was only recovered in a general way in the nineteenth century through the writings of Alfred Tennyson and Algernon Charles Swinburne and the paintings of the Pre-Raphaelite Brotherhood.

In the early fourteenth century, when the 1303 Rennes manuscript was written—and became the foundation of the later 1498 book published by Vérard, presented here—the passion for all things Arthurian, among them the prophetic utterances of Merlin, was at its height. We do not know with any certainty the identity of the man who compiled the first extraordinary collection—upon which all that followed it was, to varying degrees, based. It is possible that he could be someone called Robin Boutemont, who left his name in one of the copies of the original Rennes manuscript. It seems most likely that he was not himself a member of a religious order but rather a professional copyist of books and texts, probably for a rich patron.

Other, internal evidence suggests that the compiler of the 1485 manuscript might be a monk who had access to a library such as that once held by the Franciscan monastery on San Francesco del Deserto, one of the many islands that makes up the archipelago of Venice. We do not know for certain why he felt impelled to collect the many fragments of Arthurian lore and vision. The existence of the library, which may well have included some of the dozens of romances then emerging from France and German, is further attested to by another great collection, the *Codex Marciana*, currently held in the Marciana Library (St. Mark's Library) in Venice. This was founded in 1468, a mere thirty years before the printing of the *Prophecies of Merlin* translated here. One or other of these collections of early medieval manuscripts almost certainly provided everything required to compile the stories included within the *Prophecies*. Our text certainly emphasises a powerful connection with Venice and its people, who are referred to as "the Good Mariners" or "Faithful Mariners" throughout.

The eventual publisher of the text, Antoine Vérard (active 1485–1512), was a late-fifteenth to early sixteenth-century bookmaker and bookseller working in Paris at the turning point between the eras of illuminated manuscripts and modern printed editions. He combined these two types of books by printing works illustrated with cheaper woodcuts, of which he then produced versions on vellum with handmade illuminations for wealthy clients. Vérard used the older, handwritten texts to create his own incunabula or early printed books, specializing in Books of Hours, stories from the Arthurian canon, including tales of Lancelot, Tristan and Isolde, and the life of Merlin, as well as French folktales. The volume used as the basis for our book is a real incunabulum from the fifteenth century. The colophon to the whole book gives us a wonderfully precise description of the site of Vérard's shop: "For Antoine Vérard on the bridge [sur le pont] at Notre Dame at the statue of St. John the Evangelist / Or at the first pillar of the palace opposite the chapel where the holy mass is sung for the monsignors of the parliament." In fact, the wooden bridge was washed away by a flood in 1499, which makes our text extremely rare. When it was reprinted in 1503, the colophon read "opposite the bridge" rather than "on the bridge."

THE MANUSCRIPT AND ITS CHALLENGES

The volume from which we have worked presents several challenges for modern readers, the most notable being the often confusing and seemingly deliberate misalignment of the text, which is at times disjointed or organised in a way that seems to have been entirely deliberate.

Writing in the latter part of the thirteenth century, the original scribe would have been aware of the sometimes heretical ideas presented in the stories of Merlin, which would have made his work likely to incur the disapproval of his brethren and masters. This is at least one possible explanation for the extreme complexity of the manuscript, and of the volume published by Vérard, which seems determined to misdirect its readers. It appears that whoever the scribe was, he copied materials from other manuscripts, some of which may have later vanished from the world, but it is also possible that he deliberately mixed up the stories he was telling to disguise their sometimes heretical or, at the very least, challenging content.

The comments of the few scholars who have examined either the original manuscript or the printed book have almost all focussed on its disjointed and confusing nature. This, as we noted above, has made most Arthurian scholars back away from what seemed to them a worthless manuscript. However, our own research has revealed a veritable gold mine of Arthurian material, some of which is only to be found within the pages of this book.

In fact, the various versions of the *Prophecies*, from the earliest manuscripts of the thirteenth century to the present collection in the 1498 incunabulum, are amongst a very few texts to combine prophetic statements with aspects of the Arthurian legends. In the instance of this edition, it seems evident that the compiler of the collection was equally in love with the romances of Arthur as he was with Merlin and the prophecies. The result makes for a very tangled web, through which we have combed with great care to separate these two strands or, where necessary, to explicate the direct connections between the two.

Lucy Allen Paton, the editor of the medieval French edition of the *Prophecies* (the Rennes manuscript), makes it clear that trying to interpret everything in the original is not only a very long drawn-out activity but also, by inference, not necessary to recognise the original power and vision of the work. The version presented here is the work of two scholars who, independent of each other and of academic circles, were brought together by a love of Arthur.

To overcome the issues that might arise for a modern audience, we have elected to create a reading version of the text, in which we have moved certain blocks of text to where they seem to make more sense and have omitted some lines or passages, the inclusion of which seem intended to confuse the reader unfamiliar with the Arthurian romances of the time or to conceal details bordering on the heretical. In addition, we have smoothed out the inconsistent tense shifts within the text, which, to a modern reader, would be difficult to follow. In each case, these changes are noted in the footnotes or the commentary.

What you will find within these pages, then, is a version of the text that we have striven to make accessible to a modern reader. It is thus not always a literal, word-for-word translation but rather a reinterpretation of the original in modern language. The anonymous scribe of the text had the unfortunate habit of starting a story, interrupting it with several other incidents, and forgetting to return to the original—a method known as *entrelacement* (interlacing) found in many medieval works. Where possible we have noted this in the commentary and supplied the missing details where these can be traced.

In addition, where the sequence of events has been deliberately misplaced, we have restored it to the narrative sequence. For example, the section numbered 5 in the subheadings clearly belongs where the remainder of references to the Crusades are gathered. We therefore moved it to section 70. We also chose to omit certain of the prophecies, which were either entirely religious or politically motivated and which have little or no relevance to a modern audience.

The numbered subheadings or rubrics are from the original text and break up the material into smaller pieces. In this edition they are important, as they are matched with the same headings in the commentary, enabling readers to easily cross-check with our interpretation. Lacunae or amplifications to the text are shown within squared backets, thus [. . .].

Our work on both the text and its associated materials has been rigorous. We visited all the best sources and consulted with those more familiar with certain areas. However, it should not be seen as definitive. This leaves the door open to alternative interpretations amongst those wishing to follow in our footsteps, but our work stands as a reasoned unravelling of the often complex material.

THE SOURCES OF *THE PROPHECIES OF MERLIN*

The earliest known surviving text on which the Vérart edition is based is the Rennes manuscript (MS. 593, kept in Bibliothèque Municipale of Rennes, France), dated from around 1303 and written in Old French. Only one scholar, Lucy Allen Paton (1865–1951), took the trouble to edit the original text, translate parts of it into English, and provide commentary on it, which was published in 1926 in two volumes under the title *Les Prophecies de Merlin*. Paton acknowledged the existence of the 1498 edition, which seems to have been the last in this particular line of Merlinesque texts, describing it as "wildly confused." This seems to have deterred every Arthurian scholar since from examining the various versions, which has resulted in the virtual loss of a remarkable text.

An earlier, and now-lost, version may have existed before 1303, but we can only guess as to its content and style. The variations contained in all the versions that followed are explained as caused by the intentions of each successive scribe to reduce the level of the romance episodes or to use these to explicate the prophecies themselves. Most of the prophecies, in virtually every manuscript, are either vague or, in some instances, nonsensical.

Considering the manuscripts consulted by Paton in her invaluable edition of 1926, we found them to be full of insertions or omissions, which either interrupt the flow of the text, such as it is, or add to it in such a way that it makes the preceding and following parts hard to understand. While we have for the most part kept to the 1498 edition, we have added a few essential sections from other manuscripts—clearly indicated in the text—where these help to restore the original meaning. We are aware that this makes the text included here something of a reconstruction, but we have included these sections to show that Vérart did what he could with the material available to him, while we have sought to make it more understandable for a modern audience.

In this context, it is important to understand the method of transcription that was followed throughout most of the medieval period.

Handwritten manuscripts were selected, usually by their owners, to be copied out by several scribes (often professional copyists or monks). They, in their determination to stamp each work with their own presence, could omit, change, or reinterpret any part of the manuscript they were working on. In the case of the Merlin prophecies, this meant that almost none of the surviving versions are more than superficially alike, with a wide variety of errors, duplications, or misreadings occurring. The Vérard text is not lacking in these but has less than some of the more fragmentary versions.

Some manuscripts show that more than one scribe was involved in copying, and it is evident from that that they often lost touch with what they were doing, and then seemed to have tried with little success to add details of their own to fill in where there were gaps in the narrative. The result is, more often than not, confusion, and we have sought to replace missing sections and rearrange others where these appear to have been split up or simply forgotten.

The prophecies themselves are in fact so complicated or corrupted after numerous rewritings and by the amendments of several generations of scribes that they are virtually meaningless. However, we were delighted to discover that the Vérard version contains more of the original structure and content than any of the previous volumes.

We have also silently corrected the many variant spellings of personal names, such as the variety of spellings of, for example, Tristan and Percival, as well as numerous versions of the scribes named throughout the text; these variants simply add confusion to an already confused text. We have, therefore, sought for the most generally recognised version of names from the world of medieval and especially Arthurian literature. For the scribes' names, we have chosen, for example, Raymon over Ramon or Raymond, Meliadus over Meliodas, and Helias over Helyas.

COMPANION SOURCES

In addition to the commentary on the hidden meanings of the work, we have set forth as much as we can concerning the sources to which the original compiler had access and that he appears to have utilised. One of the most interesting of these is a curious collection of fragmentary tales, originally compiled within the same few years as the *Prophecies*. This is known as the *Cento Novelle Antiche* (The 100 Ancient Tales) or just *Il Novellino*. Compiled by an unknown author between 1280 and 1300, this is one of the earliest collections written in the Italian language for a new audience, who were moving away from Latin texts and beginning to explore the possibility of compositions in their own tongue. The results of this extraordinary outpouring of works, in a variety of Italian dialects, between the twelfth and fourteenth centuries, includes the bawdy tales compiled by Giovanni Boccaccio (1313–1375) in his *Decameron* of 1353—published in Venice in 1492, just a few years before our manuscript was printed by Vérard—and of course Dante's *Divine Comedy*, which appeared between 1308 and 1321.

Il Novellino, which predated both of these, was a very different creation. Few of the stories are longer than two or three pages and often read like summaries of much longer works—a fact that has caused some experts to suggest that it was intended as an index of tales from which professional Italian storytellers (*giullare*) could work. In fact, they were probably gathered by their author as a series of favourite glimpses into the literature of older times, as well as some of the great romances then being composed in France, Germany, and Spain. Although the style is much plainer—and a good deal more direct than the tales included in our book—there is at least one story that immediately leapt out at us as a possible source, or at least a single point of origin, for both texts. This not only explained some of the most mysterious passages in the *Prophecies* but also added to a theme we had begun to notice in the text we were working with.

This theme, which we will explore in greater depth in the commentary, concerns the links between the figure of a largely mythical character named Prester John (the name Prester is generally accepted to mean "priest-king"), believed to rule over a vast Christian kingdom in the East, and the Arthurian legends. This is a theme that has largely remained unnoticed until recent times, but it remains fascinating for the way in which it links these two powerful mythical characters.

In the *Prophecies*, we found several references to a great King of India, who, though not named here, very clearly refers to Prester John, who is described in this way in other texts. One of these, the German romance *Der Jüngere Titurel* (The Younger Titurel), attributed to Albrecht von Scharfenberg (c. 1275), recounts the connection between Prester John and the Grail story, in which the great king and priest becomes the guardian of the sacred vessel after Arthur's time. In the *Prophecies*, he is discovered by the wise cleric Raymon who, on his flight atop a magical stone, passes over the kingdom of India and steals Prester John's cloak.

Il Novellino adds a possible source—or at least an explanation of parts of the *Prophecies*—when it tells how Prester John sent a collection of magical stones to Frederick II (1194–1250), who was king of Sicily from 1198, king of Germany from 1212, king of Italy and Holy Roman Emperor from 1220, and king of Jerusalem from 1225. He was known to have an interest in both magic and alchemy, and this story accounts for the magical stones that Merlin has in his cave/tomb. The connection between the stones, Prester John, Merlin, and Emperor Frederick is close enough to make this a reasonable conclusion. The fact that *Il Novellino* and the *Prophecies of Merlin* were composed at more or less the same time and that copies of both manuscripts were found in Venice also suggests a link between the two. *Il Novellino* also contains several other Arthurian tales, mostly drawn from French sources. A full translation of the story concerning Frederick and Prester John can be found in appendix 2 of this book, together with excerpts from the letter purportedly written by the priest-king himself and addressed to the crowned heads of Europe (appendix 3).

THE GREAT DRAGON

An element of the *Prophecies* concerns specific beliefs at the time when the books of Merlin's lore were first collected in written form. Throughout much of the twelfth and thirteenth centuries, the followers of Christianity believed in the imminent appearance of the Antichrist, who would test the beliefs of all humans but more importantly preclude the end of the world. The simultaneous existence of two popes between 1309 and 1376—one in Rome and the other in Avignon—added to the general disquiet.

One prophet in particular, Joachim of Fiore (1132–1202), wrote extensively about this. Essentially, he divided the history of the world into three periods, corresponding with the aspects of the Trinity. Thus, the first age was that of the Father, the second of the Son, and the third, which was yet to transpire, the Age of the Holy Spirit, during which humanity would be greatly reduced, allowing the survivors to fulfil the prophetic beliefs of Joachim and the founding fathers of Christianity in a more perfected life, based on love. This was based on Joachim's reading of Revelation 14:6: "Then I saw another angel flying in mid-air, and he had the eternal gospel to proclaim to those who live on the Earth—to every nation, tribe, language and people."

Against this dramatic background, which was preached and discussed by virtually every educated person in the West, spread a vast canvas upon which was depicted every aspect of history in that time. It is against this backdrop that the *Prophecies of Merlin* were written, used as a means to criticise the worldliness and greed of church and rulers of the Western world. Frederick II was himself described as the Antichrist because of his refusal to follow the demands of the Pope and the cardinals of Europe to undertaking a Crusade against the Muslim forces threatening Jerusalem. That Frederick later changed his mind and did as required resulted in his being once again accepted into the church, but his constant shifting of position on this matter gave rise to a considerable amount of criticism by the Pope and the cardinals, who perceived parallels between the life of Frederick II and that of the Dragon of Babylon, a being described throughout the *Prophecies* and who is associated with the Antichrist. Merlin himself, in a lengthy discourse, describes the coming of the Dragon, which is unique within the collection of documents relating to the Antichrist.

Lucy Allen Paton, the editor of the fourteenth-century edition of the *Prophecies*, describes the basis for all of this admirably in her own study of the work. The words uttered by Merlin in the episode of the three wise men (see section 17, pages 70–71) refer to the three central concerns of the church: the empire (as represented by Frederick II), the papacy, and heresy.

We see that the episode of the three wise men not only incidentally illustrates Merlin's typical abilities as an enchanter, but reveals his power to confound and admonish the representatives of the empire, the papacy, and heresy. Furthermore he appears as a devout believer in the Trinity and the sacraments, but unhesitating in his denunciations of the sins of the highest dignitaries of the church and of the abuses that had contaminated the religious orders. In these denunciations he in part fulfils what earlier in the interview he had announced to be the purpose of his existence:

> By our Lord Jesus Christ, it is your will that I was born on earth to shame the enemies from Hell and moreover to fight on earth against the evil miracles of the Dragon of Babylon, and to disprove the wrongful actions of the clerics.[4]

What is fascinating about this is the way in which Merlin, who is at once the son of a demon or, at best, a Pagan who accepts the light of Christianity, here describes his mission to announce the coming of the Antichrist and to denounce those who would in any way welcome the Dragon of Babylon, as well as the wrongful actions of various churchmen. It remains one of the clearest examples of the way Christianity took over so much of the teachings and beliefs of the ancients, reshaping and adapting them to prove its own doctrines—many of which derive directly from the philosophy of the classical world.

The story of the Antichrist has indeed been shown to emerge from the Babylonian myth of the war between darkness and light, personified by Tiamat, the Goddess of chaos and darkness, and Marduk, the God

---

4. Translated by Caitlín Matthews from the original French text included by Paton in her edition of the prophecies.

of order and light. This was, of course, a very ancient theme, which can be traced to much earlier times. That it was a Goddess who represented chaos and a God who stood for order fitted well into the Christian idea that women were essentially evil. This gave rise to a continuing theme, which is still with us in parts of the world and within the individual beliefs of certain men. Merlin, in the *Prophecies*, is portrayed as a fallen being whose underlying Pagan beliefs could not be completely overcome by his baptism but whose nominal Christianity made him acceptable in the eyes of the church. These matters are beyond the scope of this book but make for interesting study of the overlaps between Pagan and Christian cultures. Merlin as presented here stands somewhere between the two and represents the best of each world.

We chose to omit most of the very overt theological aspects of the prophecies because to all but serious students of the material they remain largely irrelevant to us today. The main purpose of the *Prophecies* is to instruct us in the lore of Merlin, whose unique voice weaves throughout the text like a golden thread. However, we felt we had to include the episode in which Merlin appears before a tribunal of Roman Catholic cardinals to defend his teachings and prophecies. As well as demonstrating that he sits very firmly on the fence between Paganism and Christianity, his beliefs in this lengthy discourse also describe the impending appearance of the Antichrist, against which he intended to fight.

In the 1303 edition of the *Prophecies*, as edited by Lucy Allen Paton, Merlin's powerful prophecies include the following:

> The kings of Tarsie [Tarshish], Arabie [Arabia], and Saba [Sheba] will come to the Dragon with gifts, even as their ancestors came to Jesus. They will see the sign of the Dragon in the heavens at his birth, even as the magi saw the celestial sign at the epiphany, and will leave their homes to follow it. It will guide them to the desert of Babylon, and there they will wait for 30 years until the Dragon begins to preach. Then they will appear before him bearing gifts, the king of Tarsie a knife, the king of Araby an olive branch, and the king of Saba a box of ashes. Of these gifts the Dragon will accept the knife alone, explain-

ing to the people that he takes it as a token that he will bring death to each king; the olive branch he rejects, because it is a sign that he will be at peace with all who believe in the Son of Mary; the box of ashes he refuses, because it signifies death. Then he will bid the kings return to their countries, but he will give them devils as guides, who will lead them far into the desert of Babylon, from which they will never issue forth, nor will more be heard of them. Many a man will go forth in quest of them, and will encounter more adventures than befell the Knights of King Arthur in the quest of the grail.[5]

Another thirteenth-century book, now lost and enigmatically entitled *The Sayings of Merlin*, is quoted by Joachim of Fiore and the chroniclers Matthew Parris and Salimbene. The latter wrote about the lives of Frederick I and II and added to the identification of both men with the Antichrist.

The First Frederick "will seem like a lamb with shorn hair, but is truly a lion with a mane. He will be a destroyer of cities. Despite acting justly he will die between a crow and a crow. Henry shall survive him, who will die at the gates of Milazzo."[6]

The Second Frederick will be an unhoped for miracle.[7]

The lamb will seem to be torn apart by goats, but they will not devour him. His marriage bed will swell and provide fruit in the Moorish neighbourhood, who will relieve him. After this he will drown in his own blood, but not be dipped in it for long. Nonetheless he will nest there. From a third nest will come the one who will devour his sons like a raging lion.[8]

---

5. Paton, *Les Prophecies de Merlin*, vol. 2, 201–2.
6. This refers to Frederick Barbarossa, who died on Crusade in 1190. The reference to two crows is obscure but may refer to different sites.
7. Fredrick II was deemed a miraculous birth as his mother, Constance, was elderly when she gave birth.
8. A possible reference to the children, subsequently disinherited, by Frederick Barbarossa's second wife, Constance of Aragon, who continued to make war with their father.

The second Frederick,

will believe absolutely in his own prudence. He will plant the sons of Gaetan and threaten to divide the province of Rome. He will be the sole possessor of Jerusalem's spirit.[9] He will fall at 32 years, but live in prosperity another 62 years.[10]

He will be regarded kindly only twice in 50 years. He will look upon Rome with a fierce eye, and his sons will rise up against him. Then will the sea be stained with holy blood, and his enemies advance upon Naples. When he has gathered together a garrison from the north, he will avenge the blood that has been spilled. Woe to those who cannot return to their ships.[11] After 18 years he will be anointed and will hold the monarchy despite those who envy him. When he dies all who cursed him will be frustrated.[12]

Reading this we can see how the idea of Frederick as Antichrist originated and how the compiler of the *Prophecies* incorporated it in his collection.

THE CRUSADES AND MERLIN'S PROPHECIES

We might be surprised that the Crusades are given a place in Merlin's prophecies. King Arthur and Merlin date from the sixth to seventh centuries, while the Crusades took place in the eleventh to thirteenth. The man (probably a monk) who wrote the first version of the *Prophecies* in the early fourteenth century used his writings for more than just stories about King Arthur and Merlin, however. As we have noted, he also

---

[9]. Frederick's second wife was Isabella II of Jerusalem, so this may refer to her.
[10]. This ties in with the dates of Frederick's life—his coronation and death.
[11]. Reference to a sea battle in which Frederick's navy captured a group of prelates on their way to a council in Rome, which intended to disown him.
[12]. Translated from the German by John Matthews from Holder-Egger, "Italienische Prophetieen," 175–77. Further information and a variant translation can be found in McGinn, *Visions of the End*.

took the opportunity to expose corruption within both government and the church.

The monk wrote his *Prophecies* during a time when two crusading armies passed through Venice on their way to Sicily, where they embarked for Tunisia and from there travelled to the Holy Land. As well as religious reasons, there were also economic and political reasons to go on a Crusade, but the impact on society was great. This was certainly the case for Venice, though which several Crusades passed.

The impact of the Crusades can be outlined as follows: in the short term, they caused a dip in trade, since war and commerce do not go hand in hand. But in the long term, they led to economic growth in Europe, especially among the merchant families of the Italian cities. This was certainly true of Venice, which was an international trading center at the time when the Venetian monk wrote the original thirteenth-century manuscript. The Crusaders brought with them products that were very popular in Europe, such as limes, soap, perfumes, ceramics, glass, jewellery, medicines, and textiles. The merchant families in the Italian cities stimulated this trade.

Another effect was that the power of the Pope and the church increased greatly, since the Crusades required a vast amount of money, enabling the Church of Rome, which raised huge sums, to strengthen its financial hold over society. Already in the original manuscript we see papal messengers arriving in Britain with letters calling on the Pope to recruit Christian knights and foot soldiers to go on a Crusade to defend the Holy Land, these stories are entwined with King Arthur and the Knights of the Round Table, and the presence of Frederick II dominates much of the text, particularly focussing on the part he played in the Crusades.

TIMELINE OF SOURCE TEXTS

1134: *Prophetiae Merlini* by Geoffrey of Monmouth (Latin)

1135: *Historia Regum Britanniae* (which includes prophecies of Merlin) by Geoffrey of Monmouth (Latin)

1150: *Vita Merlini* by Geoffrey of Monmouth (Latin)

1170: *Erec and Enide* by Chrétien de Troyes (Old French)

1177–1181: *Yvain* by Chrétien de Troyes (Old French)

1181–1190: *Perceval: The Story of the Grail* by Chrétien de Troyes (Old French)

1190–1215: *Didot Percival* by anonymous author (Old French)

1279: A supposed Franciscan Venetian monk compiled Merlin's prophecies and translated them from Latin to Old French; this compilation was later published by Antoine Vérard in 1498

1280–1300: *Il Novellino* compiled by anonymous author (Italian)

1303: Rennes manuscript compiled by Robin Boutemont (?) (Old French)

1498: *Les Prophecies de Merlin*, volume three of *Romans de Merlin*, compiled by a Franciscan Venetian monk (?) (Old French), published in Paris by Antoine Vérard

MERLIN'S SCRIBES

There has been a good deal of speculation over the years as to how many scribes Merlin employed to write down his prophecies. The numbers range between 70, 160, or even 320.[13] In the Vérard edition there are four named scribes:

> Maistre Tholomer
> Maistre Antoine
> Maistre Raymon the Wise Clerk
> Maistre Rubens the Chaplain

In addition there are several additional, retrospective figures drawn from other texts, specifically Blaise and Helias, who were present at the beginning of Merlin's prophetic life, and Maistre Richard of Ireland, the supposed author of the 1303 manuscript on which the subsequent editions are based. All of these served both as locators in the Arthurian world and enabled dialogues between Merlin and each different scribe—a method central to the recording of prophetic and philosophical materials since Plato, thus ensuring that a number of prophetic collections were couched in this format, our text included. The constant switching about between Ireland and Wales as a setting for the various

---

[13]. See Paton, *Les Prophécies de Merlin*, vol. 2, 302.

scribes again indicates that more than one edition went into the compilation of each successive book of Merlin's prophecies. That some of the scribes were familiar outside the range of the *Prophecies* is shown by a quotation from *The Story of England* by Robert Manning of Brunne (1275–1338).[14]

> Then said Merlin many things
> That in his land should happen unto kings,
> That are in Blaise's books written
> And in Tolomer and Sire Amytayn [Antoine]
> Who knew him well and more could write
> And from these they wrote his prophecies
> And were his Maisters in all things.

MAISTRE BLAISE

First and foremost amongst the named scribes of Merlin's prophecies is Blaise, though he is not actually present as a character in the Vérard text. First mentioned in the twelfth-century text of the *Huth Merlin*, he is said to have compiled a great book of the prophet's words and deeds. This is presented as a recollection of Merlin, since Blaise was his mother's confessor (and hence a priest) who was responsible for christening the infant, thus preventing his birth as an Antichrist. Blaise seems to have been commanded to collect everything he could find or recall about Merlin by Uther Pendragon, Arthur's father, following a famous episode in which Merlin prophesied the triple death of a member of the royal court (see Geoffrey of Monmouth's *Vita Merlini*).

This was so impressive that King Uther ordered that everything concerning the child prophet should be written down—presumably including the detailed prophecies later gathered by Geoffrey of Monmouth in the *Historia Regum Britanniae*. This followed an episode

---

14. From Manning, *The Story of England*, 288. Translated from the Middle English by John Matthews.

in which Vortigern, a tyrant who sought to be crowned High King of Britain, having failed in this attempt, fled to Wales and to a hill known as Dinas Emrys (Emrys being an alternate name for the seer). When the tower he sought to build there as a refuge failed to stand, he was told by his druids that a child without a father should be sacrificed there. The child turned out to be Merlin, who showed that two dragons, one red, who represented the Britons, and the other white, representing the Saxons, were fighting below the foundations of the tower. A pit was dug, from which the dragons arose and fought in the sky above the hill. The red beat the white—signifying that the Saxons would be beaten—and this prompted Merlin to burst into tears and prophesy for some time, tracing the future history of Britain from the Roman occupation to the period of Norman history in which Geoffrey lived. This enabled the author to strengthen the links between Britain and its new Norman overlords. This same incident and some of the prophecies can be found in appendix 2 of this book.

The essence of Maistre Blaise's book concerned itself with the life, deeds, and death of King Arthur, and this is referred to in more than one romance of the time. Sadly, the *Book of Blaise* has not survived—assuming it ever existed—but we must see it as the point of origin, fictitious or not, of all the subsequent collections of his work up to and including our own volume of 1498.

Just who Blaise might have been is the cause of speculation by scholars over the last hundred years. Some believe him to be identified with the mysterious Bledhericus or Bleheris, who appears in the little-known text of the *Elucidation*.[15] Another possibility is an identification with the fourth-century saint Blaise, patron of throat ailments, who began life as a physician in Armenia and later turned to the church, becoming revered as a saint sometime in the thirteenth century AD. Sometime after this, as the cult of the saint grew in popularity, a nineteenth-century scholar, Émile-Henry Vollet, wrote down this account, which summarised his life as follows:

---

15. See Matthews and Matthews, *The Lost Book of the Grail*.

Blaise, who had studied philosophy in his youth, was a doctor in Sebaste in Armenia, the city of his birth, who exercised his art with miraculous ability, good-will, and piety. When the bishop of the city died, he was chosen to succeed him, with the acclamation of all the people. His holiness was manifest through many miracles: from all around, people came to him to find cures for their spirit and their body; even wild animals came in herds to receive his blessing. In 316, Agricola, the governor of Cappadocia and of Lesser Armenia, having arrived in Sebastia at the order of the emperor Licinius to kill Christians, arrested the bishop. As he was being led to jail, a mother set her only son, choking to death of a fish-bone, at his feet, and the child was cured straight away.[16]

Apart from the advantage of having exactly the same name, we might note that he had a relationship with animals, which is something also attributed to Merlin, and that as the patron saint of throats, he could be said to have had something to do with the preservation of Merlin's voice!

HELIAS THE HERMIT

This is the hermit who once again falls outside those listed as active in our text but who appears chronologically as a character in sections 85–87 of the edited text. Like Blaise, he is seen as a contemporary of Merlin, who knew the sage personally and compiled one of the earliest collections of the prophecies. In the *Livre d'Artus* (Book of Arthur) of circa 1230, he appears not only in relationship to the prophecies but also as one who had great skill in the interpretation of dreams. Helias (or Helyas) appears in our text as someone who, like Blaise, knew Merlin as a child. We even hear that he not only had a copy of Blaise's collection of prophecies but also possessed a copy of a book written (or dictated) by Merlin himself, aged only eighteen months!

---

16. Vollet, sv. "Blaise," 993.

The Hidden Gospel of Childhood remains only a title in the listing of Merlin's works, but it offers a wonderful glimpse into the imagination of the time, suggesting how the infant prophet was perceived.

Beyond these supplementary figures, those who are active in the Vérard text are the scribes Tholomer, Antoine, Raymon, and Rubens, along with Petroine, the Abbé d'Orcanie, and Richard. We need to look briefly at each of them to understand both the shape and style of the text and the suggestion that more than one collection of prophecies and stories may have gone into the compilation.

MAISTRE THOLOMER

Tholomer is the first of the scribes to appear in the Vérard text. He is probably named after the great visionary author and astronomer Claudius Ptolemy, who lived and worked in Alexandra from about 100 to 170 AD. His work was well ahead of its time and continued to be read and copied throughout the Middle Ages. According to the *Prophecies* of 1303, he visits Ireland with a fictitious pope named Clement whose clerk he was. Little more is known of him from the various editions of the prophecies. He features as Merlin's scribe, following Blaise, and ends his work when he becomes a bishop, which makes it inappropriate for him to continue as described to Merlin. He appears to have been Merlin's scribe for the shortest period of time, due to his swift rise through the ranks of the clergy to become a cardinal. He is clearly a devoted man and perhaps something of a scholar, who even rebukes Merlin when he suggests that Arthur might be a better king than Uther Pendragon. Finally, at Merlin's request, Tholomer calls upon "a Clark of Normandy," Maistre Antoine, to be his successor.

MAISTRE ANTOINE

Master Antoine, who follows Tholomer, is described by Lucy Allen Paton as "entirely colourless," a fair judgment since he has little or nothing to say on his own account and serves merely as a simple recorder of

Merlin's words. Ironically, he is the longest serving scribe, continuing to serve the seer until his retirement to a hermitage, where he appoints the Sage Clark (Wise Clerk) of Gales (Wales)—Maistre Raymon—who is thus named only in our 1498 edition.

MAISTRE RAYMON

Again, little or nothing can be said about this scribe—for the most part referred to as "the Wise Clerk," though his adventures on the flying stone, or Pierre Ronde, make for lively reading and allow him to converse with the demon locked within the stone. Since this demon is the supposed father of Merlin, we are thus introduced to further details of the demonic plot to create an Antichrist. It also gives the compiler an excuse to include prophecies concerning most of the lands over which Raymon flies on his journey. It also introduces the figure of Percival and the matter of the Grail, while at the same time mentioning the emperor of India, who is later identified with Prester John—a figure about whom we have more to say in the commentary.

MAISTRE RUBENS THE CHAPLAIN

This scribe appears only in the closing pages of the book, and nothing further is known of him.

MAISTRE PETROINE AND THE ABBÉ D'ORCANIE

Maistre Petroine is an extra scribe, not mentioned in the *Prophecies* texts but identified in the *Prose Lancelot* as one of the founders of a school in Oxford. The unlikeliness of this is, of course, clear, since the actual establishment of the university did not take place until the twelfth century, some six hundred years later than the supposed Arthurian period.

A further additional scribe, the Abbé d'Orcanie, also referred to in the *Prose Lancelot*, is otherwise unaccredited, and nothing further is known or heard of him elsewhere.

Lucy Allen Paton perfectly sums up the purpose and nature of all the scribes in her magisterial edition of the original collection of 1303, as follows:

> The scribes are fictitious authorities for whom we have no actual prototypes. They stand as imaginary descendants from Maistre Blaise in a presumably honoured line of succession. They were suggested to the author by the other scribes of Merlin that have a less conspicuous place in the legend, and he created them the better to spin out his formidable list of prophecies.[17]

MASTER RICHARD OF IRELAND

We are left with one more significant name in the list of those deemed responsible for the creation of the *Prophecies of Merlin*. In most, though not all, versions of the prophecies, Master Richard (Maistre Richart) is proposed as the author of the work. In each instance he is said to have translated the text from the Latin to the French, specifically at the request of Emperor Frederick II, who, as we have seen, was believed to either be the Antichrist or its father. The fact that he is also said to have had the work translated into Arabic is a very curious notion of the time when most of the Western world was at war with various Saracen forces. However, it should be remembered that Islamic scholars retrieved much of the classical world's writings and that this ensured the transmission of texts back into a European corpus of learning via the interrelationships of religion and culture known as the *Convivencia* in the still-Islamic areas of southern Spain.

All the evidence we have been able to gather points to the same conclusion as that reached by the only editor of the original text of 1303, Lucy Allen Paton, that Maistre Richard is entirely fictitious, one of many named characters who lent a form of authenticity to a variety of medieval books. The possibility that the chosen name is reflected in

---

17. Paton, *Les Prophecies de Merlin; Part Two: Studies in the Contents*, 327.

that of Frederick II's confidante Riccardo, a Sicilian of possibly noble dissent, is unlikely. However, Frederick is known to have had contact with Ireland following his marriage to Queen Isabella, sister to King John of England, so the name and origin of Richard could have been suggested by historical events since John's brother was the redoubtable Richard Lionheart. However, it is doubtful whether we can consider Richard of Ireland to be the actual author of the work upon which the present text of 1498 is based. The fact that his name appears only in some of the various manuscripts of the prophecies collected between 1303 and 1498, the date of the present edition, suggests that his name was added or dropped according to the wishes of each individual scribe or compiler.

The facts, as outlined earlier, indicate that the prophecies, in this form, originated in Italy, almost certainly in Venice, and that at the monkish scribe who garnered his book from the many editions of Merlin's prophecies was in all probability of Franciscan origin. He did his best to disguise his apparent love for Merlin and the Arthurian legends, deliberately muddling them to prevent any hint of heretical belief, while at the same time referencing the possible heretical beliefs of Frederick II and others, following such outlawed or heretical groups such as Cathars, Ghibellines, Johannites, and others. The work thus became a remarkable combination of many things: Arthurian romance, prophetic utterance, and Pagan belief. It opens many doors into as yet to be explored regions within the vast edifice of the Arthurian legends.

CENTRAL CHARACTERS IN THE PROPHECIES

The commentary to the *Prophecies* in part three provides details about characters and events, necessary for a modern reader to understand the translation. However, certain characters are so important and are mentioned so frequently that they deserve a fuller treatment.

THE LADY OF THE LAKE

To understand the history of the Lady of the Lake, who looms large in the text of the *Prophecies*, we need to be aware of her relationship not only with Merlin, but also with other figures from the legends of Arthur. Of course, her primary function in the *Prophecies* is that of Merlin's nemesis, but in older texts within the Arthurian canon, her role is that of foster-mother, specifically of Lancelot, whom she steals away from his mother. In the *Prophecies*, she performs the same role in the bringing up of Meliadus, who becomes a major player, acting as a go-between for Merlin and as one of his scribes, as well as becoming the Lady's lover.

In the twelfth-century text known as *Layamon's Brut*, which follows Geoffrey of Monmouth's book chronicling the early kings of

Britain, including Arthur, Layamon draws from a more ancient faery tradition:

> There Uther the king took Ygerne for queen; Ygerne was with child by Uther the king, all through Merlin's craft, before she was wedded. The time came that was chosen, then was Arthur born. So soon as he came on earth, elves took him; they enchanted the child with magic most strong, they gave him might to be the best of all knights; they gave him another thing, that he should be a rich king; they gave him the third, that he should live long; they gave to him the princely virtues most good, so that he was most generous of all men alive. This the elves gave him, and thus the child thrived.[18]

The child is, of course, Arthur, and according to Layamon, the elves who fostered him dwelled in Brittany. He writes of a lake, dug by the elves, where four kinds of fish swam apart from one another. When Arthur eventually lies mortally wounded, he wills his kingdom to Constantine ap Cador (son of King Cador) and says: "And I will fare to Avalun, to the fairest of all maidens, to Argante the queen, an elf most fair, and she shall make my wounds all sound; make me all whole with healing draughts."[19]

Nowhere but here, in this single text, does the name Argante appear, yet it seems to have been an ancient name for the Lady of the Lake. Layamon may have been thinking of the French word for silver (*argent*) when he wrote this, or it may derive from a more distant Celtic name.

The character of Argante described by Layamon immediately strikes us as close to the Celtic Morgain or Morgen, who in various texts takes Arthur to Avalon to heal his wounds with her own hands. If one places an *M* before Argante, one arrives at Margante—not a world away from Morgan or Morgain, who is sometimes called Margan or Morcant. As we see in our text of the *Prophecies*, there is a very evident rivalry

---

[18]. Wace and Layamon, *Arthurian Chronicles*.
[19]. Wace and Layamon, *Arthurian Chronicles*.

between these two figures, who may once have been one and the same.

The most likely point of origin for her is the Celtic Goddess Modron, who appears first in one of the four branches of the *Mabinogion*, a compilation of Welsh lore and myth assembled in the fourteenth century (not far from the date of our copy of the *Prophecies* but based on materials from at least eight hundred years earlier). Her name, literally, means "mother," and her son Mabon son of Modron means "son of the mother"—an interesting title for someone who brings up two heroes, Lancelot and Meliardus. An older title is Matrona, a Goddess worshipped in Gaul and around the area of Hadrian's Wall, where her son was known as Maponus.[20]

The major text, which deals with the Lady's fostering of Lancelot, is the *Lancelot-Grail*, written about 1225. It draws upon earlier German and French traditions, which tell a similar *enfance* story. We learn how the wounded King Ban of Benoic and his Queen Elaine fled from their besieged castle, and how, when Elaine was tending her dying husband, the Lady of the Lake unswaddled their young son, Lancelot, from his cradle and bore him into the lake, pressing him to her breast. Elaine pleads to have him back, but the Lady of the Lake says nothing. The text continues:

> The Lady that nourished him abided only in woods and forests that were vast and dense, and the lake whereunto she sprang with the child was naught but enchantment, and it was in the plain at the foot of a hill . . . in the part where the lake seemed widest and deepest the lady had many fair and noble dwellings . . . and her abode was so hidden that none might find it, for the semblance of the lake covered it so that it might not be seen.[21]

The Lady sets a master to teach him archery, games, and riding. She also sends one of her women to rescue Lancelot's cousins, Lionel

---

20. For a detailed exploration of this figure see Matthews, *Mabon and the Guardians of Celtic Britain*.
21. Quoted in Paton, *Studies in Fairy Mythology of Arthurian Romance*.

and Bors, from imprisonment, which she does by shape-shifting them into hounds. Together, the children grow up, until at the age of eighteen Lancelot desires to go away. At this, the Lady instructs him in the duties of a knight, itemising the qualities of the shield, horse, helmet, and sword. She bids him have a heart as hard as diamond against enemies and a heart as soft as wax for the oppressed. By presenting Lancelot to Arthur, she not only gains a protégé at Camelot, but she also invests Camelot with the knight whose heart will always follow the values of Faeryland. Interestingly, the name of the attacking king who sets these events in motion is given as Claudas, who also features in our copy of the *Prophecies* (see sections 69 and 82).

In *Le Morte D'Arthur*, Sir Thomas Malory's fifteenth-century reworking of parts of the *Lancelot-Grail* (or Vulgate) Cycle and other texts, the confusion amongst the Lady of the Lake, her handmaiden Nimuë, and Morgain becomes profound. The Lady and Morgain, whose functions are so similar in early tradition, become mutually antagonistic. The Lady of the Lake and Nimuë are also frequently taken to be one and the same person. In fact, Malory refers to the Lady of the Lake by that name on only two occasions. In the first of these we read how Arthur received his famous sword. Journeying with Merlin to a lakeside, Arthur sees

> an arm clothed in white samite, that held a fair sword in that hand. . . . With that they saw a damosel going upon the lake. What damosel is that? said Arthur. That is the Lady of the Lake, said Merlin; and within that lake is a rock, and therein is as fair a place as any on earth, and richly beseen; and this damosel will come to, you non, and then speak ye fair to her that she will give you that sword.[22]

Arthur does as he is bidden and gets the sword in return for a promise to grant the Lady anything she asks. This rather rash promise is claimed under curious circumstances soon after, when another lady named, interestingly, Lile of Avalon, comes to Camelot bearing another

---

22. Malory, *Le Morte D'Arthur*.

sword, which is a great burden to her but which only a knight of outstanding prowess can draw. He who does so is the ill-fated Balin le Sauvage, who draws forth the sword from its scabbard but then refuses to return it to Lady Lile when she asks for it back. At this moment the Lady of the Lake herself enters and demands her payment for the gift of Excalibur—the heads either of the Lady Lile or of Balin himself, whom she blames for the deaths of both her lover and her brother. Arthur, naturally enough, is none too keen on this idea, but before any further discussion can take place, Balin, recognising the Lady of the Lake as having been the cause of his own mother's death, takes the sword and cuts off her head. For this crime he is banished from the court, but he takes the head with him, leaving Arthur to bury the Lady with great sorrow, even though Balin defended himself by describing her as a sorceress who had destroyed many good knights.

This curious and conflicting account of the Lady of the Lake is unique. In almost every one of the texts in which she appears, she is seen as beneficent and, since she is clearly an otherworldly personage, presumably immortal. Yet here, she takes advantage of Arthur's rash promise by demanding that he perform an unreasonable act and then meets her death at the hands of a mortal. Malory's immediate source for this story, the thirteenth-century *Roman du Graal*, tells the same story, omitting the names of both ladies, though the implication is still, clearly enough, that the second lady is the one who gave Arthur his mighty sword.

In all probability this confusion arose from a conflation of stories, one of which was a human tale of strife and vengeance. The fact that it is part of the account of the spiritual Grail quest may also account for the negative presentation of the Lady of the Lake. What is interesting is that both women are sword bearers, whose weapons can only be acquired by the best of knights. Arthur earns his, in part, via Merlin; Balin, seemingly, through his own merits. The fact that the first lady is described as coming from Avalon seems almost to suggest a rivalry within the otherworldly realm. Throughout the remainder of Malory's book—though we find frequent references to either "a lady" or "a damosel of the lake" and although Nimuë (also known as Niniane) is thereafter sometimes referred to by this title and in some instances seems to take over from the Lady following her death at the hands of Balin—there is no further information to add to what we have already learned from the French texts.

The general namelessness of the Lady of the Lake is a feature of Celtic faery lore, but this anonymity has troubled more than one storyteller in the Arthurian tradition and has led to her conflation with both Morgain and Nimuë at different times. In fact, as noted above, the only text in which she is given a name is Layamon's *Brut*, where she is depicted as a powerful faery queen. It is reasonable to assume therefore that the title "Lady of the Lake" was borne by more than one person.

That the Lady is indeed a doublet of Morgain has been surmised more than once. The two characters have caused a single role to split into two: Argante retains the nurturing, foster-mother symbolism, while Morgain takes on the role of faery mistress and prime adversary of Arthur. Both women tend to retain their lovers and offspring in the otherworld, making it very difficult for the men to get back into the mortal realm. In this, Argante is more generous than Morgain, equipping both Arthur and Lancelot for their earthly tasks. Arthur is fostered in the magical motherland of the lake. Merlin sets up the test of the Sword in the Stone, which only Arthur can pull forth, but it is the Lady of the Lake who gives him the sword by which he is empowered: Excalibur.

Even this mighty weapon is as nothing when compared to the scabbard, which preserves its bearer from loss of blood and thus guards Arthur's life. The sword given by Argante is a symbol of the contract between Arthur and the Goddess of the land: the theft of the scabbard by Morgan later on points to a breaking of faith in this mystical marriage between land and king.

The Lady of the Lake is a prime mover of events, one who takes a wider and sometimes prophetic view of the Arthurian world. The fact that the *Prophecies* describe her as being taught magic by Merlin breaks somewhat with older traditions but gives her a reason to hate him. He gives her his wisdom but only in return for her sleeping with him and is punished by having his own power used against him. This is very much in keeping with the later Arthurian literature, where a figure of Pagan magic can only be tolerated when described as the son of a devil, while the Lady becomes a motivator behind some of the major events in the saga, giving magical gifts and advice but seldom appearing in person. She is the foster-mother of heroes, dwelling in the withdrawn and hidden home of the west. She remains a faery queen in medieval dress.[23]

MORGAIN LE FAY

In the *Prophecies* Morgain[24] is an implacable foe of both Arthur and Merlin but appears at different levels of the Arthurian tradition as a Goddess, an enchantress, and a mover and shaker of events. While her incorporation from Celtic origins into medieval text is gradual, it is nonetheless complete. She begins as a shape-shifter, but the transitions that she undergoes thereafter are at times bewildering.

Geoffrey of Monmouth does not mention her at all in his *Historia Regum Britanniae*, the style of which is strictly that of a chronicle. Instead Morgain appears in his *Vita Merlini,* which informs us that she dwells with eight sisters on the island of Avalon. She is noted for her healing powers, her shape-shifting, and her learning. She receives Arthur after the Battle of Camlann and undertakes to heal him.

Later, the twelfth-century poet Chrétien de Troyes mentions her in his *Erec and Enide* as Morgan le Fay (the Faery) and says that Guingamar, lord of the Isle of Avalon, is her friend. She is said to have made an ointment that heals wounds for her brother, Arthur. In *Yvain*, also by Chrétien, she is called Morgan the Wise. The German author Hartmann von Aue calls her a Goddess, an appellation that is repeated in both the medieval English poem *Sir Gawain and the Green Knight* (author unknown) and again in *Diu Crône* (The Crown) by Heinrich

---

23. For a more detailed exploration of the figure of the Lady, see Matthews and Matthews, *Ladies of the Lake*.

24. Or Morgan. The names are interchangeable, but we have followed the spelling used by our scribe. Also, Morgan is a masculine name in Welsh.

von dem Türlin in 1220. The chronicler Étienne de Rouen, writing before 1169, calls her "an eternal nymph."

There are many other texts, some independent of the mainstream Arthurian tradition, in which Morgain figures as a major protagonist. These establish her reputation as a woman of enchantment into whose faery realms she guides the men whom she desires as her own. Several of these texts derive from Norman sources, and it is by this means that she was transplanted into Sicilian and Italian texts such as *Tavola Rotunda* (Round Table), finally becoming the Fata Morgana of *Orlando Furioso* and *Orlando Innamorato*. Her presence in these last named may also account for her appearance in the *Prophecies*, as these feature a number of Italianate themes and make several references to Frederick II, the basis of whose kingdom was Sicily.

The *Lancelot-Grail* Cycle gives us a lively portrait of Morgain:

> She was the sister of King Arthur, very gay and playful; she sang agreeably; though dark in the face, very well made, neither too fat nor too thin, with beautiful hands, perfect shoulders, skin softer than silk, engaging of manner, long and straight in the body: altogether wonderfully seductive and, besides all that, the warmest and most sensual woman in all Britain. Merlin had taught her astronomy and many other things, and she studied them so well that she became an excellent scholar and was later called Morgan La Fée because of the marvels she wrought. She expressed herself with gentleness and delightful sweetness and was more good-natured and attractive than anyone else in the world when she was calm. But when her anger was roused against someone, she was very difficult to appease.[25]

In the *Lancelot-Grail* Cycle, Morgain appears as an adversary to Guinevere, seeking to imprison Lancelot in her otherworldly Valley

---

25. Quoted in Markale, *King Arthur, King of Kings*, from the *Suite du Merlin*, part of the collection known as the *Lancelot-Grail* Cycle.

of No Return. She created this valley, from which no knight false in love can escape, because of a former lover of hers, Guinevere's cousin, Accolon, from whom the queen separated her. All who enter the valley have to undergo perilous adventures. Lancelot enters it and, aided by the ring given him by the Lady of the Lake, destroys the place, rescuing the many knights imprisoned there. Morgain attempts to imprison Lancelot once again, luring him to a tower by means of a maiden. While languishing there, he paints a picture of the Lady of the Lake and Guinevere—the two women of his life. Morgain keeps him imprisoned because she loves him and wants to change his affections from Guinevere to hers, but Lancelot finally escapes her clutches. Morgain here appears very much as a foil to the Lady of the Lake.

That Morgain began as a Goddess is in little doubt. Giraldus Cambrensis (Gerald of Wales) in his *Speculum ecclesiae* ridicules the British for considering Morgan as *dea quaedam phantastica* (some kind of fantastic Goddess). He calls Morgain "a noble matron," a blood relative of Arthur's, who took him to Glastonbury for the healing of his wounds. But Morgain does not appear as a member of Arthur's family until the twelfth-century romances of Chrétien de Troyes.

The etymology of Morgan's name has been much disputed among scholars. The Gaelic name Muirgen, which means "born of the sea," has been identified as a possible source, but more likely Morgan is derived from Morrighan or Morrigan, meaning "great queen," the name of the Irish Goddess of war and death. Morgan shares many attributes with this Irish Goddess, as we shall see. The Welsh Goddess Rhiannon similarly derives her name from the proto-Celtic name Rigantona or "great queen." Regan is a name of British tradition.

Morgain is truly one of the paramount ladies of the lake. She rules over the land of Avalon, which lies over an unnamed lake, on the margins of this world. Looking more closely at the *Vita Merlini*, we read the following description of Avalon:

> The island of apples which men call "the Fortunate Isle" gets its name... because it produces all things of itself; the fields there have

no need of the ploughs of the farmers. . . . Of its own accord it produces grain and grapes, and apple trees . . . and people live there a hundred years or more. . . . There nine sisters rule by a pleasing set of laws those who come to them from our country. She who is first of them is more skilled in the healing art, and excels her sisters in the beauty of her person. Morgen is her name, and she has learned what useful properties all the herbs contain, so that she can cure sick bodies. She also knows an art by which to change her shape, and to cleave the air on new wings like Daedalus; when she wishes she is at Brest, Chartres, or Pavia, and when she wills, she slips down from the air onto your shores. And men say that she has taught mathematics to her sisters, Moronoe, Mazoe, Gliten, Glitonea, Cliton, Tyronoe, Thitis, Thetis best known for her cither. . . . Thither after the battle of Camlan we took the wounded Arthur, guided by Barinthus to whom the waters and the stars of Heaven were well known. With him steering the ship we arrived there with the prince, and Morgen received us with fitting honor, and in her chamber she placed the king on a golden bed and with her own hand she uncovered his honourable wound and gazed at it a long time. At length she said that health could be restored to him if he stayed with her for a long time and made use of her healing art.[26]

This Morgain rules over an Island of Women like that to which heroes such as St. Brendan sail on their voyages to the Blessed Isles. Geoffrey's *Vita Merlini* draws upon many established features of the Celtic sisterhood tradition. The Fortunate Isle on which so many apples grow is an earthly paradise. The apple, which in Judeo-Christian tradition is the fruit of the fall, is the fruit of restoration in Celtic tradition.

British tradition abounds in ninefolds. They appear again in the sisterhood of the cauldron of Annwn, who breathe over it and cool it with their breath, or the ninefold sisterhood called "the Nine Witches

---

26. Geoffrey of Monmouth, *Vita Merlini*.

of Gloucester," who give Peredur, the Celtic Percival, his weapon training. While Greek classical tradition also has its ninefold sisterhood of the Muses, Celtic tradition has its nine sisters, each of whom has a special quality or gift. In the case of the sisterhood of the underworld cauldron, which will not boil the food of a coward, they each bestow a gift of inspiration upon the food within. Geoffrey is annoyingly terse in his enumeration of the sisterhood. We note that the main features of Morgan remain constants within later legend: her ability to heal, her shape-shifting, her great learning. Although she loses her ability to fly, her ubiquity throughout many of the texts is remarkable.

Although Geoffrey of Monmouth gives us the first textual source for Morgain, her influence in Celtic tradition precedes his writing. Behind the figure of Morgain stretches a venerable Celtic lineage. As the Celtic and native understanding of Morgain broke down, she became the enchantress of literary tales and reverted to being the Queen of Faery among the unlearned—Argante, the figure whom, as we saw, the Saxon writer Layamon made into the faery godmother and receiver of Arthur. In this role, Morgain and the Lady of the Lake are fused into a single entity, but we can see that Morgain's independent nature—the characteristics that differentiate her from the Lady of the Lake—derive from her mortal persona as Arthur's half sister.

The German and Italian Arthurian romancers brought the myth of Morgain into contact with that of the Sibyl. Morgain, like Merlin, became the mouthpiece for assorted prophecies, both becoming incorporated into local stories as token Arthurian characters. The continuing popularity of both Morgain and Merlin testifies to their otherworldly natures, which allows them to appear at will, under most shapes and guises.

Morgain has the power to both heal and harm. She seeks lovers only to destroy them. She has an island paradise to which few come and from which she does not allow visitors to leave. Such features continually recur in her mythos, and it seems difficult to reconcile them. Celtic tradition supplies the answer in Morgan's prototype, Morrigan, from whom Morgan inherits her role as raven queen.

Morrigan and her sisters, Badb and Macha, collectively known as the

Morrigna, are a triplicity of Irish Goddesses who represent the important functions of victory, battle, and prophecy. They frequently appear at battlefields in the shape of crows. With the triple Brighid, responsible for healing, poetry, and smithcraft, and the major Goddesses of sovereignty, Eriu, Fodla, and Banba, the Morrigna form a ninefold sisterhood of Goddesses within Irish tradition. The character of Morrigan is more distinct than either of her sisters, and she appears more often in an independent way.

The *Gesta Regum Britanniae* (Deeds of the Kings of Britain), written between 1235 and 1254 and attributed to William of Rennes, a Breton Monk, confirms Arthur's true relationship with Morgan in Avalon: "Wounded beyond measure, Arthur took the way to the court of the King of Avalon, where the royal virgin, tending his wound, keeps his healed body for her very own and they live together."

Despite the wealth of earlier Arthurian traditions with their deep roots in Celtic antiquity, it is the Morgain of later tradition who is best known. We may not recognize the earlier figure, lost as she is in the shape of an enchantress. The shadow of Morgan in Arthurian literature stretches longer than the figure who casts it. She represents a potentiality that is feared: sexuality, intrigue, and enchantment are the features that have given her power. The medieval motivation of Morgain is only comprehensible as a sorceress because she has been demoted from Goddess to mortal woman in Malory. All of this is in keeping with her appearances in the *Prophecies*.

The incorporation of Morgain the Goddess into Arthur's family presents problems. Deities adhere to cosmic principles rather than parochial concerns. There is no human rationale or motivation to the deeds of Morgain when she is stripped of her original identity. She becomes a bitter, hate-filled woman, determined to stop Arthur at all turns. This implacable hatred of Morgain for Arthur and his court is worked up to furious heights in Malory. Morgain is the younger daughter of Igraine and Gorlois, put out to a nunnery and then requisitioned for marriage to one of Uther's vassal kings, Uriens. Her attempt to kill off first Arthur and then Uriens shows that she wishes to assume power herself, and her various bids for power always involve her acquisition of dangerous knights, who subsequently become her lovers and champions.

The lovers of Morgain are clearly important to her tradition. While in Avalon, she must always have a partner, it seems. Arthur, according to later tradition, is related to Morgain as half brother and so cannot be her lover. The only alternative is that of challenger, but another of the children of Uther and Igraine, Morgause, takes over this role and gives birth to Mordred in a forbidden incestuous union.

Morgain may have begun as a shape-shifting Goddess, but her own form is shifted by the Arthurian romancers. The darkening of her character is gradual and is the result of a series of romancers who reframed the myth to their own purposes. Morgain is thus given many different treatments that render her less and less sympathetic. Instead of portraying the healing sister, Morgain becomes the skeleton in Arthur's family cupboard. In the end, just as Merlin survives in the otherworldly retreat of his *esplumoir*, so the real Morgain remains hidden within the realm of Avalon.[27]

MELIADUS

Meliadus, also known as Meliodas, is an important character in the *Prophecies*. He acts as a go-between from Merlin to the various recorders of his words, particularly after the sage is entombed. He alone, apart from the Lady of the Lake, knows the exact location of Merlin's tomb and frequently visits it to listen and copy the words of the prophet. He is also the lover of the Lady of the Lake herself, replacing Merlin, once she has rid herself of his clearly tiresome presence.

The choice of this figure in the *Prophecies* again points to the importance of the work in Italian Arthurian literature. At least one long romance of the thirteenth century has Meliadus the elder as a hero, and the younger man is again referenced both within the sagas of Tristan

---

27. For a more detailed exploration of the figure of the Lady, see Matthews and Matthews, *Ladies of the Lake*.

and other, more general Arthurian texts.[28] As we will see in the main text of the *Prophecies*, a reference to Meliadus as a descendant of Troy brings to the fore the whole question of the mythic connection between the ancient city and the world of medieval romance. In an as yet unpublished work found in a fifteenth-century manuscript in the Biblioteca Nazionale Centrale die Firenze (National Library of Florence), which bears the lengthy title of *The Vengeance that the Descendants of Hector, the son of King Priam of Troy the Great, with the aid of King Arthur Pendragon and other kings and barons and knights errant of the Old Table, took up on the Greeks*, we see that in the medieval period the two literary strands were seen as closely adjacent.

In the *Prophecies* Meliadus is described as the half brother to the great Arthurian hero Tristan, son of King Meliadus of Léonois (Lionesse) and the Queen of Scotland. Following the death of his father, Meliadus was found floating in a small boat by the Lady of the Lake and raised by her, along with Lancelot, Bors, and Lionel, who were similarly abandoned following the death of their guardian (father to Lancelot and uncle to Bors and Lionel) at the hands of King Claudas, who also features in our text.

The *Prose Tristan* and its many recensions, along with the French romance of *Palamedes*, feature Meliadus as a central figure, considered amongst the best knights of Arthur's Round Table, but this is almost certainly the father of the character presented in the *Prophecies*. Several other men bearing this name appear within the vast range of Arthurian texts, so while he is largely a forgotten character in well-known texts such as Thomas Malory's *Le Morte D'Arthur*, he was clearly a popular hero throughout the period when Arthurian romances dominated the literature of the Western continent.

PERCIVAL

The introduction of Percival as a central figure towards the end of the *Prophecies* is interesting. Percival is one of the most important

---

28. See Gardner, *The Italian Legend in Arthurian Literature*.

characters in the vast cycle of Grail romances, appearing first in Chrétien de Troyes's *Story of the Grail* (or possibly earlier as Peredur in the Welsh mythbook of the *Mabinogion*). He remained the key seeker for the Grail until the appearance of the saintly Galahad, son of Lancelot and the Maiden of the Grail, in the *Lancelot-Grail* Cycle. But it is to a very different text, the *Didot Percival*[29] (named after one of its owners), that we must turn to, to discover why Percival appears in the *Prophecies*.

In this text, composed sometime between 1190 and 1215 and thus available to the author of the original manuscript of the *Prophecies* dating from 1303, Merlin acts as an otherworldly guardian to Percival, whom he has long-since foreseen to be the destined Grail winner. It is for Percival that the Round Table was created, along with the Perilous Seat, at which only the destined Grail bearer could sit. In addition, Merlin follows Percival throughout his career, reproving him for his weaknesses, guiding him to the Grail castle, and even bidding him to ask the needful questions that lead him to achieve the quest.

He is thus a guiding hand throughout Percival's career, and we should not perhaps be surprised that the colophon to the *Didot Percival* gives the title of the work as the *Prophecy of Merlin*, and at the end of the work it is said that Blaise put into writing the history of King Arthur's expeditions to France and Rome, his battle with Mordred, and his passing to Avalon following the Battle of Camlann. Blaise then takes the *Book of Prophecies*, not to Helias the hermit, but to the castle of the Grail itself, where he explains its contents to Percival. Once again, in this, we see how the medieval romancers strove to connect Merlin, an archetypal Pagan seer, begotten by a devil, into the realm of the quest for the sacred cup of Christ.

The *Didot Percival* ends with the withdrawal of Merlin rather than his entombment:

---

29. Skeels, *The Romance of Percival in Prose*.

[A]nd then Merlin came to Percival and to Blayse his master, and he took leave of them and told them that Our Lord did not wish that he should show himself to people, yet that he would not be able to die before the end of the world. . . . "and all those who will see my lodging will name it the Esplumoire (or moulting cage) of Merlin."[30]

---

30. Skeels, *The Romance of Percival in Prose.*

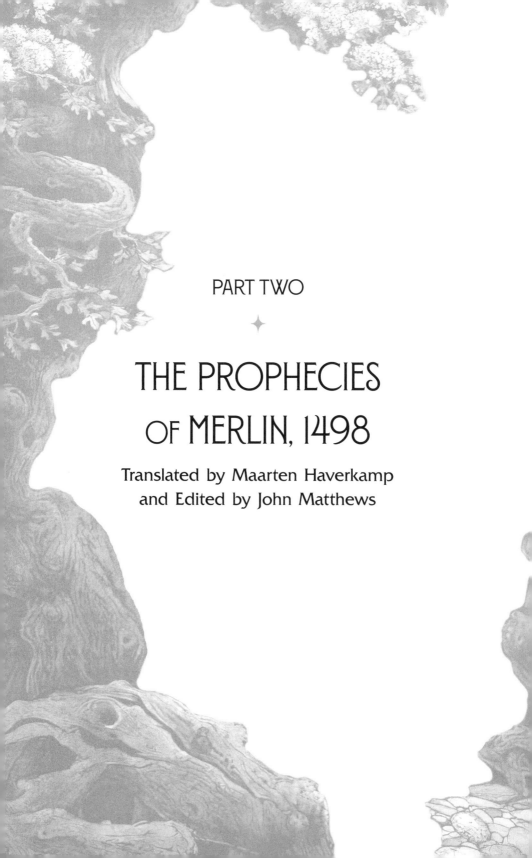

PART TWO

THE PROPHECIES OF MERLIN, 1498

Translated by Maarten Haverkamp
and Edited by John Matthews

What follows in part two is our rendition of the text, omitting some of the more theological or political materials and those prophecies that have little or no relevance to our understanding of the text. Such omissions are indicated by an ellipsis in brackets, thus [. . .]. Additional words added for the purpose of sense are also in brackets. We have presented the text here in part two as one cohesive unit so you can appreciate the flow of the story. Part three contains commentaries on each of the corresponding numbered passages so you can learn the complexities behind the words and symbolism in the text. Brief references are contained in the footnotes here in part two; longer interpretations are in the commentary in part three.

Colophon from the Rennes Manuscript, 1303

Here begin the Prophecies of Merlin and his works and his marvels, which happened in Great Britain and in many other lands. For those who attest to the story of this matter, the words of the Prophecies of Merlin are here translated from Latin into French, by the command of Emperor Frederick, for the knights and other people who would thus hear it better and take more from each example, so that they can better understand the story.

1: Merlin Begins His Prophecies

Merlin was one day with Tholomer[31] in a room in Wales. Merlin was lost in deep thought. Master Tholomer asked, "I beg you, Merlin, God bless you, tell me what you have been thinking about for so long."

Merlin answered him: "Write down everything I say, Master Tholomer. Listen well! I think of the people of the world who left Jerusalem 277 years ago.[32] God be merciful to them, for they will not keep the doctrines of their ancestors. But they will follow the works that have been and will be made by tyrants, and they will follow their discourse, and with them there will be a governor whose door will be forced open by the power of money, which the tyrants use to bribe him. Tholomer, write down that on this earth there will be discord between two clerics, that he who will have the power of money will appear, and there will be a battle between good and

---

31. Only in the 1498 edition is Tholomer the first scribe to be named.
32. We assume this refers to the Hebrew nation as a whole.

evil. Whoever does not have money will lose, and bad habits will overcome them."

"God bless you, Merlin," said Tholomer. "Will everyone's habits become bad?"

"Indeed," said Merlin, "they will not look at the good works that the holy governors and holy servants have made. But they will look at what the bad tyrants and the bad ministers have done, who will devalue gold with iron and will open doors with their money."

"Merlin," said Master Tholomer, "what will the people say in that time?"

Merlin replied: "They will say that the clergy have altered the Gospel of the Lord St. John. Know that nothing can resist the power of money."

"So," asked Master Tholomer, "has the book of the Gospels been altered?"

"Certainly," said Merlin, "by money. For judges can only keep justice through money. And if the evil work in this time begins, I will tell you. Before that it will be shown forth at the governor's court, but not as clearly as I will tell you. The Lord Jesu Christ will show a sign for this."

2: Of the Sea That Will Grow above the Shore as High as the Mountains

"What sign will that be?" asked Master Tholomer.

"He shall make the seas grow as high above the banks of the water lily as the mountains are above the plains. And were it not for a terrestrial angel,[33] they would all be drowned, for they are not fish. But the sea will rise very far above the shores."

"Explain, Merlin," said Tholomer. "When will this be?"

"Continue writing," said Merlin. "It will take two years for the Dragon[34] to appear."

---

33. An angelic guardian of Earth.
34. The first of many references to the Dragon of Babylon, a name given to the Antichrist.

"Tell me," said Master Tholomer. "How long will the sea be like this?"

And Merlin replied, "Forty days."[35]

"What month will it be?" asked Master Tholomer.

Merlin replied, "It will be in September. So it is indicated. Write on, Tholomer.

"That God will give neither food or drink to the fornicators, and that the doors of Hell will never be closed against them. They shall not want to be born, for the gates of Paradise will never be opened to them, and they shall die in their sins.

"And I tell you that at that time the clerks in Telz[36] will sin as I said. Yet I wish you to put in writing that the governor's court will not administer justice if they have no monetary power. And with money, all bounty will be given to the clergy.

"And know that when the time comes for the evidence to be faced, two clerks will be required to go to court, one good and the other bad. The rich will be bad and have a bad reputation, and so it will be desirable that the unlawful clerk should carry with him four or more barrels and a chest full of money.[37] And the poor clergyman, serene in shabby robes, will say to the clerk: 'Please pay the governor, Sire, for I have nothing unless God and you give it to me.' When he has said this, the tyrants will say to the governor: 'Sire, such a clerk beseeches you in the name of God, and we also beg you to give it to him, for in him is the best use for it.'"

"Merlin," said Master Tholomer. "The other people of the world, how will they be at this time when things get worse? Because even their temptations are written in your prophecies."

"I have told you many times," said Merlin, "and again I tell you, that when a leader takes pity on man, all the people feel it. The governor's court will grow worse from that time until the

---

35. The same number of days as the great flood in biblical mythology.
36. Telz is a township in Lithuania, associated with sects regarded as heretical in the Middle Ages.
37. Merlin returns to this theme again towards the end of the book in section 83.

Thing[38] that once left Jerusalem shall be one thousand, one hundred, and twenty-three years old—not in the knowledge of all men, but amongst the clergy.[39] And when it is discovered, evil will begin for everyone. And know that the people will improve if the sea rises in the way I have told you, and in many countries the bad example that the clergy will set will be changed in that century."

"Explain, Merlin," asked Master Tholomer. "Is there hope of Heaven in the sky?"

"Yes," he said. "And I can hear the words that are said in the Holy Church, to which the firmaments under Heaven give structure."

"Dear God!" said Tholomer. "I believe that you are so perfectly full of knowledge that no man in the world would dare dispute these celestial facts."

"Of course," said Merlin. "None of the clergy from this century have dared to do this. It must be done only for those on whom the Holy Spirit takes pity."

"Merlin, can you tell me where the blessed lady, Holy Mary, is?" asked Master Tholomer.

"In Heaven," said Merlin, "above the angels and above the archangels, above the towers and the dominions, above the cherubim and seraphim, and above the principals and their superiors. As Holy Mary was above all others in the high age, so she and Heaven are above all other celestial beings. She was a mother on Earth where we are, and now she is a mother in Holy Heaven."

"Explain, Merlin. What glory will people have when their souls are in the Paradise of the Saints?"

"They will have no greater glory than to see the face of our Lord Jesu Christ."

"Explain," said Master Tholomer. "What punishments will they receive when their souls are judged and sent to Hell?"

---

38. The Thing, also Abomination. The Hebrew nouns *sheqez* (abomination, something abominable) and *shiqqutz* (disgusting or detested thing) come from the root *shaqats*, used in the sense of abomination.

39. Only the church knew all truth, according to the beliefs of the time.

"They will have no alternative but to see the devils, and they will be on fire and suffer other pains so cruel that all the tongues that are and will be cannot tell of their misery."

"That will be a bad time indeed," said Master Tholomer.

"Write down," said Merlin, "that Arthur, who will become King of Greater Britain,[40] will ride through the perilous woods to test the knights and be honoured wherever he goes. They will show the wonders and power of their weapons."

"Explain, Merlin. Who will risk his life or be the plaything [of the Dragon]?"

"I have told you what will happen," said Merlin. "For many it is not clear, for they do not know whether or not I am telling the truth."

"Explain, Merlin. Will God kill you if you tell me when my life will be ended?"

"I will not tell you anything more," said Merlin. "But I see you being consecrated bishop at Pentecost in the city of London and King Arthur being crowned king."

"Is that true?" asked Master Tholomer.

"Of course," said Merlin. "You should say you heard me testify to this."

"I shall be there," said Master Tholomer, "as you wish."

"Write that King Lot of Orcanie will be killed because of his pride after the coronation of King Arthur. That he killed his son out of treachery. Those who will kill their father are sons of the same King Lot."

Now the account says that Merlin and Tholomer were together and that they wrote that the son of King Uterpendragon would be richer in the age than any earthly royal house had ever been before or after.

And Tholomer said to Merlin: "That may not be true."

"Are you sure?" said Merlin. "There will be a knight who will be so full of kindness that he will put an end to the adventures that

---

40. So-called to distinguish it from Little Britain or Brittany.

come to Britain. And there will be another so worthy and so benevolent that Our Lord God will make changes for him in time and put an end to all that the other knights cannot see. And the water from the fountain will stop flowing when he puts his hand in it."[41]

"Surely," said Tholomer, "if you say this, you will believe anything! Explain, Merlin. Will we ever have such a good king in Logres as King Uterpendragon?"

"His son will be even better and more graceful than he," said Merlin [. . .] He will be a hundred times braver than his father was, his fame will never waver, and his kingdom will be so great that he will recalibrate the lineage of the other kings of England and that of Gaul and of other countries, and many will dedicate themselves to him."

"I hope you also write down," said Merlin, "that with the granting of judicial equality, there will be less kindness and courtesy for all of the knights from the king."

"By God!" said Tholomer. "[Does that mean] there will no longer be knights of faithfulness or courtesy?"

"Write down," said Merlin, "that from then on the knights will deteriorate in their faith as a man who approaches death. Because of the great destruction made at Salebiēres,[42] complaints will stain the honour of chivalry, since in this place both good and bad knights will die."

3: About the Dragons That Live Underground

One day, Merlin was summoned by King Uterpendragon. He asked Merlin: "How did the dragons of Vortigern's tower live underground?

Merlin said: "Come with me."

---

41. This refers to the Grail knights Percival and Galahad; for the fountain reference, see the commentary.
42. Salebiēres is almost certainly Salisbury, in which case the reference here will be to the infamous "Night of the Long Knives," which took place at Stonehenge and in which many British chieftains were killed after being lured there by the Saxons under a flag of truce.

He led the king to the valley where there was a round block of stone, without locks or wire mesh and therefore completely closed.

Merlin said: "A small snake is trapped in this stone and is gnawing at it."

Uterpendragon gave an order for the stone to be split. The snake flew out, and Merlin caught it and showed how sharp its teeth were.

Then Merlin said: "These teeth are sharp enough to gnaw their way into the stone. They can fly over the Earth and cause harm to everyone, people and animals."

Then Merlin said: "There is a sword in the serpent-stone at Monte Gargano, and from the mountain no one can take it out except the chosen one."[43]

4: The Queen of Brequehem Visits Merlin

One day Merlin received a visit from the Queen of Brequehem,[44] and he said to her: "There will be natural disasters and unusual events in the Holy Land, and wars, and famine in Treviso.[45] Write on, Tholomer, write that government and the church will become corrupt and follow a false religion."

5: How the Emperor of Rome Came before the Pope with a Hundred Knights

[Editor's note: this section is moved to section 70, where it clearly belongs.]

6: The Death of King Arthur

Merlin said: "God bless you, Master Tholomer, I'm going to give you a prophecy that I don't really want to make. King Arthur, the son of King Uterpendragon, will be killed by his own son, who is also his nephew. It pains me, God rest his soul."[46]

---

43. This is a reference to the Sword in the Stone, which still exists at Galgano; see the commentary.
44. We assume this is meant to be Bethlehem, but we have retained the original spelling.
45. A city in Northern Italy.
46. Mordred, who was Arthur's incestuous son by his half-sister Morgause.

7: Of the Damsel from Wales Who Came to the Room Where Merlin and Tholomer Were

A damsel from Wales entered the room where she knew Merlin was staying. When Merlin saw her, he began to smile and said: "My lady, I will write your life and deliver an important prophecy."

Then Merlin said to Tholomer: "She has the mark of the supernatural. Put on parchment that this damsel will have a child as soon as a year has passed. That after the death of the King of Ireland, the child shall become King of Bellistans, a city just above the sea around Sarrazin, and that in time King Arthur shall crown this child king. This lady will acquire great fame."

What shall I tell you? How did Merlin banish this beautiful damsel? Know, readers, that Merlin would have loved to play with her as he had so often done with others. But he held back. Her child would be a descendant of the royal family of Ireland. From her would come such a good-natured child as Bellic. The damsel from Wales made overtures to Merlin, but he rejected her. At which she was so embarrassed that she asked Merlin to send her away, which he did. The damsel spread her arms to hug Merlin, but he remained behind in the room.

"I see," then said Merlin, "the Holy Grail traveling from Jerusalem to Babylon and again back to Jerusalem, and I see it wandering many times afterwards, and many will go in search of it. Eventually, I see that the Holy Grail will be guarded along with a bleeding spear in an inaccessible castle, guarded by the Grail king and the Grail knights. The Grail is said to provide happiness, eternal youth, and food in infinite abundance.

"Now write down that because of the Thing that came out of Jerusalem one thousand, two hundred, and seventy years ago, there will be heavenly miracles. Our Lord wants us to know that he will be angry, and when you say this, the world will tremble with love, and when you say that innocent blood will suffer evil, it will be there. Our Lord will utter his lamentation before all and will gather the blood of Abel when his brother Cain spills it on the earth.[47] Know that those will be judged who show no pity for the shedding of his blood. And even more men and women will suffer and become bitter because the grains of wheat they sow on the earth will yield nothing.[48] And everything will be done by Our Lord in this place where evil has been done."

"Where is this?" asked Tholomer,

"It shall be," said Merlin, "among the people whose ancestors came from the great city of Troy,[49] and it shall be exactly at the time when I told you that there shall be heavenly wonders. Write that some of Isaac's ancestors, the sons of Abraham, used to go to an island in the sea, and that they drowned in that sea. As for what they have eaten, it will be as human flesh. After the death of those who will destroy Armenia, more than a hundred thousand men and women will drown at sea."

"Won't God be with [even] one of the women?" asked Tholomer.

"Yes," said Merlin. "For the women will hurt men as if with spears and swords."

"Tell me, Merlin," asked Tholomer. "Will the Dragon of Babylon[50] throw some kind of great feast?"

"No," said Merlin. [. . .] "I want you to write that a man will come to Babylon, and it will be that man who was born a minor in a place near the Indies. That man will calculate the coming of the Dragon to be thirty years. He will make many people believe that the Dragon is the Messiah."

"Explain, Merlin," said Tholomer. "What happens next to this man?

---

47. Theologically, Christ is seen as a type of Abel because, like him, he was put to death as an innocent.
48. A reference to John 12:24: "Unless a grain of wheat falls into the earth and dies, it remains alone; but if it dies, it bears much fruit."
49. Now Turkey. The descendants of Aeneas of Troy were believed to have peopled Europe according to legend. Brutus, Aeneas's grandson, was believed to be the founder of Britain.
50. It was a common medieval practice to refer to the Antichrist as the Dragon of Babylon.

"Many will pray to him in the city before the palace of the Good Mariners,[51] and he will preach before that palace."

Merlin and Master Tholomer went into the room [to talk] many times until the day came for Merlin to depart from there and go far away.

"Master Tholomer, God be with you! You will never see me in Ireland again. Other words I shall say to you, but these you will write down in Wales."

Then Master Tholomer wept openly, and Merlin said: "Now I pray you go live as you promised me. I shall not come to Wales just to speak. I want you to say that you heard me crying loudly."

And Master Tholomer answered and said: "I will seem to be on fire [with inspiration] while you are with me, for I have found nothing in the present that goes against Holy Church. And if there comes no other prophet to proclaim this, you alone will have declared this. To confirm these things, another scribe must take my book, read what is written there, and decide whether or not you truly foretold these things."

"Master Tholomer," said Merlin, "I am not telling anyone I'm dying. But if anyone wants to believe in [the Dragon], he will believe in him, and if he does not want to believe, then he will not believe. Such belief would not affect him greatly but could be harmful to God, for if they do not believe that God is mighty in all things, so they sin. And if anyone says he does not see that, but that Merlin knows what he is saying, and that he has no power to change his form, he is wrong, then he will fail to believe that God is mighty in all things."

"I want so much to speak directly to God, just like you," [said Master Tholomer].

"Soon you will go to Wales," said Merlin. "Eventually, you will become bishop there. But you will never see me again."

Then Master Tholomer kissed Merlin good-bye, and Merlin went

---

51. The people of Venice.

straight to London and found all the men there lost and wars starting all over Greater Britain. And the next day when Master Tholomer arose, he went straight to the king[52] and told him all that Merlin had said to him. And the king grew wondrously wrathful when he heard that Merlin was gone. The king was so angry that he could not promise Master Tholomer he would be at peace with Merlin's prophecies.

The next day a galley from Wales arrived directly at the port of Ireland. The barons and clergy had come to persuade Tholomer to become the Bishop of Wales. When they came before him, a minister began to speak:

"Sire, our Lord Jesu Christ, from whom all graces descend, gave his blessing to the clergy of Wales, who make their household like you, lord and master, and to the governor of Eulz,[53] and finally to grace the coat of arms of Wales.

"Since our Lord Jesu Christ suffered, he alone is Lord and God of all things, and he can give death and life according to his good pleasure. All the choral precentors[54] of Wales have died suddenly. Now, good lord, concerning this damage, which is as great as you can see in this land, we have all come, and we pray to you and my lord the king, and to all of Wales, that you come to this country."

"Know that we all long and strive to see you, lords," said Master Tholomer. "It is most regrettable what has become of the clergy of Wales. I am angry and sorry. I express my regret every day. You think of our lord the king and all of Wales, and you have come here to ask me to come and live with you there. This ought to be, and through your prayers I will do so. Set your sails ready at this time, for tomorrow I will be with you on the sea."

When they heard that, they were very happy; they thanked the

---

52. This probably refers to the King of Ireland, but it could equally be Uther or Arthur.
53. Unknown character or place.
54. Precentors lead monastic communities in the divine office, which is chanted seven times a day.

Great Father: "We must now return to Wales." Master Tholomer went to the King of Ireland and told him that he must depart. "I am at your service every day of my life and in all the places I am commanded to enter."

Then Master Tholomer and his companions went to the port. They entered the galleys with all those who were to go to Wales.

"I beseech you," said Master Tholomer, "to tell the King of Ireland that I mourn all the dead. [. . .]"

Master Tholomer entered the galley with all those who came for him, and they sailed so swiftly that they arrived in Wales in the morning. When people heard the news of his coming, there was some opposition, but also a lot of honest belief that he should be well received. He was not consecrated bishop until sometime later, and after a long life devoted to God, he finally died in the Holy Land. But before he left, he gave the *Book of Prophecies* to Master Antoine, who wrote down everything in a new book.[55]

8: Of Master Richard, Who Translated Merlin's Prophecies

Now I will tell you that when Master Richard translated the prophecies, a knight was with him who came from the Holy Roman Emperor.[56] He read all the great words Merlin had said. Master Richard told how all the things he wrote about Merlin's prophecies were true. "I beg you," said Master Richard, "speak of it no more. The prophecies are written on parchment and shall be sent to the emperor. I will send my servant to carry the bundle."

And at that time poor people began also to speak more about Merlin's prophecies.[57]

---

55. The second of Merlin's list of scribes.
56. Frederick II.
57. This section is from the Rennes manuscript, included here for its reference to Master Richard.

9: Of the Crown of the Emperor of Orbance

"Tell me, Merlin, God bless you," asked Master Antoine. "Will it rain [on] men in Orbance, or in the city called Anceris?"[58]

"It will be in Orbance," said Merlin. "For my part I will tell you, that as soon as my prophecies are translated from Latin into French, a golden crown will be found at the bottom of the Dead Sea, four precious stones of which would be worth more than two bars of gold.

"And know that this crown belonged to the Emperor of Orbance, which hitherto was buried in a ship wrecked on the high seas. After that, illiterate men and children forgot his fame.

"And see you put in writing that the King of Arians, who was once mighty and notorious, went to war and then lost everything, including his heirs and all the Islands of Slavonia.

"And write that as soon as the Dragon of Babylon is slain, the ocean and the eastern sea will dry up. And men will plainly see what I have said, and so I shall be silent on this matter, for the evidence shall indeed be shown to all."

10: Of the Crown of Orbance That Shall Be Found

"I see and know," said Master Antoine to Merlin, "that you are the wisest man of the age."

"I am indeed a wise man," said Merlin. "But not as wise as the apostles and prophets and many other saints."

"Tell me Merlin, God bless you," asked Master Antoine. "According to our Lord Jesu Christ, there will be wicked men who will follow evil ways. Is that true?"

"Of course," said Merlin. "It will be even worse than everything I have told you."

"God bless you," said Master Antoine. "Will the crown of the

---

58. This appears to be a reference to the flood Merlin prophesied earlier. The city may be Ankara.

Emperor of Orbance, who drowned at sea during a storm, also be seen in this century, as you told me?"

"Yes," said Merlin. "A poor fisherman will find it. When he sells it in Saragossa to the chieftain of that time, he will give the precious stones to the stonecutters, who will take the stones and gild a golden crown with a hundred stones. Put in writing that these master stonecutters will go to Messina, the place where these prophecies will be translated from Latin into French,[59] and there they will buy these jewels."

"Tell me, Merlin, God bless you," said Master Antoine. "Will the emperor place these four stones in his crown?"

"Surely!" said Merlin. "And he will send the crown with the stones to discover what these prophecies are about. The stones should be kept, for they will cause great miracles throughout the country."

11: How a Large Part of India Will Melt

"Know also that on that day much of India will melt."

"Tell me Merlin, God bless you," Master Antoine said. "Does this not make you weep?"

"Of course," said Merlin. "It would kill any man in the world [with sorrow], and every one ought to mourn that harm, when something so beautiful must be brought down by the command of so vile a man as he shall be, of whom I see this is written.[60] And the Good Mariners will triumph in battle by their courage and through the prayers of the emperor."

12: Of the Evil Lady of Falone

"I will tell you," Merlin said, "how I came to a city on the Grecian Sea, which was called Falone. Many people lived in a castle near this city. The Lady of Falone, who lived there also, had a neighbour

---

59. Messina was a major city of Sicily, then ruled by Frederick II.
60. We assume this is a reference to the actions of the Antichrist, but the text is unclear.

with whom she waged war over both land and sea. Because of this there was such a famine that her enemies even ate their dogs and were so weak that they could not beg. They spied and gave information to a man named Cymphones,[61] asking him to come and take the castle in such a way that they would not be harmed. And Cymphones came and took the castle and freed the men that were within. But when they went to the city of Falone, the Lady said they were traitors and ordered that they be hanged."

13: Of the Macedonian Wolf and Other Things

"Master Antoine," said Merlin, "write down that towards Macedonia there will come a wolf who will enslave all the beasts in the country."

"When will that be?" asked Master Antoine.

"It will be," said Merlin. Then he spoke more of goods that were deposited in Sinople[62] and of a man who would dig a cave and find quantities of silver.[63]

14: Of Muhammed Who Built a City in Three Days

"Write down that Muhammed built a city in three days and that it will be destroyed in one day."[64]

15: Of the Good Mariners

"See that you put in writing," said Merlin to Master Antoine, "that honour shall belong to the Good Mariners, who shall settle on a great island in the sea and shall improve their lives above all other peoples of the world. And when you have put this in writing,"

---

61. Another unknown character.
62. The Bulgarian city of Plovdin was called Sinople by the Crusaders of the Fourth Crusade.
63. This is probably a reference to the story of Merlin's laughter. See commentary for more on this.
64. Very typical of the kind of Crusading fervour that gripped the West at the time the *Prophecies* were originally composed.

Merlin said, "write of he who is the last governor, and of the fight against the enemy upon the sea. From the Good Mariners a new governor will be born."[65]

16: Of People Who Go on a Pilgrimage to the Sea with the Emperor of Rome

What am I telling you? When Merlin and Master Antoine met in the room, Merlin spoke and said: "Master Antoine, write down, that of all the people who shall be on pilgrimage with the emperor upon the sea, they shall not return from it."

"How will that be?"

"Write down," said Merlin, "that they will not return. However, the people will avenge them so that their death will not be in vain."[66]

17: Of Merlin Alerting Master Antoine to the Arrival of the Three Ministers

This part of the story says that Merlin sent word to Master Antoine that three wise men were coming to see him. He said: "Make haste to the docks. There will be three of the wisest men there. As soon as you see them, tell them that I will speak about perfecting the laws of Holy Church."

As for Master Antoine, he obeyed Merlin, whose wishes agreed with the wishes of the whole clergy of Wales, and rode to the port. And when three ministers [almost certainly churchmen or cardinals] came ashore they saw Master Antoine. And these clerics [who included Bishop Tholomer, Bertous of Germany, and one named Phellis] said they would not leave until they were sure of Merlin's allegiance. Then Bishop Tholomer and Bertous, after being greeted, said: "Master Antoine, tell us how it is that you and your clergy are against us?"

---

65. Possible reference to the doge of Venice, but the word is *governor*.
66. This probably refers to a Crusade led by Frederick II, or it could have to do with the Crusaders, who invariably went to the Holy Land via Venice.

"Sir," said Master Antoine, "I have never heard that said before. Merlin told me that you are Bertous, born in Germany and therefore called Bertous of Germany, and he told me that you will seek him out so that you may discuss the functioning of the laws of the Holy Church."

"God help us!" said Phellis to Master Antoine. "He guaranteed it before our arrival!"

Then they made the sign of holy faith to their leader, and mounted their horses, and set themselves in motion, and rode back until they came into Wales and went separately to the inn [where they were to stay].

18: Of the Lady Who Came to Antoine's Room

Now the story says that Master Antoine and Merlin were in the room where they were used to be and that a young lady of high quality came to the door. And you should know that Merlin had taught her a great deal about the dark arts and enchantment [in the past]. She and several other damsels came from Léonois.[67] They asked about Merlin, and said he was fickle, and that he had told both her and the other damsels that they could learn magic in exchange for their virginity.

Then Merlin said to Master Antoine: "This lady will die after she has enchanted King Meliadus of Léonois." Then he said: "Sometimes I do not know the difference between the White and Black Serpents.[68] I will never learn unless I understand the innocence she possesses. So I will be careful not to talk to fleas, or to hold a meeting, or to talk to others. Master Antoine, seal your mouth, [for I will be secret]."

This came about after Merlin had already deflowered the lady.

---

67. Lionesse, the drowned land off Land's End in Cornwall, once ruled over by the family of Sir Tristan of Lionesse.
68. The Black Serpent is probably a reference to Mordred, King Arthur's incestuous child.

19: Merlin Speaks Regarding the Lady of the Lake

"Tell me, Merlin, God bless you," said Master Antoine. "Which of the ladies you have known in the world do you think the wisest?"

"Put it in writing," said Merlin to Master Antoine, "that all the glory of the world should be hers, for she is the wisest, and all the beauty of the world lives in her. She is called the Lady of the Lake. [. . .] I am fearful of the White Serpent I just mentioned. It is taking my life."

"My God!" said Antoine. "Is this true?"

"Close your mouth!" said Merlin. "I believe this mixture of fire and lust will bring me to my death. The beauty of the Lady of the Lake borders on Paradise. And I was in her company at night in the forest of Avrences."[69]

20: Of the Lady of the Lake and of Lusente

"Now look what you write down," said Merlin to Master Antoine. "The Lady of the Lake will be loved by all people more than anyone else in the world, for she has a good reputation. She will be spoken of as Lusente[70] used to be by Virgil, the Swan of Mantua, who was born about October 15, 70 BC. He was a Latin poet of the end of the Roman Republic and the beginning of the reign of Emperor Augustus. This lady often spoke to Virgil.

"Listen carefully, Master Antoine: I am going to tell you about my disappearance in the forest of Avrences. This disappearance will be caused by the Lady of the Lake. I know it is going to happen, but I cannot escape it."

21: How Merlin Went to the Forest of Avrences

In this part, Merlin speaks of events that happened after Master Antoine was consecrated as a bishop. Merlin came to Master Antoine

---

69. In Manche, a département in Normandy, Northwest France, near Brittany.

70. An unknown lady, possibly a punning reference to a phrase used by Virgil in the *Aeneid* to describe the dawn.

and said: "Bishop, the feast of Saint Michael is approaching. God asks me to go to the forest of Avrences where the Lady [of the Lake] will be. I have one task to accomplish there. Bishop Antoine, after my death I will prophesy more than before it. There will be two kingly knights in this century. There will come to the forest a knight-king, who will be crowned in Aubiron.[71] He will place himself in the forest of Avrences and will not ride far until he has news of the month of my death. God bless you, Antoine, I cannot escape my fate."

22: How Merlin Bade Master Antoine Farewell and Entered the Forest of Avrences Where the Lady of the Lake Was

Merlin got on his knees before Bishop Antoine, who gave him his blessing and ordered him not to seek fame but to remain humble. Merlin stood again and left the city of Palagre[72] and walked to the forest of Avrences.

He wandered for many days but came at last to the entrance of the forest. It took a very long time for the Lady of the Lake to come that way, but great was the joy of their meeting. Merlin made a meal, and the Lady, needing nothing else, feasted with him as if he were a new knight.

Then with great joy they went into the woods. Merlin loved the Lady of the Lake with all his heart, but the Lady of the Lake hated him intensely.

23: How Merlin and the Lady of the Lake Got to the House Where Merlin Felt at Home

They wandered through the forest of Avrences until they came to the entrance of a cave and to the tomb over which the Lady of the

---

71. Aubiron (Oberan) was first mentioned in the *Romance of Huon of Bordeaux*. It is probably the same place as referred to by Merlin later in sections 75–76

72. In Middle Norman French, *pellagra du mal* meant "high seas" or "open water," but this may well be a reference to an unknown city.

Lake had so often prayed. And know this, ladies and gentlemen, that the place was so hidden that if all the knights of the world had set out to find it, they would never have succeeded. Merlin spoke to the Lady, saying: "Lady, this place shall never be found, and know that the Kings of Aubiron shall buy this grove just to see my tomb, but it shall be in vain."

"You will find me, however distant," said the Lady.

Know that the night came and the Lady of the Lake slept but little. She was disappointed that Merlin had so many stones that glowed so much the night was as bright as day.[73]

"Merlin," said the Lady. "If the anger of the Gods fall upon you, will there be a knight in Little Britain who can look after me?"

"No one can save you here," said Merlin.

Then they came to a house and entered it, where they found all the comforts they needed for a great lady and a rich man.[74]

"Answer me, Merlin," said the Lady of the Lake. "Will these stones ever be removed from here?"

"Lady," said Merlin. "No, because I do not want you to leave."

She swore then that she would not leave. "I swear I will remain just like a mother who gave birth to a child in bitter labour."

24: How Merlin Lived with the Lady of the Lake for Fifteen Months

No one asks me how long the Lady of the Lake was with Merlin, but I would say it was fifteen months, and every month Merlin sent a message to Master Antoine, who was by then Bishop of Wales. And it would have been even longer they were together if it had not been for Morgain, who had gone into the woods in search of Merlin and often approached the cave where he and the Lady of the Lake were.

The Lady doubted she could hold Merlin securely. Many dam-

---

[73]. Probable reference to the magical stones from the crown of the King of Orbance; compare also to the flying stone.

[74]. Possibly a reference to the house built by Merlin himself or by his sister, Ganeida (see commentary).

sels had learned magic from Merlin. To do so, they had to sleep with him. The Lady thought that no other damsel would suffer this fate because she believed Merlin slept with her alone.

25: Of the Lady of the Lake, Who Fooled Merlin While She Slept with Him

The next day a knight who served the Lady of the Lake was attacked by a knight who served the Lady Morgain. Merlin heard of this and quickly came to the Lady of the Lake. When he arrived, she told Merlin what had happened and begged him not to lie naked with her again.

Merlin replied: "Forgive me, White Serpent, I shall never speak of it."

He wanted the Lady of the Lake carnally, but as soon as he got into bed with her, she cast the spirit of her soul upon him, so that he went to sleep until daylight. And when the day came, she awakened him and deceived him, as she often did.

How could it be that Merlin, who was so wise, was so easily fooled? I think you know, gentlemen and knights. If you have ever met a woman, be it a lady or a damsel, all you see is how good she looks! I see you agree to love every young lady. No one can resist a woman's attraction. The Lady of the Lake always tried to disappoint Merlin, for she hated him with a deadly hatred, while he loved her with all his heart.[75]

She wanted to hide him in such a place that he would never be seen again. Meanwhile, Merlin strove to be with her. He taught her to anoint herself with herbs, and other things with which to bathe her body and wash her limbs so that she might live until the day the world ends! But her flesh was so polluted by this, she washed until she was white again.

He taught her everything he knew about the arts of black magic and all the other arts and sciences, so subtly that in the end he knew

---

75. A very typical view of churchmen and others throughout the Middle Ages.

no more than she. But the Lady of the Lake made him believe he knew better. He taught her to know the virtues of gems and herbs and the power of words, so subtly that she wonderfully united all three subtleties.

Then one day she said: "Merlin, you say that you only seek to sleep with such a beautiful lady as me, then you sleep with other ladies and girls and that sickens me."

Merlin swore to God that he would not touch anyone but her alone, but that same week he broke his promise. What shall I tell you? Merlin stayed with the Lady of the Lake for about fifteen whole months.

26: Of the Lady of the Lake, Who Decided to Cheat on Merlin

The Lady of the Lake determined to deceive him but never spoke of it. In her heart she knew she would get no help. Who would suggest that Merlin had all his ladies illegally? I would say no, because they got magic in exchange for their flesh.

The Lady of the Lake prepared to complete her plan and asked Merlin if he was going to leave, to which he replied that he was not. "No," he said to the Lady, "I am so tied to you that there can be no other. I am here to be with you throughout this age. In time my bones will be laid here, but if you die also, I pray that our bones will be united and our souls meet again."

27: How Merlin Went with the Lady of the Lake to the Tomb in the Rock

"Lady," said Merlin, "you know verily that I shall soon be buried."

"My God," said the Lady of the Lake. "What do you mean?"

"It will be as I tell you," said Merlin.

"Since you must be buried before me," said the Lady of the Lake, "I beg you to lie here."

When Merlin saw what he would come to in such a place, he knew there was no way in the world he could escape.

"Merlin," said the Lady of the Lake. "Do you think I am the White Serpent you have often prophesied—she who comes from Little Brittany and mingles with the demi-man[76] in the forest of Avrences?"

And Merlin said it was so.

28: Of Merlin Lying in the Tomb, He Died More Each Day

Merlin went into the tomb and lay down in it, then spoke and said: "Lady, take care of yourself!"

And when the Lady of the Lake saw that he was in the tomb, she pulled down the lid and made it unbreakable. Merlin knew no human could get out, not even he.

"Merlin," said the Lady of the Lake, "you are going to say that your prophecies are false, but they are real. You are going to die in here. This is what you yourself prophesied. This White Serpent takes revenge on you for the foul game you played with me. Remember the first lesson you gave me on the art of magic?"

"Yes," said Merlin. "It was to put a man to sleep and wake him up whenever you want."

"You showed this to me and then took my virginity. I hate you intensely for this. The second lesson was to know how to lock a place so no one can open it. Merlin," said the Lady of the Lake, "I will kill you and then awaken you. This is my revenge. You knew I was still a virgin, yet you put me to sleep and overpowered me."

"I beg you now," said Merlin to the Lady of the Lake, "go to Master Antoine, the Bishop of Wales, and tell him he should write down that I am dead and ruled by my senses. I am slain by my own lust."

"Merlin," said the Lady of the Lake, "because it is your wish [I will do so]. But only if you tell me, if you know how long you can keep your spirit in your body."

---

76. Merlin himself—half demon, half man.

29: Of Merlin's Ghost,
Who Will Speak to All Who Come to His Tomb

"Madam," said Merlin, "my body will be rotten in a month, but my spirit will continue to speak."

"Tell me," asked the Lady of the Lake. "How many knights shall I know in my life?"

"Lady," said Merlin, "you will see only one knight until you die, and he will be coupled with you. This knight will please you very much and have many adventures."[77]

30: Of the Departure of the Lady of the Lake

What shall I tell you? The Lady of the Lake asked Merlin where her chariot was, and he told her.

"Merlin," said Lady of the Lake, "I am indeed the White Serpent who came from Little Brittany and met the demi-man in the wood of Avrences."

Then the White Serpent, not at all ashamed of her conduct, departed from the wood and set out on the path that would lead her to Vincestre.[78] She rode so far that she came to the port where she found a ship that would take her to Wales. There she met with Master Antoine, who was bitter, for he knew that the prophecy of Merlin's death had been fulfilled. And the Lady of the Lake told everything as we have told it here. [Then she departed again in the ship.]

The sailors unfurled the sails, and the ship arrived at a port within three days. The Lady of the Lake gave ten pieces of silver to the sailors, then disembarked and went ashore and lay in the grass for a time. Then she arose and wandered for many days before she came home to the Lake, where she found many children, including

---

77. This will refer either to Meliadus, who is the Lady of the Lake's lover in our text, or to Accolon of Gaul, who has the same role in other Arthurian texts.
78. Probably Winchester, in Hampshire, long famed as the original site of Camelot.

the children of King Ban of Benoic and his nephews.[79] The Lady of the Lake was very happy. She embraced everyone and kissed them a thousand times. They made a great noise when they celebrated her homecoming.

Thus was Merlin's own prophecy of his death fulfilled.

31: Of Merlin Speaking to Meliadus, Friend of the Lady of the Lake

Now the story tells that Meliadus,[80] who was a friend to the Lady of the Lake, came to the tomb where Merlin lay. And Meliadus saw the Lady through the spirit of Merlin. He felt that his love for her was very strong and that her love for him might be even stronger. And Merlin said to Meliadus: "You shall love her with all your soul until death shall part you."

32: Of Merlin Telling How His Father Killed His Mother

Now tell the stories and now keep the truth. Let the testimony of Merlin live, that speaks of his friendship with Meliadus. They were both at the rock where Merlin was trapped in the tomb.

"Meliadus," said Merlin, " I am the son of a demon. I am half human. My father was a demon who impregnated an innocent virgin. After I came into the world, and my mother baptized me, my father killed her in revenge."

33: Of Tristan, the Brother of Meliadus

Merlin then testified that Meliadus was left alone after his father's death and that Tristan was his brother. "Know that there will still be issues between you and him, but if he knows that you are his brother, he will be as happy as anyone who discovers blood relations."

---

79. These were Lancelot, Bors, and Lional, who were all fostered by the Lady of the Lake.
80. So we meet the next of Merlin's scribes; this time a knight rather than a clerk.

Then Merlin said to Meliadus: "Tell me how much money must go to Cornwall so that your brother Tristan will not be killed. I see that you have written on your parchment that you are indebted to King Ban of Benoic. Through him a great company of knights will come from across this sea and burn all of Cornwall to ashes. Your brother will be brave, and King Arthur will take revenge."

34: How Meliadus Went to Church and Found Letters Testifying to What Merlin Had Said to Him

"Ha!" said Meliadus. [And Merlin replied,] "Your name is the same as your father, King Meliadus of Léonois. Your mother was the queen of Escoce.[81] Go to the church and find the evidence."

Meliadus went to the church and found proofs written on parchment.

35: How Meliadus Left Merlin and Came to Wales

With Merlin's permission Meliadus departed from the tomb and travelled to Wales. He visited Antoine, the Wise Clerk of Wales,[82] who received him with joy, and Meliadus told what he had heard. Raymon put everything in writing, and on the third day Meliadus mounted his horse. He rode out in the morning as God had commanded him. He rode day and night and finally arrived at the court of King Arthur, where he was received with joy, for everyone knew him well, and when the queen was sure that he was a friend of the Lady of the Lake, who alone was with Merlin, she greeted him with as much joy as if he were her own brother. She asked him about Merlin's soul, and Meliadus told her much of what Merlin had said, and about an evil lord who would come to the court of Arthur, and of Slatix and the Pagans.[83]

---

81. An early name for Scotland.
82. Another scribe of Merlin's prophecies. He and Meliadus seem to share the work.
83. Another reference to an unknown character.

36: How Meliadus Departed from King Arthur's Palace and Met the Lady of the Lake

What shall I say? Fifteen whole days passed, full of joy and celebration, and after that rejoicing Meliadus departed, leaving behind King Arthur and Queen Guinevere and the people of his court. He rode as long as he could to the sea where he found a ship equipped to sail away.

He embarked, and the sailors raised their sails to the wind and set out on the high seas. The wind was good and strong. As a result, they crossed the sea in two and a half days. When they arrived at the land, Meliadus mounted a horse and rode until he came to Lake Dyane.[84]

He knew the way very well. He rode the pathways and kept his course. He drove onwards so long that he came to a hostel where the Lady of the Lake received him joyfully. [. . .]

And Meliadus told her how Merlin had told him many times that women make men worse, and how he had asked him how this might be, and that Merlin whimsically replied that all the women of the world have the subtlety of teasing men, just as she teased him. All the men in the world are plagued by this. But women are not as wise as men, and men notice this, so that it becomes hard for the women.

Then the Lady of the Lake began to laugh and said: "Yes indeed. I will not be entertained for long if we do not find a better feast here than anywhere else."

"According to Merlin," said Meliadus.

Then the Lady of the Lake kissed him and said: "Beautiful, kind friend, will you ask Merlin about my three children: Lancelot, Lionel, and Bors?"[85]

---

84. Possibly a corrupt form of the Goddess Diana. The lake bearing her name is recorded in the Middle English *Prose Merlin* (see commentary).
85. Not her actual children but the sons of kings whom she had rescued.

37: Of a Knight from the Land of the Indies Who Came before the Chaplain

Meanwhile, the Chaplain of Wales [whose name was Raymon][86] looked into the *Book of Prophecies*, and at this time a knight from India arrived. "Sire," he said, "God bless you!"

The Chaplin saluted back and said: "What do you want?"

The knight replied: "Sire, I am from India. I have seen many great wonders of the world in that country. There is a sea in that land so high no one can conquer it. There was a city that was threatened by Pagans in this Christian land. Merlin told them that he had driven all the heathens out of the city and that this sea rises no more."

"God help us," said the Chaplain. "Is Merlin [known] in India?"

"Absolutely!" said the knight.

Then the Chaplain gave fifteen clerks a lot [of money] and prayed that they put everything they could find from Merlin in writing in a great book. The next day the fifteen clerks departed and went their way, and the Chaplain remained. He was very pleased with the great treasure of the *Prophecies of Merlin*, which he loved to read.

What shall I tell you? The Chaplain went everywhere and gathered clerks who liked to write, and he gave them money for parchment, and they made a great book. And in that great book were recorded stories that were brought hither. Gentlemen, I want you to know that four hundred clerks were sent around the world without assistants.

The Chaplain of Wales thought he did well to take this work very seriously, and you must know that he certainly would not have spent a penny on any work other than that he commissioned.

So, as I tell you, the strange wonders of Merlin were collected and put in writing in a book, including the prophecies, the adventures of the knights that took place in the Holy Land, the hard and

---

86. Later to be yet another scribe.

bitter battles fought in the world in the quest for the Holy Grail, and the gatherings of the knights and the battles—all were put on parchment and collected in a great book.

38: Of the Woman Who Did Evil to Her Husband

Now the account testifies that the Chaplain of Wales [. . .] looked at the things the Wise Clerk had written in Merlin's service. He looked at the book Blaise, the master of Merlin, had given to Merlin's mother, and he wrote down the prophecies he found there. And he learned that when the mother of Merlin was delivered from evil, she took her child and put her breast in his mouth and gave him milk. And when she had said a prayer, she went to the convent where there were many nuns. At that time there was a lady in a solitary cell who had done bad deeds and let her body be used by both her husband and a servant. After hearing Merlin's stories, she was released by the judge of Norbellande.[87]

39: How the Lady Rambarge Pretended to Feed Merlin but Wanted to Kill Him

What would I tell you? This lady's name was Rambarge, and she was dressed very neatly and very nicely. But she wanted to kill Merlin. She went to the convent and said to the abbess who was with her: "Lady, it is not proper that a male child should be fed in this holy place." The woman said to the abbess: "For love of you I will let him eat, give milk to him, and let him defecate."

"Mercy, lady," answered the abbess. "Take him and feed him as you dictate."

Then Merlin said: "Lady, you take me to feed me, but rest assured that you or I will die."

"Be silent, little child, for none of us will die from it."

Then Merlin started laughing. The lady ordered her maids to take the child and bring it to her house. They did what they had to

---

87. Norbellande, probably Northumberland.

do, and then the lady said good-bye to the abbess and the other ladies and went to her house. Then came her husband, and he was very pleased with the coming of Merlin, and said: "Lady, take care that you feed the little child well, for he has not come to this world at this time without great wonder and without great commission."

40: How the Lady Rambarge Tried to Strangle Merlin

"Sire," said the lady, "I will give him enough to eat."

And Merlin spoke up and said: "Know, my lord knight, that my coming shall harm either me or your wife."

"Please not!" replied the knight, whose name was Naymar.

The statement was supported by one of his servants—he who slept with the lady.

And when the lady heard these words, she got up from her husband and went straight to the cradle where Merlin lay and took him in her hands to strangle him, but the knight was very careful and had put a greyhound on guard. However, the greyhound was asleep, and she grabbed it and strangled it with a chain. Then she went back to bed with her husband. However, the next day when the sun rose, the knight saw that his greyhound was dead and Merlin was not. He was sad and amazed and exclaimed: "Now I have lost my beloved dog!"

41: Of Merlin's Message to Naymar

Then Naymar heard the words of Merlin: "Sir," said Merlin, "know that your enemy has slain your friend. Wicked will be your enemy when you get to his place. He will totally hate you if you see him or listen to him. He will shame you, Naymar, in turn, if you are not careful."

"God help me," said Naymar. "Who is my enemy in this hostel?"

The knight was very angry about the loss of his dog. When he found his wife again by the cradle with her hands around Merlin's neck, he pressed her down and laid her on her back and said: 'Wicked thing, what are you doing?'

She replied: "I do not know where I am, or what I am doing."

Then he said: "You did not strangle him?"

And Merlin said: "You will not know prosperity if you do not retaliate."

42: Concerning the Lady of the Lake, Who Sent a Reply to the Queen about a Dream She Had Dreamed

Here is the story of how one of Queen Guinevere's damsels visited the Lady of the Lake. When the damsel saw the Lady, she knew her, for she had already seen her several times in Little Britain. She knelt before the Lady and showed her a letter that the queen had sent her. The Lady took this and broke the seal and began to read what was written within.

"Greetings, Lady of the Lake. Queen Guinevere greets you as the wisest lady in the world. I beg you by all means that you send a letter stating where you have hidden Merlin the sage. I need him to interpret a dream."

In this letter everything was written that the queen had dreamed. The Lady of the Lake thought for a while, and then said: "Beautiful maiden, God save your lady and her honour. Tell her from me that Merlin has returned to the forest of Avrences, and as for the dream she dreamed, tell her she should not be surprised in any way by the world, which knows the truth. And whatever happens, know that she will be feared by all."

"Ah, Lady of the Lake," said the damsel, "I beseech you to work with us on behalf of my lady, Queen Guinevere, and that everything you have to say should be sent through your letters."

Then the Lady's chaplain came and said that Merlin had told him how a knight from the Caledonian royal line would leave Benoic and go to the kingdom of Logres, and that the Crowned Serpent would leave the kingdom of Logres. And also that the Lion that comes from Benoic would fly over the sea and rule the kingdom that once belonged to King Evalac.[88]

---

88. This is all about Lancelot, whose home is at Benoic and whose (*cont. on p. 86*)

43: Concerning the Dream That the Queen Dreamed

"Lady of the Lake," asked the damsel, "tell me, if God is with you, if you know who the knight is that is looking for Merlin, and whether he will find him or not. It seems he wishes to search forever."

"He will not find it," said the Lady. "Nor will he see it." [But she did not say who the knight was.][89]

"Lady," said the damsel, "Queen Guinevere sends you the content of her dream, which she dreamed the first night she lay in King Arthur's bed. And if you want me to tell you what happened—my lady the queen, after being carnal with King Arthur, saw a serpent coming out of his belly, and the serpent wanted to bite him.[90] And afterwards the king did not speak to her of this, at which she was dismayed."

"Damsel," said the Lady of the Lake, "such dreams are always dreadful to hear. But many people know that I have suffered great harm from the fact that Merlin is lost, and that all the learning that came from him is also lost. So tell your lady that I do not know how to interpret her dream at this time. Yet I believe that I will be able to speak the truth one day, and then I will know what to tell you or the queen myself."

Then the Lady of the Lake began to laugh loudly, and the damsel asked why she was laughing. She told her that she laughed at the Queen of Logres,[91] who will be fearful of one knight, Galeholt, the half giant, who will conquer all.[92]

(*cont. from p. 85*) heraldic device is a lion. He is also "of the Caledonian line" and eventually rules over the kingdom of Evalac. We assume the Crowned Serpent, who is referenced throughout these texts, is Morgain le Fay—though we should not forget that the Lady of the Lake is referred to as the White Serpent by Merlin himself.
89. Presumably Percival.
90. This is probably a reference to Arthur's incestuous son, Mordred.
91. This seems to refer to Morgain despite the fact that Guinevere is the Queen of Logres—the old name for Arthurian Britain.
92. Galeholt, or Galehaut the Haut Prince, is a companion to Lancelot who dies by his own hand when the latter fails to acknowledge his love. Some of his adventures are told within the 1303 text of the *Prophecies*.

44: Concerning the Stone the Lady of the Lake Gave to the Queen

The damsel said: "Lady of the Lake, the queen beseeches you that, however much she may be advised by you, Morgain the Unfaithful should have nothing to do with any of this."

Then the Lady of the Lake opened her dress, exposing her breast, and showed a most virtuous gem that she wore and said: "Maiden, take this, and tell the queen from me that she should hold it. And know truly that as long as she has it in her possession, or has it in her mind, Morgain will have no power to harm her."

The damsel took the virtuous stone in her hand and thanked the Lady of the Lake for receiving her so well. Then the damsel went to an inn for four days, where she was well served and provided with all the things she needed.

And on the fifth day she bade farewell to the Lady of the Lake, and went from the inn to the road, where she mounted her horse. The damsel rode so swiftly that she soon reached the sea where she immediately found a suitable ship to cross to Vincestre,[93] which took her back to Little Britain.

45: How the Queen's Damsel Asked Sebile the Sorceress to Explain Her Mistress's Dream

Samide[94] the damsel went in search of the other damsels of the world who had learned magic from Merlin. She came upon Sebile the Sorceress, who was one of these, and asked on behalf of the queen to interpret her dream. Sebile knew the queen was afraid of Morgain [. . .] and sent words of comfort, telling her that a certain knight would challenge Morgain and would cause her great fear.

The dream had frightened the queen so much that she had turned pale. And when Samide asked what worried her, the queen

---

93. Probably Winchester.
94. We assume this is the same damsel, though she is not named in the previous section.

said: "I believe I dreamed of putting myself to death, or that the serpent wanted to destroy my marriage."

"God help you!" said Samide "May your dream be interpreted in such a way that you are no longer afraid but are encouraged by it."

"Samide," said the queen, "what explanation was sent by Sebile the Sorceress?"

"Lady, she says it is about Morgain."

Samide then gave the letters from the Lady of the Lake to the queen and said: "Madam, read what the Lady of the Lake sends you."

The queen broke the seal and began to read the letters, comparing them with her dream. As she read them, her anger and fear began to subside, and her color returned to normal. What shall I tell you? All the color that was lost returned to her face, and she laughed and said: "Sebile has told me what is in my dream."

The queen said that through her lady, Samide, she now knew the interpretation of her dream, which Sebile the Sorceress had sent to her, [along with the letters from the Lady of the Lake].

The king saw that all the color had returned to her face, and the queen said: "I know it is about Morgain. She is the serpent that crawled out of your belly in my dream and wanted to bite you."

46: Prophecies Found by a Knight on a Stone Written by Merlin

The next day, the Wise Clerk Antoine asked Meliadus to go to the rock where Merlin was trapped, as had been foretold. Meliadus set out, and the Wise Cleric beseeched God to keep him safe. Meliadus wandered for days through the forest of Avrences until he came close to the rock beneath which Merlin lay.

He then encountered a knight whose arm had been cut off. Meliadus saluted him and said: "Knight, if you do not want to die, do not ride any further." Another knight came with a stone he had brought down from the mountain, which he showed to Meliadus. It was full of inscriptions.

47: Meliadus Was So Serious That He Swore to Kill Any Knight Who Passed through the Forest

"My God," said the knight whose arm was cut off. "Since you are the one who saved me, I will turn and distract the knight so that he will not know of your arrival in this place." But the knight had already arrived with the stone. The one-armed knight told him what Meliadus had said.

48: Of the Letters Merlin Carved in the Stone

Meliadus looked at the rock where Merlin had carved the inscriptions. He had ink and parchment with him and wrote down the inscriptions. Then he made his way to the entrance of the tomb, which he knew very well. And when he came there, he cried out, and Merlin answered and said: "Meliadus, I know you have received the letters from the Round Stone, which the knight found in the burial place of King Hugon Sachies,[95] [who lived very long ago] and which I myself cut."

49: The Importance of the Letters on the Stone

"The first testimony is a blessing from Jesu Christ, who is Lord of all things. And the second is about the things He does that He wishes everyone to have their share of. And the third testimony speaks of a merchant who managed his affairs without involving others and collects sulphur for the fires of Hell."

Meliadus relayed the importance of the letters to the knight. He wrote everything down and gave him the manuscript. The knight began to read. And when the knight saw that the work was reverential, he said that he would have no more bad habits for the rest of his life and that he would get rid of those he had now. The knight then rode off to his court and with him the knight whose arm was cut off. They rode until they came to Saufine. There the

---

95. An unknown character only mentioned in this text. It literally means Hugo the Wise.

knight gave [. . .] half his wealth to the knight whose arm was cut off.

Now Meliadus returned to the rock and spoke to Merlin, who said: "Meliadus, I see that you will go to King Arthur's court before you cross the sea to Wales."

50: Of Meliadus's Meeting with the Wise Clerk and His Departing from King Arthur's Palace

With Merlin's permission, Meliadus went first straight to Antoine, the Wise Clerk of Wales, who received him with esteem. From that day to the next and to the third, Meliadus told him all that he had experienced and what the cleric had missed. On the quarter of the third day, Meliadeus departed and went to do what God had commanded him. So much did Meliadus ride, by day and by night, that he soon came to the court of King Arthur, where he was lovingly received. The Wise Clerk studied every detail of the writings again.

51: How Meliadus Was at Merlin's Tomb, and of the King's Son, and of Tristan

Meliadus, the friend of the Lady of the Lake, went to the tomb where Merlin was imprisoned. The spirit of Merlin spoke. "Meliadus, collect all that you hear in this place and that is written on the tomb and take it to Master Antoine, who is now a Bishop of Wales."

Then said Merlin: "I see you leaving here, and it is for the king's son's need that you do this. His name is Tristan, and he will eventually be important at King Arthur's court. He has come to realize that he must be a knight and knows that his wanderings are important to the adventures of Greater Britain. He will eventually transform part of the dangerous adventures, though the sin of lust will take root in him.[96]

"I still wish you to know that it is by the acceptance of lust that the court of King Arthur will be destroyed, though the Table

---

[96]. This presumably refers to Tristan's desire for Queen Yseut, King Marc's wife.

will be replenished despite your brother's poison. I hope you know that Tristan will come into contact with the King of Longes and will experience many bad practices and many dangerous adventures where good knights have failed.

"The son of the king will not be known until his chivalry is spread throughout the world. From then on, when he has fought the most bitter battle for the proudest castle, his name will spread abroad. In many places his name will be feared for years."

52: Of an Angel Who Will Take Water from a Fountain and Extinguish a Fire at the Castle of Morgain

At this time knights in all parts of England collected old books to enable King Henry to see the miracles that might be written therein. If anyone wanted to meet the good king and searched all the forests, he would find [him in] the residence that formerly made King Uterpendragon [Uther Pendragon] proud and that would be completed after his death by his son King Arthur.

[Merlin said that] "Once again the fountain that belonged to Constans, the father of King Uterpendragon, will be seen. A lion will be seen to enter, that will emerge as a man. A miracle will be seen here, when a knight of the family of Galehas, who is the mighty King of Wales, appears at the fountain, and an angel will be seen coming from Heaven that will place a container by this fountain. The castle that once belonged to Morgain will be guarded because her fame has diminished. Meanwhile, the castle will not be forgotten. Know that the angel will be willing to go through dry land to tell the knight he is alive and will follow him to the castle. Angels will intervene to extinguish the fire that evening, and because the angel is sacred, he will take that knight, who will be called Synaublans, and lead him into the castle, where he will see the earth and the abyss openly. Again, tell Master Antoine that all men, and all distinguished people who come from the sea, will see this miracle. And tell him that I will win hearts in Gaul, and others will show them miracles, and they will see the depths [of the earth] filled with sulfur."

53: How There Will Be Much Rain in Brittany

Master Antoine, Bishop of Wales, wrote down everything he knew from Merlin's mouth, whether it had been written before or not. In the manuscript Meliadus presented to him, he found that Merlin had said that there would be a rain in Brittany that would destroy all wheat, and the famine would be so merciless and so severe that many thousands of men and women would starve.

Then [Merlin said that] a champion would go to an island in the sea where there were Pagans. He would subdue it and see that its people were baptized. And from this place they would bring food and flesh to England, where currently people have to beg. "And if you want to know what [the champion] is called, I will tell you it is Sadaine."

Seeing that his arts did not match Merlin's qualities, Antoine began to study, so that he could share his [wisdom and skill] and understand the heavenly things that formed the firmament, the moon, the sun, and the stars and the place where it was changed. From the moment of his awakening, Merlin's prophecies were true, for he knew the choices that would be made in the future, as the Holy Spirit revealed in the firmament.

54: How King Henry and One Hundred and Fifty Knights Will Go to the Forest of Avrences

"I see that you still write everything down, Master Antoine," said Merlin. "Now write of King Henry,[97] who will take himself into the forest of Avrences, with one hundred and fifty knights. They will be searching for my tomb but will be afraid to find it. They will gather before the roaring mountain, but they will not find the entrance to the rock.

"In front of the mountain, the king will make a tower. The book that Blaise wrote about my science testifies that I spoke it. And know that King Henry will create a serpent that, when the Dragons

---

[97]. Impossible to say with any certainty which King Henry this is.

of Babylon begin to hunt, will cross the land, and their eyes will grow great with fear, and they will fly to the deserts of Babylon.

"King Henry, who wants to discover the entrance to the mountain, knows that, when he is before the mountain that roars, he will be buried. Know that he will be destroyed. He will never return to his court."[98]

55: On the Death of Tristan and How Meliadus Cannot Harm the One Who Killed Him

"Now write on, Meliadus," said Merlin's spirit. "Your brother Tristan will be slain by the meanest and most disloyal king there is."[99]

"Tell me, Merlin," asked Meliadus. "If I set out to find the one who killed my brother Tristan, am I harming him in any way in the world?"

"Certainly not," said Merlin. "He must have no future, as I tell you, and know that I cannot be distracted by anyone. Know also that Tristan's death will make you very sad."

What shall I tell you? Meliadus had ink and parchment, on which he wrote down all that Merlin told him, as he also wrote all that he found written on the stones that were around the rock. Then he handed over the parchment at the port of Wales to Master Antoine, the wise Bishop.

56: Of Raymon the Wise Clerk of Wales

After a long life dedicated to God, Maistre Antoine decided to retire and become a hermit. He passed on the task of compiling the prophecies he had received from Tholomer to a Wise Clerk of Wales by the name of Raymon.

Meliadus, meanwhile, constantly travelled back and forth with ink and parchment between the cave where Merlin was trapped and the Wise Clerk's workshop. Meliadus, [by this time], was the lover of the Lady of the Lake. A prophecy revealed his identity,

---
98. The end of this story continues in section 54.
99. King Marc.

of which he knew nothing. He was the son of the Queen of Scots and King Meliadus de Léonois, abandoned at birth by his mother, exposed in a small craft at sea, and rescued by the mother of the Lady of the Lake, who raised him in secret.

Meliadus brought the prophecies he had heard directly from the mouth of Merlin to Raymon. He also copied the inscriptions scattered around the tomb. Raymon, who was an adherent of the occult arts, tried to verify Merlin's prophecies using magic and was very eager to visit Merlin's tomb. On a clear night with an exuberant, starry sky, he cast his spells to test the truth of the prophecies. The following night, Antoine's ghost appeared in a dream to confront him about his pride. He invited him to confess as soon as possible:

"You came here to talk to Merlin. You want to be serious, but you are like a sheep. You have no knowledge of the Mysteries of Jonah[100] that were written down. Go to confession as soon as possible, for you have no real faith in the Lord God."

Meanwhile, Meliadus descended to the cave where Merlin lay. As he did this, several knights approached him with swords raised. The knights said they would kill him if he did not lead them to where Merlin was trapped. Meliadus said: "Come, follow me."

The writer of this knows that Meliadus led King Henry's knights to the mountain where he and Merlin spoke. When they got there, the mountain started to make more and more noise, then broke apart and swallowed the knights. They are dead now. I'm telling you this so that you know and in case the stories of this adventure fade and Merlin's prophecies are no longer heard.

57: Of the Damsel Who Visited the Chaplain

A damsel came with letters. These letters said that chivalry and the Order of Saint Peter would be terminated, and that the land would

---

[100]. These prophecies were supposedly made after Jonah was recovered from the belly of the whale.

be changed, and all trade, all goods, and all evil, would be set right. But before that happens, it said in these letters, evil would be seen by all the people of the world. Holy men will face the great mountains and will say:

"Climb up. Rise above us and enchant us, for through our eyes we have never seen such great wonders from Heaven.

"And it is written that above this island the bearer of this will be a woman. Write it down and add it to Merlin's other prophecies."

At that point a damsel came and stood before the Chaplain[101] and said: "Sire, a miracle has happened in my country, for a letter written on a marble stone testifies that Merlin the wise prophet said that the birth of the Abomination that used to be in Jerusalem will be prevented, that all debts will be paid off, all sins forgiven. And there will be an island in a place that has been under water for a long time, and that island belonged to Cir and Pol."[102]

"Lady," said the Chaplain, "do you have the letters that testify to what you say to us?"

"Yes," said the damsel. "It is all in these letters."

58: From the Clerk Who Came before the Chaplain

While the damsel was talking with the Chaplain, it happened that one of the clerks whom he had sent to find Merlin's writings came before him. "Sire, I have [not] failed. You sent me to Norbellande[103] to seek the things of that wise prophet. There are many great sorrows, pains, and marks that I bring you. Many of his works that will enable you to see great miracles, according to his prophecies."

"Make haste with this task," replied the Chaplain. "For I am very anxious to see his works."

---

101. This must be Rubens, who is the next compiler of the *Prophecies*, but he is not named until later.
102. Possible references to Sancerre and Saint-Pol-de-Léon in Finistère, west Brittany.
103. This is either Northumberland or the Netherlands; these are used interchangeably in medieval manuscripts.

Then the cleric showed a letter testifying that with the Guardian of Merlin's possessions would come an image of brass, which would speak for him as a man of flesh speaks and which shall want to know that the death of the Wise Clerk will take place a year later.

"God!" said the Chaplain. "When shall I see such a great miracle?"

Then the clerk pulled out the brass image and said: "Sire, here, let me show you an enemy of Hell."

59: Of the Enemy Who Broke the Brazen Image

"You are not telling the truth," the statue said. "I have never been to Hell. I have never set foot there."

"God help us!" answered the Chaplain. "Who are you that speaks from this image?"

"I am," he said, "an angel who was once in the company of the Most High God, and for the pride of Lucifer I fell from Heaven to the Earth and know surely that all those who converse with Heaven on Earth have not died at all, but those who are in the abyss and who obey Lucifer are damned."[104]

"Tell me," said the Chaplain. "Who put you into this image?

"He was the son of a woman," said the Enemy.

"And what is his name?" asked the Chaplain.

"His name is Merlin," replied the image.

"If it is true that Merlin put you in there," the Chaplain replied, "I, who am here in his stead, would like you to come out and let all who are here see you."

What shall I tell you? There was no other force but that of the Enemy, who broke the brazen image and stood before them with the face of an angel, but all blackened, and spoke and said: "Sir Chaplain, we have lost Merlin and will continue to lose him. He is considered part of the Supreme God."

---

104. According to later folklore, this is the origin of the faery race.

And when he finished, he took off from them like lightning. And though the Chaplain left with his companion, the image of what had happened was etched into their souls.

60: Of the Sad March of the Lady of Caiaphas

The letter that the Chaplain held in his hand said that during a sad march to support another lady, she will cross the sea and will do so much good she will be proclaimed a Lady of Caiaphas. And if you want to know when it will be, the letter said it will be at the time when the Abomination departs from Jerusalem.

Then a clerk came and when he reached the Chaplain and had greeted him, the Chaplain said to him: "You come with other writings?"

"Yes," said he. "I bring it from the forest of Avrences, and I tell you that first I rode through the forest, then stood upon a step on which all of this was written. If you start reading you will find everything you want to know."

Then the Chaplain began to read and found out that in this letter it was written that, in time, the greatest Abomination ever born in Jerusalem will be slaughtered by many serpents.

61: Of Those Who Cannot Be Buried until the Third Day

It was also said in this writing that within a mountain surrounded by ridges, which will be called Hole, a hermitage will be made. At that time, the Abomination in Jerusalem will openly reveal a miracle to those who have watched for it, and it will mean that, when they die, they cannot be buried under the earth until the third day, and it will be through prayer of that holy hermit, who lives there, that it becomes possible.

62: Meliadus Alone Has Access to the Tomb

Raymon the Wise Clerk was very eager to go to Merlin's tomb. [He said to Meliadus:] "Tell him about me, and that I promise to write down all the things he has spoken of, including the truths of Jonah's prophecies spoken in the past.[105] I can see signs of these prophecies touching all the world."

Meliadus reported Raymon's wish to Merlin, and Merlin said to the Wise Clerk: "The one who says this is so stubborn it seems as if [his mind] is set in stone!"

Then Merlin sent a message to Raymon asking him to go to King Arthur's court and wait there for Percival le Gallois. He said that Percival would lead him to a place where he would find a round stone, and that if he cast a magic spell, he would be able to speak to Merlin's father, who is trapped in the stone.

Meliadus asked Merlin if only the Wise Clerk could do this. Merlin confirmed it.

"Tell me, Merlin," asked Meliadus. "Of all the vain and earthly men in the world, is he the best [for this task]?"

Merlin said: "It is best to let him go, for no other will be approved by me in this world. By giving him the right instructions, he will do what is desired in the right way. Furthermore, it is better to make friends than have enemies.

"Again, I foresee that if the Wise Clerk of Wales decides not to leave his possessions, his soul will go on an adventure and his enemies will give away his possessions."

"Will he survive?" asked Meliadus.

"Through Percival's prayer, he will escape alive," Merlin said.

Then Merlin added: "If he climbs upon the stone, it will fly through the air at high speed, and from there he will see not only the cave where I am buried, but the whole world under the sky."

"And where shall he descend?" said Meliadus.

"In King Arthur's court," said Merlin.

From Merlin's tomb, Meliadus went straight to the Wise Clerk

---

105. Biblical reference to the Prophecies of Jonah, as follows. "God then once again commanded Jonah to travel to Nineveh and prophesy to its inhabitants. This time he reluctantly goes into the city, crying, 'In forty days Nineveh shall be overthrown.' After Jonah has walked across Nineveh, the people of Nineveh begin to believe his word and proclaim a fast."(Book of Jonah, 3:5) of Wales, who greeted him affectionately. Meliadus told him everything he had experienced [with Merlin] and what was hidden in the future. For three days Meliadus stayed with the Wise Clerk, and on the fourth day they mounted their best horses and went to do what God had commanded them to do. [. . .]

63: Of the Wise Clerk of Wales, the Enemy, and Percival

The Wise Clerk of Wales [sought out the Round Stone] and mounted it. Immediately, it shot out across the sea and then further into the sky. Powered by an evil force, it flew over the countries, cities, and castles of the world. Meanwhile, the devil imprisoned in the stone by Merlin's magic conversed with the Wise Clerk. It told of Merlin's miraculous birth, his lust for women that sealed his fate, and how he was murdered by the Lady of the Lake. This had been predicted by Merlin himself. Meanwhile, the Round Stone passed the north side of St. Mark's Basilica [in Venice], and the Wise Clerk saw there the Byzantine relief depicting Alexander the Great riding in his griffin-drawn chariot on his aerial journey.

Then the Wise Clerk said to the Enemy that was in the stone: "Tell me that you know the place of Merlin's tomb."

The devil replied: "Lius, an important devil, knows it well. [. . .]"

"Tell me," said the Wise Clerk. "Is he, Merlin, safe or not?"

The devil replied: "I cannot know whether my enemy is safe or not. But I know that despite my strength and that of the other servants of Hell, he cast me into this stone."

"How is it," said the Wise Clerk, "that you have no chariot? And how is it that you were shut up in this stone? Is it the same as when I was shut in stone by my stubbornness?"

"I do not know," the devil said to the Wise Clerk. "Just as you do not know how Merlin was conceived. Only Merlin has power over all things, and he knows that this stone, though it is heavy, is like a fish when it is in the sea and like a bird when it is in the air."

"Can you tell me how Merlin was conceived?" asked the Wise Clerk.

"No," said the Enemy. "[Even] Lucifer would not speak of this, nor would those who are with him in Hell. Know that had not lust caused Merlin to rob the Lady of the Lake of her virginity, he would have done many good things, more even than the apostles could have done in an age. But the Lady of the Lake has taken his life, and only his spirit continues to prophesy."

"Will he be present on Judgment Day?" asked the Wise Clerk.

"Yes," said the Enemy. "He will be there, along with all the souls who were called before. You may reach Heaven through the [intercession of the] Virgin Mary, and all the angels of Lucifer's company will have their place. When the judgment is pronounced, at the end of the days, the angels of Heaven will remove all false men, who will be given to the angels of Hell. Lucifer will rule by fire in the Second Age, and their torments will be endless."

"How did you get into the stone?" asked the Wise Clerk.

"I won't say that," answered the Enemy.

Then the Wise Clerk cast a spell that compelled the Enemy to speak. It said: "I was sent by Morgain to the Lady of the Lake to break the glass floor the Lady had constructed, but Merlin spied on me and conjured me into the Round Stone where I must remain until the day of judgment."

64: The Round Stone Goes to India

Now the Round Stone set course for India. The story says that, as it passed the palace that St. Thomas built there, the Wise Clerk took the opportunity to seize the mantle of the King of India, which was at that time ruled over by a mighty Christian emperor.[106]

When the Round Stone reached Burma,[107] the King of Burma saw the stone with the Wise Clerk of Wales seated on it. The king fell to his knees and begged Our Lord to grant him understanding

---

106. Prester John, as we shall see.

107. Although both India and Burma were known by this time, the actual name should be seen as a reference to Berne in Switzerland.

of the miracle. The Round Stone immediately stopped, and the devil explained that it was trapped there by Merlin. Whereupon the King of Burma wanted to search for the great wizard.

[Now the Round Stone flew on], and on its way above Antioch,[108] Raymon dropped the cloak of the King of India into a fire. The cloak remained intact because the servants of the Priest John always used fire to cleanse it.

Then the stone flew straight to Camelot. Arriving there, it flew over the square in front of the palace, put Raymon safely on the ground, and then was swallowed up by the earth, which gaped open to receive it. When Percival saw this, he fell to his knees and began to pray: "Lord Jesu Christ, let those men and women who are created in your image, and for the grace that is in you, let the Wise Clerk live, I beseech you."

Then he arose and went straight to King Arthur, to whom he told what he had seen. What shall I tell you? Among those at court were King Arthur and the High Princes, the Fathers of the Islands of Lointaines,[109] Lancelot of the Lake, the Baron of the King of Longes, and Knights of the Round Table. All who were there saw the miracle and how the earth worked to swallow the stone.

Then the story says that the Duke [of Antioch] took the cloak [dropped by Raymon the Wise Clerk] out of the fire undamaged and went in search of the one he saw wearing the coat.

One night a palanquin, carried by porters, arrived at a hermitage. The moon shone brightly. In the palanquin sat the Duke of Antioch. He who lead the procession called at the door, and the priest opened it. The bearers saluted the priest, and he greeted them back.

"Priest," the Duke said, "I found an inscription on a marble stone, which mentioned the name of the master who owned this coat, and the inscriptions showed me the way to this place."

Then the priest let the porters in with the palanquin. And when

---

108. Now Antakya in Turkey.
109. *Lointaines* means "distant," so the distant islands.

the hermits saw the duke, they thought he was a practitioner of black magic and plotted against him. But Percival called upon them to respect him.

What shall I say? The duke told them: "I met a clerk on a marble stone in the sky! A part of my soul emerged that I never found in my own barren land, and so I renounced the black arts. Now I have found him, the one I have been seeking for a year and a half."

Now the Wise Clerk told everyone that it was he who met Percival le Gallois and how he said: "God bless you, Sir Knight. I knew for sure that the Saviour of the World would find me worthy of escape."

"I beg you," said Percival. "Tell me how it was that this stone carried you so perfectly between the sea and the sky?"

The Wise Clerk replied: "An Enemy from Hell sat in the stone. He showed me the whole world from the air in just three days."

65: The Wise Clerk Goes to Meliadus

After this the Wise Clerk mounted a strong horse and rode until he reached Meliadus. Their meeting was cordial. They hugged. Raymon told of his adventures and begged him to visit and talk to Merlin.

Then Meliadus asked the Wise Clerk if he would like to see the place where Merlin was hidden, and that it was the most glorious place of all the beautiful places in the world he had ever seen. The Wise Clerk begged to go with Meliadus to the rock where Merlin was trapped so that he could talk with him. [But to this Meliadus said no.]

Then he rode four days until he came to the mountain that roared like the sea when it was angry. Meliadus arrived at the tomb in his chariot and entered the cave where Merlin was imprisoned. He knew the entrance very well, and after removing the magpies that were there, he continued into the cave.[110] Merlin's flesh had

---

110. Magpies then, as now, were considered unlucky.

already softened, and he could see the bones. Meliadus sensed Merlin's ghost approaching.

"Speak to me," said Meliadus.

"Meliadus," said Merlin, "as the wisest man in the world, I place my prophecies in your hands. Know there will be a joust between good and evil, and that war will be caused by the Dragon of Babylon.

"When will that be?" said Meliadus.

"It will be," said Merlin, "after the destruction of Burma."

"When will Burma be destroyed?" asked Meliadus.

"It should be written down that Burma will be destroyed before the Abomination leaves Jerusalem. And if anyone asks me when this must end, I answer that it will be after the Dragon of Babylon is put to death by two holy men, Helias[111] and Enoch, who will witness the coming of Jesu Christ."

"Merlin," asked Meliadus, "when will the quest for the Holy Grail begin?"

"The knight who will begin the quest has not yet been born," Merlin replied.[112]

"Now I want you to tell Percival that he must go to Cornouaille[113] to help his brother Tristan," said Merlin. "I know he hates going there, but Tristan is in need, and it is God's command."

"Why does Percival have to go to Cornouaille?" Meliadus asked.

"Because you want to know, I'll tell you," Merlin said. "Know that King Marc is holding Tristan captive. I'm sure Percival will free him, and I'm sure he will imprison King Marc. Tell him he must go faster than he can actually go. This is what God commands, Meliadus."

It is now time to tell more about the plots of King Marc against

---

111. The text says Helias, but in biblical tradition Elias and Enoch are paired as foreseeing the coming of Christ.
112. This must refer to Galahad, the final Grail winner, since Percival and Bors are already alive. The timeline here is incorrect, but the author was clearly referring to several manuscripts.
113. Cornwall.

Tristan. I am going to tell you this, though the story has been translated from Latin into French by others.[114]

66: The Plots of King Marc against Tristan

"King Marc desired to imprison Tristan and put Sadoc[115] to death. Sadoc, when he learned that Tristan was in prison, put out to sea with two nephews," [said Merlin].

"He preserved complete secrecy as to his movements but kept a spy on shore to inform him of the doings of King Marc and the traitor Meliagrance, who consorted with him. One day Sadoc overtook them as they walked together by the sea. He hailed them, and King Marc at once took flight. Sadoc, with the aid of his nephews, killed the traitor Meliagrance and four companions, who were kinsmen to King Marc.

"Sadoc then went to the castle of Léonois and roused the people to fury by the story of Tristan's imprisonment and his own encounter with King Marc. The chatelain of Léonois betook himself to Albrac[116] and told the news to the seneschal, who vowed that if he found King Marc before Tristan was released, he would surely behead him. Nor would he ever set foot on the ground in front of Tristan, if he could set Tristan free before he found King Marc and [even if] Tristan refused to come with Yseut to Léonois. His retainers prepared to go with him to take vengeance upon King Marc. Yseut vowed that if Tristan was freed she would indeed accompany him to Logres.[117]

"Meanwhile, King Marc's followers went to the court and found the bodies of the four knights [slain by Sadoc] but no signs of Sadoc himself, until they came to the road leading to Léonois. They returned with their tidings to King Marc, who at once made ready for war after burying the traitor Meliagrance and his own kinsmen."

---

114. It is not clear whether the section that follows is in the voice of the author. We have assumed it is still the voice of Merlin.
115. Sadoc is an important character from the romances of Tristan; see the commentary.
116. An unknown location, probably derived from the *Prose Tristan*.
117. The old name for Arthurian Britain. Cornouaille, King Marc's realm, is part of it.

67: The Release of Tristan by Percival

"King Marc now received letters from the Pope entreating him to go on a Crusade to the Holy Land. He therefore sent a chaplain to Tristan in prison and offered to release him on condition that he took the cross in the service of the church. Tristan replied that if he were free and the Pope bade him go, he would obey, but he would not set out at Marc's suggestion. When he does so, it must be on pilgrimage with all the chivalry of Léonois in his train. Accordingly, King Marc sent him a forged letter from the Pope, bidding him undertake the Crusade," [Merlin continued].

"Tristan recognized the source of the letter and dispatched a defiant reply to King Marc, agreeing to go but telling him that no knight of Cornwall who was not also a king would accompany him. For he was himself the son of a king and had a realm no smaller and no less honoured than that of King Marc.[118] If he did not depart, he would be hated forever. [And, he said:] 'Tell Marc he is forcing me go.'

"While King Marc reflected upon this message, four wounded knights were brought before him in litters, who told him that they have been set upon by knights of Léonois, who had entered the land and were attacking whomsoever they met. King Marc ordered his men to arms, forgetting to exempt the guards of Tristan's prison, who came to Tintagel with all his company. Percival arrived in the kingdom at this juncture and released Tristan.

"It is my duty now to tell what will happen to Tristan and Yseut and what will be the ending of their love for each other."

68: The Deaths of Tristan and Yseut

"Tristan and Yseut drank a magical potion and fell deeply in love with each other. Precisely where love is not allowed to grow, it

---

118. This is Lyonesse or, as it is here, Léonois.

blossomed. When the two lovers met in King Marc's castle garden, they were betrayed," [said Merlin].

"Tristan was mortally wounded, and out of sheer despair and inexhaustible love, Yseut also gave up the ghost. She fell dead upon the body of her soul mate, and they are now together forever.

"Write this all down carefully. Forgive me, I am now going to tell you about the plot of Claudas[119] against Lancelot."

69: The Plot of Claudas against Lancelot

"Claudas [the enemy of Lancelot's father, King Ban], upon hearing of the prowess of Lancelot, determined to destroy him. He called his allies together, announcing to them that he was going on a pilgrimage to Rome and begging them to guard his land in his absence. They went to Berri and doubled the guards throughout the country. Claudas took with him a wise clerk, who vowed to himself that he would let no harm come to Queen Guinevere for she once did him a great service. Claudas, disguised as a pilgrim, arrived before the Pope, delivered a sermon in Latin concerning the Holy City of Jerusalem, and then told the Pope that he was a hermit who, knowing the sore need of the Holy Land, had come to reveal that the war with Lancelot was deterring the men of the Terre Déserte from taking the cross. He persuaded the Pope to give him a letter that he could send to Lancelot, bidding him go on a Crusade to Jerusalem. Claudas then returned home," [said Merlin].

"However, King Arthur declared war on him, and [Claudas] was never heard from again. His son became one of the Knights of the Round Table."

Now I have to tell you another story. I must tell you this prophecy of Merlin's before I forget.[120]

---

119. Claudas is the king who attacked the kingdom of King Ban, Lancelot's father, which results in the fostering of the future hero by the Lady of the Lake.
120. Here we find ourselves listening to the voice of the narrator.

70: Of the Damsel from Avalon Who Came in a Boat

Here the story tells of a damsel of Avalon who came ashore in a barge with full sails. And the wind hurt the barge a little more than the boat could bear, for it seemed as if the barge was thrown into the maelstrom at the end of the world.

And whoever asks me how strong this boat was, I answer that the wise Merlin, when he was alive, described this boat as if it were a creature with stone fists and a temper! The ship had sailed safely from Wales with Merlin to India, where he had lived for several years and selected the damsel to be further taught in magic by the Lady of Avalon.

What shall I tell you? When the ship landed, a huge crowd gathered to witness the great miracle. The crowd was so large that the great city of Vitré[121] in Brittany, where King Arthur's palace stood, was half empty. And if you asked me where this young lady came from, I would say she was from India and that Merlin sent her from there to get in touch with the people here [in Logres].

When she approached the palace, she took a ladder from the boat and rested it on dry land, and the boat rose [high in the water]. And having previously had a fish as a guide, a fisherman now took its place. The fish was sent to King Arthur, who cooked it whole and ate it. The young lady who came out of the boat prayed and was taken to the Church of Saint Stephen. And know that King Arthur wished to delay the damsel's arrival, for he still wanted to pray, and so the people left the church. And when the damsel, after prayer, found him whom she sought, like a beast pouncing upon its prey, she opened her arms and ran to King Arthur, saying: "Sire, I have found you!"

The king took her immediately in his arms and then pushed her away: "Madam, you don't greet everyone this way, do you?"

---

121. This version of the story seeks to transpose Arthur's realm to Brittany. At the time many British storytellers had fled to that area, taking the native stories of Arthur with them. Vitré would translate as "city of glass," a term often used in the romances for a faery castle or city. Vitré is, however, an actual place in northwest Brittany.

"Sire, where is Merlin, the wisest in the world?" asked the damsel.

"Merlin?" said the king. "Why should he be here?"

"Do you not know that he sent me to Tous Saints?" said the damsel.[122] "This while he was in India for twenty years preparing the country for the coming of evil, since it had previously been very pious under a Christian king."

"Lady," said King Arthur, "do you know me?"

"Ah," she said. "Are you not King Uterpendragon?"

Then King Arthur laughed and said: "Damsel, you have come to my court by a strange twist of fate. I do not think your mother can have seen King Uterpendragon very often. And yet you, damsel, though not yet thirteen years old, say you have seen him."

"No!" she said. "It is as I told you. And if you want me to prove it, I saw you on the day the Round Table was founded."

"If you want to find the writing I shared with other damsels who were at the feast," said the king, "I can show it."

He was chivalrous and offered her the charter and said again that she did not know him.

"So be it," said she. "I am Aglentine, damsel of Avalon."

"Of course, I am not the one who was described to you. I am not the one you expected to see," said the king.

"Tell Merlin I want to return his barge," said the damsel.

"Dear God, he is lost!" said the king. "He has been dead more than fifteen years."

"My God!" she said. "Merlin has not been in my life for so many years."

71: King Arthur and the Maiden of Avalon

Then the king took the damsel by the hand and led her to his palace. And the damsel felt compelled to lay down on the table letters she had with her.

"Why have you come at this time?" asked the king.

---

122. All Saints. Another unknown location.

"I am come to bring you these letters," said Aglentine, handing him a bundle wrapped in silk. "They are from the Christian Emperor of India. His wisdom is great, and the Lady of Avalon asks that you read these and remember what is to be found within them."[123]

Then she told how Merlin himself had journeyed many years before to the kingdom of India and there had spent many days talking of all manner of things with the emperor.

"Damsel," said King Arthur, "I beg you to stay here till you are at least twenty."

"No, Sire," she said. "Since you and the others only remember me as a little child, I will return to Avalon, where I came from, before I went to India with Merlin along with other chosen ones."

Then the ship turned back and set its sails to the wind. King Arthur, who had stayed in the same place, saw the letters she had left behind. [. . .]

King Arthur wanted to stretch out his hand to stop the barge. However, the wind billowed the sails, causing it to set course and drift away. It didn't matter that the ship was leaving. There was such noise from the direction of the palace, as if one of the greatest miracles in the world was happening. As the people looked on, there came an iron griddle with four fish upon it, and they were cooked by lightning. This happened in the evening, and when the griddle came to land, the fish were eaten by King Arthur and his court.

The ship kept course, and King Arthur followed it [on land] with many companions and knights as it went out to sea. As it approached the Black Chapel, the ship was reflected in it, and the king and all his companions did not know what was reality and what deception.[124] And when his wish for the damsel to stay did not come true, the king was very sad that he had not been able to stop the boat by force.

---

123. This section was moved from within the next section, as it clearly belongs here.
124. It is unclear what is meant here. There are several black chapels in Arthurian romance, but the passage makes no sense as it stands, unless the chapel is made of obsidian, which is highly reflective.

72: Of the Letter that the King of India Sent by the Maiden of Avalon to King Uterpendragon

When he saw the crowds and that everyone was having a good time drinking, King Arthur asked if anyone had taken the letters that the lady had placed on the table. And a maidservant said: "Sire, I have them."

And then King Arthur said to the knights [who were assembled there]: "These letters, which this lady brought for King Uterpendragon, my father, I can legally open, according to the law, since he is dead."

And then King Arthur broke the seal and found what was in the letters:

"To King Uterpendragon, to whom the Mother of God grants to see the sage [Merlin] as the one who from India sent a damsel in a barge, by sea, then by land, then by sea to Vitré. The King of India greets you and prays for you. And since he has had holy baptism and believes in the Father, the Son, and the Holy Spirit, St. James will not be forgotten."[125]

The damsel returned to India in a month and a half and stayed in the sacred palace Saint Thomas had built there long ago. She travelled so far to see the great virtue bestowed by our holy Jesu Christ through the works of the saint.

The king gave what was intended for Merlin to a knight of Tennes and said he should travel to the Gates of Wales and give gifts to the Wise Clerk whom he would find there. The knight understood the message and mounted his horse and did well what he had been told to do.

Now I'm going to stop talking about this adventure and talk about another prophecy. This is a very important and fulfilled prophecy. I am telling you this now because I am afraid of forgetting it.

---

125. This is a reference to James, the half brother of Jesus.

73: Of the Proud Damsel of the White Kingdom and King Arthur's Wedding

I will tell you now that the nephew of King Arthur, who had met the Wise Clerk of Wales, who had told of Merlin's many wonders, ran to Uterpendragon, knelt before him, and said: "Sire, I am from Wales and know that Merlin's prophecies are true."

Uterpendragon, hearing this, said to King Arthur: "It is certain that within half a day there will come a footman that everyone will talk about.

"A large crowd, young and old, will come to us. In this company is the lackey, and they say he has no belly. He has a torso and no legs, he has good working hands and no arms, he has a good head and no mouth. This my cousin who told me, who heard it from the Wise Clerk who heard it all from Merlin."[126]

King Arthur wanted to respond to what Uterpendragon had said, but he saw that many people passed by, until all that remained was a damsel who knelt before him, and then stood to one side. [A servant said:] "Sire, a damsel comes to greet you."

Then King Arthur said: "Mother of God, [I believe] Merlin sent her to me! Or maybe the Wise Clerk sent her. See how she hesitates. She can't put her foot forward."

The damsel said: "I beg you to ask your men to allow you to come to me."

The king took his staff and came down from his throne and ordered everyone else to leave the room.

Then the damsel came to him, and King Arthur took her by the hand and led her upstream along the river and through the valley. And when King Arthur stood in the mud by the bank, the damsel said: "Sire, though I am only a girl, as you see me, I am the

---

126. This section is very confused. Uther was already dead before Arthur became king. The "nephew" could be Gawain or any of the Orkney Clan. The mysterious footman sounds very much like one of the monsters who appear in other Arthurian romances.

daughter of a king. The White King was my father, and the Queen of the Aryans was my mother. I prayed and swore to the Mother of God that, although I am beautiful, I will not give myself to any man unless he is true. Sire, the knight named Gruira has dozens of times ordered my father to be killed and our country to be invaded. I do not speak of what he had done to me, but I have my pride."

While she spoke thus, an old man came by who turned out to be a hermit. He had a gold ring with a gemstone in it. The hermit must have followed her. He gave her the ring and said that Merlin asked him to give it to her when he was one hundred years old, so that the ring would bring her fame. Then they returned to King Arthur's palace, and the maidservant led the girl to her room.

What shall I say? The damsel was clad in the king's relined mantle.

When the king went to the damsel, he took the ring in his hand and put it on his finger. What Merlin had said while imprisoned in the tomb is fulfilled: King Arthur and Guinevere were married.[127]

On the following morning the High Prince Galeholt prepared for the tourney, which began when the knights were armed and Queen Guinevere and her ladies were in their places. After a fierce battle between the Knights of the Round Table, Lancelot emerged victorious.

In the city of Vitré the good knights began their quest for the Holy Grail.

74: Of the Emperor of Rome, Who Came before the Pope with a Hundred Knights[128]

[The story now tells that] the Pope spoke of truces broken in Jerusalem. As he did so, the Emperor of Rome entered with more than a hundred knights. The emperor went straight to the Pope and

---

127. The implication here seems to be that the "damsel" who came to see Arthur was actually Guinevere. The ring, sent by Merlin via the hundred-year-old hermit, seems to be the symbol of their wedding. This story appears nowhere else.
128. This section was originally at section 4, but it clearly belongs here.

fell on his knees, hands folded in reverence, head bowed to the ground, and cried: "Forgive me!" The Pope spread his arms and said to him: "Emperor, instead of penance, will you take up the Holy Cross and go over the sea to guard the Holy Land where our Lord Jesu Christ was crucified?"

"Sire," said the emperor, "I understand what you want to achieve."

Then the Pope sent for the cross, and the emperor knelt before it and kissed it, accepting the commission along with the barons who were with him. The Pope then forgave the sins of all who would go to Jerusalem.

The emperor left the council and gave his command that all should drink with him and that he would give them everything they asked for. But there was a bishop at the council who pretended to be very religious and a good Catholic—but in truth he was not. So completely was he burdened with fear that all could see it. If you brought him before you and begged the emperor to test his virtue, he would only say that he was true, and thus deceive the whole world by his evil works.

75: Of the Aid Sent to Jerusalem

Now I must tell you a prophecy about the King of Sessoines[129] coming home in chains and receiving from his tributary kings acceptance of the terms imposed by Galeholt. He was accused of waging war against Christian kings. He agreed to pay tribute to King Arthur and swore never to make war against Christian kings again.

King Arthur was very pleased and called the Knights of the Round Table together. When the knights were assembled, Bleoberis[130] told of having killed two giants in the forest. He displayed their heads.

---

129. Saxons, or in this instance perhaps it might be better understood as Saracens.
130. A very famous knight of the Round Table, Bleoberis was the son of Nestor, godson to King Bors, brother to Blamor, cousin of Lancelot, and lord of Gannes. He also fought against the Saxons and King Claudas, which may account for his presence here. His appearance probably derives from one of the manuscripts in the possession of the compiler of the first *Prophecies of Merlin* in 1302.

Next, the King of Sessoines made his promise and left the council chamber.

A long debate ensued. Galeholt opened it and advised that mercy be shown to the King of Sessoines. Gawain approved his sentiments and added that while King Arthur was in Carmelyde the Pope had in vain sent the Bishop of Galice and the son of the King of Jerusalem to Britain to ask aid for the Holy Land. The Pope was now writing letters calling for help against King Baudic, who was threatening Jerusalem. Gawain advised, therefore, the tribute from the Pagans be applied to the protection of the Holy Land.

At the request of Lancelot, the letters were read, first of all that in which the Emperor of Rome who, at the bidding of the Pope, had gone to Jerusalem [and] had written to His Holiness asking for aid. Next from the King of Ireland, who was also in Jerusalem at this time, in which he had authorized the Pope to sell Ireland: "Sell everything: all the land with men, women, children, cattle, castles, houses, and farms. Use the money to send forces against the King of Baudic."

A letter was also sent to King Arthur stating that his sins would be forgiven and that he was summoned to travel as a Christian King to Jerusalem to fight. At Lancelot's suggestion, it was proposed to lessen the Pagan's tribute and demand that it be paid in one lump sum so that it could be immediately sent to the Pope.

King Arthur took up this suggestion. The Pagans accepted the conditions, and the tribute was sent to Britain, where it was employed to pay a large force of men to go to Jerusalem under the leadership of Henry the Courteous.[131] After a long journey by sea, they landed at Japhes,[132] where the news of their arrival and of the treasure they had brought with them was joyfully received by the Emperor of Rome.

Merlin said: "I now take the opportunity to speak of the adventures and words of Richard of Jerusalem."

---

131. Unknown character.
132. Jaffa, modern Tel Aviv.

76: Of Richard of Jerusalem

"The Bishop of Galice and Richard of Jerusalem returned to Rome from England bringing with them the treasure they had been given. The emperor had been crowned by the Pope and had gone to the Holy Land. The Pope proclaimed an indulgence for all those who would join in the Crusade, and a large company embarked for Japhes, near which the emperor was encamped in the plain of Burtinuble. Richard followed the host, and on the day of his arrival, the Christians won a mighty victory over the Pagans. As a tribute, the emperor had a chapel built, about which the Crusaders passed barefoot.

"He quickly undertook an expedition against Sarras,[133] where the ruling lord had been killed by another nobleman, and the followers of both sides were fighting day and night. The two factions united against their Christian assailants. When the opposing armies met, Richard, making the sign of the cross, felled to the ground a Pagan champion who advanced against him, and then led the way in a tremendous conflict, which lasted all day.

"At nightfall the Pagans lit fires on their towers as a signal of distress, and their neighbours from the surrounding country came to their rescue. The King of Ireland, seeing the fires from the meadow near Jerusalem where he was lodging, ordered his men to the aid of Richard. They met the Pagan forces who were bound for Sarras, took them prisoner, and proceeded on their way.

"The people of Sarras saw them coming but were helpless to withstand them. The giant Alchendic, who had put to death the former ruler of the city, called the people together and gave them the choice of remaining beside him or leaving the city in safety. They decided to remain with him. Alchendic then advanced towards the

---

133. Sarras was later known as the home of the Grail; before this it was a Pagan city. The giant Alchendic is unknown in any other existing romance, but the story of Galahad becoming king after achieving the Grail is found in the *Lancelot-Grail* Cycle.

Crusaders and offered Richard four sets of spears, each of which was to be given to a Christian, who should use them in single combat with him. If he was overthrown, the Crusaders could enter the city, and he would offer a just peace. Otherwise, he proposed a truce of ten years.

"Richard accepted the spears but said he would leave the granting of the truce to the emperor. In the combats that followed, Alchendic proved invincible, and the emperor accordingly granted the truce. At the end of the month Alchendic was baptized."

Then Merlin said: "I am going to tell you about the King of Ireland and King Baudac. Write it all down carefully so that it is not forgotten."

77: Of the King of Ireland and King Baudac

"The King of Ireland, with a large party of Crusaders from England, set out from Jerusalem to aid Richard at Orberice.[134] However, he had already taken the place. On his way, the King of Ireland met a company of Pagans from Sarras who were bound for Orberice to relieve their fellows.

"He and his forces ranged themselves against these men and succeeded in defeating them. He then returned to Jerusalem, since Orberice was already in Richard's hands.

"King Baudac heard that the Christians had resolved to leave no fortress in the possession of the Pagans and accordingly held a council of war to deliberate on a plan of action. After a lengthy discussion, in which many Pagans spoke of their options, it was decided to send messengers to Jerusalem, under the leadership of Ulfal, offering defiance to the King of Ireland.

"When they reached the gates of Jerusalem, through a miracle

---

134. This place name comes from the river Orbe, a tributary of the Rhine that rises in France and flows to Switzerland, where it forms the river Thielle at its confluence. The similarity of the name to Orbance may have suggested this.

of Christ, they were rendered unable to alight [from their horses], and the King of Ireland, in the absence of Richard, came out to meet them. Ulfal, believing they were bespelled, addressed him as an enchanter and announced that his master, King Baudac, commanded him and his hosts to depart, under the threat that he would destroy the city. The King of Ireland dismissed him, bidding him reply to his lord that the Christians had a helper far more powerful than he and that they do not fear him. Richard, on hearing of the defiance of King Baudac, set fire to Orberice and returned in haste to Jerusalem."

Merlin said: "I am now going to tell a story that takes place in the court of King Arthur."

My honesty compels me to say that I copied this from other, sometimes older, manuscripts.[135]

78: Of King Arthur and the Knight of Carmelyde[136]

Savariz, a knight of Carmelyde, came to the court of Arthur and defied him because it had been established at the court of Logres that no judgment given by the barons of Carmelyde was valid. Therefore, he called King Arthur a traitor and threatened that if he failed to acknowledge his baseness, the barons would cut off his head on the field of battle. Gawain offered to take the combat upon himself, but the knight would do battle with no one but King Arthur. They engaged in a fierce contest, in which, at length, King Arthur unhorsed Savariz, snatched off his helmet, and threatened to behead him if he did not call himself vanquished. When Savariz refused to admit that he had been justly conquered, King Arthur smote off his head, and then himself fell exhausted to the ground. Physicians were summoned to tend his wounds. He thus proved that the barons of Carmelyde were false.

---

135. Here the copyist tells us clearly that he has access to older manuscripts.
136. A name generally associated with the kingdom of Leodegrance, Guinevere's father.

79: How a Lady from Abiron Put Merlin to the Test

Know that Merlin sent word to Antoine to write the story of the lady of Abiron, who would have been the wisest lady in the world, but she was wisest in the dark arts and not in the other sciences. When Merlin first saw the lady, she greeted him: "I want you to know that I have come here from Abiron to see you, Merlin. It is good of you to see me."

"Lady," said Merlin, "you are welcome, but do the people of the city of Abiron know you are here? I promise you I could tell you many times before midnight why you came from Abiron. It has taken six months for you to come hither, but know this: when you return, the third day after that Abiron may be taken, and their inhabitants slain, and their possessions thrown into pits."

"My God!" said the lady. "What are you saying?"

"That you shall be delivered from Abiron and from the hands of your enemies."

This is what Merlin said, and Master Antoine put it in writing.

"Merlin," said the lady, "who will do so much damage to the city?"

"I hope Master Antoine puts it in writing," Merlin said, "that it is because Acloas cannot find you in Abiron."

"Is he unhappy?" asked the lady.

"Certainly," said Merlin. "Because you are not in Abiron."

"Merlin," said the lady from Abiron, "love me and follow me into the dark arts."

80: Of the Ring Merlin Gave to the Lady of Abiron

"Merlin," said the lady, "I tell you I will have a golden image made in your honour, a meter above the main gate of Abiron in honour of the love I have for you."

Merlin was wearing a ring. He took it from his hand and gave it to the lady, who took it in her hand. It gave her great joy, especially when we consider that the lady was taken by the henchmen of Hell, carried to Abiron at night, and placed naked on a tower. She was released there three days after Acloas destroyed the city. She was saved by Merlin's magic. The father of the lady of Abiron afterwards retook the city.

I will keep silent about this adventure and tell you further of Merlin's prophecies, for there is much to tell. I have yet to tell you about Esglantine,[137] the damsel of Avalon, the lady of Avalon, the queen of Norgales, Sebile, and Morgain.[138]

81: Of the Lady of Avalon, the Queen of Norgales, Sebile, and Morgain

A message was conveyed to the Queen of Norgales and Sebile, who were in the castle of Norgales. They were told that Morgain had brought a wounded knight to Belle Garde.[139] They decided to travel there at once. As they were leaving Norgales, a damsel approached. "I come from the Lady of Avalon. I urge you to meet her at once. You will see a miracle."

Aglentine, one of the maidens of the Lady of Avalon, was sent to India in a miraculous barge made by Merlin shortly after he erected the Round Table. Now she returned, looking just as she had been in her youth. She told the story about a huge, opulent palace in India. She brought two rings for her mistress: one made the wearer invisible and the other made them irresistible.

"My mistress, the Lady of Avalon, wants to introduce Esglantine to her three powerful friends: Morgain, the Queen of Norgales, and Sebile. Please," begged the damsel, "come to the harbour where the barge of the Lady of Avalon awaits."

Morgain was also informed of the request of the Lady of Avalon. The Queen of Norgales and Sebile escorted the damsel to Belle Garde. However, Morgain, who was afraid of betrayal, hid herself.

"Behold the barge," said the Lady of Avalon. "See how powerful it

---
137. Esglantine is probably the same as Aglentine, who appears earlier in sections 70–71.
138. Once again, we hear the voice of the compiler.
139. This probably refers to Lancelot. In a famous episode from *Le Morte D'Arthur*, he is captured by the three queens, each of whom attempts to seduce him.

is. It will carry us [all] to Avalon." When the two faeries saw Aglentine, they were astonished at her age: "Your youthfulness amazes us!"

The damsel decided to wait for Morgain to arrive, while the other faeries travelled to Avalon. The barge bore an inscription that it would carry Arthur to Avalon if [he was] mortally wounded, as Merlin's prophecy foretold. As they sailed across the water to Avalon, the Lady of Avalon challenged the other two queens: "You cannot overcome the power of my rings," she sneered. She put on a ring and the miracle happened: she became invisible.

"We will break the spell!" cried the Queen of Norgales and Sebile. The two faeries tried with all their might to break the spell, but the Lady of Avalon alone could make the palace tremble and rain down swords.

Then she put on the second ring. "Undress yourself!" she commanded the other two.

The spell was [such that they obeyed, but] did not notice their shameful state. Then the Lady put on a third ring brought to her by Aglentine. Behold the spell was broken, and the Queen of Norgales and Sebile discovered their plight. Sebile burst into rage. "We cannot help but recognize the power of the rings," they both said.

The Lady of Avalon was now convinced that she had power over them as well as over Morgain.

Morgain, meanwhile, received the message from the damsel of Avalon. Arriving at the harbour she heard from the harbour master what happened to the other faeries. "Come, lady, come with me to Avalon," said the damsel. "Look at this barge, it will carry us over." They set course for Avalon.

Nearing Avalon, Morgain summoned a troop of devils, sending them ahead in the form of birds and dragons in order to capture the Lady of Avalon, convinced that the rings would have no power over them. Morgain followed them reading from her book. The Lady put on the rings that made her invisible and irresistible and commanded: "Morgain, undress yourself!" Morgain took off her clothes. A devil took her cloak and hung it from a tower.

"If Merlin had been alive, surely he would have taught me an incantation stronger than these rings," said Morgain. Then the Queen of Norgales and Sebile appeared, and I tell you that since the Lady of the Lake was there also, all the subtlety of the world was in that place! The Lady led her guests to the tower where Morgain's garments were, but sent ahead a flame that burned them. "I learned this magical spell from Merlin," she admitted.

Morgain said: "If this is so, then Merlin has deceived me. He said that he had taught me all the magic he taught the others."

The faeries then decided to sail north in search of Merlin's tomb.

82: On the Rescue of Breuse Sans Pitie[140]

The Lady of the Lake went to Galles, where she found Meliadus her lover waiting for the Wise Clerk, who had left the country for a time. The Lady expressed surprise that Meliadus had lingered there, but he replied: "There is no one else in the whole world who is better able to understand the words of Merlin and to confer with him so often."

King Urien and his barons welcomed the Lady to Galles with great acclaim. It chanced that two years earlier Urien had been bespelled by a maiden from Little Britain and lured to her castle, where by her enchantment she had compelled him to do battle with the neighbouring knight, Margondan, who was attacking her domains. Urien killed him and was being attacked in revenge by four of Margondan's cousins, when the Lady of the Lake appeared with ten of her own knights and stopped the combat. She then bade Urien put on his finger a ring that freed him from the maiden's spell. She then dispersed his assailants, explaining to them that he was under her protection, and escorted him to the port, where he set sail for Vincestre.

News of the honour the Lady was giving to Urien aroused the jealousy of Morgain le Fay. She travelled with fifteen knights to

---

140. The story of the feud between the faery women is continued in the 1303 Rennes manuscript of the *Prophecies* as edited by Lucy Allen Paton. The following sections are drawn from Paton's summaries of the episode, found in Paton, *Les Prophecies de Merlin*; "Part Two: Studies in the Contents."

Vincestre and, after having set up her pavilion on the coast, sent her followers throughout Logres in search of the Lady of the Lake. Claudas de la Terre Déserte, Morgain's ally, was at this time fortifying Benoic against a possible attack from Lancelot, his fear of whom was increased by the friendship between Lancelot and Galeholt of the Distant Isles. Morgain told him of her plans against the Lady of the Lake and begged him to do his utmost to take her prisoner.

Claudas offered his followers large rewards for her capture, reminding them that she occasioned the death of his son, Dorin, and that she was protecting three of his mortal enemies, namely Lancelot, Lionel, and Bors, and that she desired his own destruction. The men accordingly sought for her all along the coast and through the forest, as a result of which many travellers fell into their hands.

At this time Thomas, the Count of Miaus, came to Britain. His daughter had sailed with her husband, Guillaume du Pas Fort, to Vincestre. After landing they lodged with Breuse Sans Pitie,[141] who threw Guillaume and his attendants into a dungeon and did violence to his wife, before allowing her to leave the castle. She returned with the story to her father, who at once went into Logres with two squires in search of Breuse. He met him one day in a narrow pass, unhorsed him, and took him prisoner to Vincestre, intending to deliver him to his daughter at Miaus.

On their way they encountered a company of Morgain's knights, some of whom Count Thomas killed in battle. From those who escaped Morgain learned all that had occurred and rode at once to Vincestre, arriving after the Count had put out to sea with Breuse. Morgain now sent a gale across the waters, but the wind was so strong that she could not watch the ship and thus failed to interfere with its course so that it came safely to port.

While Count Thomas was leading Breuse in bonds to his castle, he offered him his liberty in return for the release of Guillaume. Breuse accepted the terms and sent orders to his wife to set

---

141. A notable villain, whom Lancelot was eventually to defeat.

Guillaume free. But presently a party of Claudas's followers overtook the Count. Despite this he made his escape, leaving Breuse in their hands. They escorted the rescued captive to Claudas, who out of respect for Morgain did him honour. He then preceded to Vincestre to join Morgain, who was overjoyed to see him.

The Lady of the Lake learned from one of her maidens that Claudas had laid an ambush for her. She laughed in scorn to this and shifted her shape into that of an old woman, thus passing in safety to her dwelling.

83: Of Berengier de Gomeret

Berengier de Gomeret, a handsome widower [who loved Sebile], came to the castle of the enchantress in search of his child, who had been stolen from him. Sebile knew that one of Morgain's maidens, Flor de Lis, had carried the child away to a castle belonging to her mistress in Norgales, where, since the destruction of the Valley of No Return by Lancelot, Morgain had kept all her treasures. Flor promised Berengier that his child would be restored to him if he would marry her mistress.

To this he agreed, and Flor took him to Norgales. There, Morgain, seeing his beauty, bade her handmaid to refuse to return the child unless he gave up Flor de Lis and, in the presence of the other faeries, promised Berengier that he would have his child in return for a boon, which he need not grant until the following day. She then secretly told him that he was doomed to become the husband of either Sebile or Morgain, but that she herself would convey him and the child to the safety of Gomeret, provided he promised to marry her. Berengier consented, preferring her to either of the other two faeries. Flor de Lis showed him the way to escape in the night, and they fled together to Gomeret.

Sebile, when she discovered that Berengier had disappeared, accused Morgain of having made away with him, and in a towering rage [made her way to Norgales and] seized her by the hair, dragged her up and down the hall of the castle, and struck her violently, before she departed, leaving Morgain half dead. On her way home she met Breuse, disguised as a pilgrim, bound for Morgain's castle, but he hid from her, not wishing to be discovered. When she reached her own dwelling, Sebile learned from some of her followers, who had returned by a shorter route, that Breuse had already arrived at Gomeret and had begun to tend Morgain's injuries. They also told her of the escape of Berengier with Flor de Lis. Sebile was filled with regret for her treatment of Morgain.

84: The Reconciliation of Morgain and Sebile

After three days of unconsciousness, Morgain revived thanks to the remedies administered by Breuse and lamented the injuries that she had sustained from Sebile. Breuse reminded her that she had many quarrels with various faeries, but permanent enmity with none, except for the Lady of the Lake. He then opposed every plan for revenge upon Sebile that she suggested, assuring her that the enchantress was powerful enough to resist her. At this Morgain burst into such a passion that Breuse left her.

Morgain forthwith sent a letter by her damsel, Morguenete, to the Queen of Norgales, announcing that she was dying and requesting the queen to come to her and propose a plan for vengeance against Sebile. In return for this Morgain would give her many of her possessions. Sebile happened to be at the queen's palace when the letter arrived and on learning its contents begged her in tears to effect a reconciliation with Morgain. The queen proceeded to Morgain's castle and induced her to forgive Sebile, reminding her how she herself had pardoned Morgain several time before [. . .]. Morgain accordingly sent for Sebile, and peace was made between them.

It is now time to move on with the story about Meliadus, Percival, and Raymon the Wise Clerk from Wales.

85: How Helias Gave the Book of Blaise to Percival

What am I saying? Meliadus took the boat to Wales. There, he rode for so long that he finally arrived in the place where he found the

Wise Clerk and Percival together, along with the King of Burma and the Duke of Antioch. Meliadus was warmly received.[142] [. . .]

Meliadus told the Wise Clerk everything the Good Mariners needed to know. He told the Duke of Antioch that he had heard from Merlin that he should return to his country, where he would experience a great miracle. Meliadus said good-bye to those present and experienced great happiness.

Before returning to the palace, the Wise Clerk told Percival all about Merlin's prodigious wisdom and all he had experienced.

"Ha! Prejudiced Wise Clerk! Why are you putting yourself in such mortal danger?" asked Percival.

"I'll tell you," said the Wise Clerk. "I have studied the arts of energy for a long time, and if I have learned anything, I believe that all the senses of the world are hidden in this cave. Merlin is so powerful that he has even travelled back in time to explain the dreams of Caesar, ruler of the Roman Empire."[143]

"Dear Wise Clerk," said Percival, "how can all the senses of the world be brought together as you describe?" Then the Wise Clerk told the story of Merlin and how he was trapped in a cave in the forest of Avrences and the prophecies he had uttered about Percival's sister and Percival himself, who would keep his virginity until the Grail was found. Also, that he would travel with the good knights to the Holy Land.

Percival, who had never heard of Merlin, swore he would look for him. Raymon [the Wise Clerk] warned him that his quest would be futile, though he would have many brave adventures along the way.

"Sir Knight," the Wise Clerk told Percival, "according to Merlin's prophecies you will experience a miracle, such as other knights have seldom experienced."

---

142. The following four lines are repeated below; we have therefore deleted them here.
143. This refers to the story of Merlin appearing before the Roman emperor in a story found in *The English Merlin*. However, there is no need for him to travel in time as, in this story, Merlin and Arthur are contemporary to the Roman Empire.

"Sir," said Percival, "you say that Merlin is so wise?"

"Sir Knight," said the Clerk, "I have experienced that in him are all the senses of the world and that we owe everything to him for the future."

"Can this be proven?" Percival asked.

"I do not know," replied the Wise Clerk. "My heart is in the forest of Avrences, that everyone has seen, and I am sure his fame is everywhere in the world where there are men."

Then the King of Burma set out to find him, and also more than a thousand knights, and also the Duke of Antioch, and with him twenty knights. And the power they gave to their search for Merlin was unspeakable. I want you to know this firsthand.

"Look who came from India," said the Wise Clerk to Percival, "the one whom I met when I journeyed on the stone in which the bloodthirsty foe was imprisoned. I came to the palace of Saint Thomas and was allowed to hold the coat of the King of India. And further, on my way back, when I passed Antioch,[144] I cast off the coat of the King of India and let it fall, and the Duke of Antioch found it, which was a great marvel."

Meliadus told Percival what Merlin had said to him. "Since no one will ask," said Percival. "I vow to the Mother of God that I will go in search of Merlin and that my search will be according to the custom of Logres."

86: Of Percival's Search for Merlin's Grave and His Several Adventures

Percival went as fast as he could for his weapons. They wished him good luck, and he went forth. Soon he found a stone engraved by Merlin. The inscription stated that widows and orphans would no longer receive alms, although this was obligatory according to the dictates of religion. The stone also had a prophetic message inscribed: "Woe to those who will not protect the widows and the

---

144. Now Antakya in Turkey.

orphans. The Mother of God, patroness of these, will give them a sign: the earth will gather itself up, the rain will destroy the wheat they grow, the men will plough and reap, and so they will have enough to give, but they will give to those who do not need it." [. . .][145]

Percival continued through the forest, where he accomplished various other exploits and in the course of time chanced upon a hermitage in which he found hospitality for the night.

The location of the hermitage was in Northumberland.[146] Percival wandered for a year and a half before he reached it. There he met an aged hermit called Helias, who remembered Merlin's childhood and the marvels he had performed. Helias lived in seclusion in this hermitage while waiting for a destined knight.

The hermit Helias, who was old and feeble, told Percival that he was waiting for the son of Pellinor.[147] Long years before, a certain knight had unjustly suspected Helias of loving his wife and was planning to kill him. But Merlin prophesied in his presence that Helias would retain his chastity to the end of his days and that he would not die until Percival arrived at the hermitage. The prediction convinced the angry husband that Helias was innocent. Merlin sternly reproved the man for the sin of jealousy, and then presented Helias with a book of his prophecies, bidding him give it to no one save Percival.

Without revealing his name, Percival lingered at the hermitage. Helias in the meantime entertained him with stories concerning Merlin from his own book. Helias told of events from Merlin's childhood and the miracles he performed.

Percival was very grateful to spend a few days with this privileged witness of Merlin's childhood. When it became evident that Helias's death was near, Percival revealed his identity. The hermit

---

145. This passage from the original manuscript is cut here as the same story in the same exact words is repeated in the following section, 87.
146. Blaise's book was written in Northumberland.
147. Percival himself.

opened his arms, seized Percival, and hugged him gently. Then he opened his fist, in which he held a small coffer, and said: "Sir, wait, as Merlin would have ordered you! I am weak and will soon die. You cannot prevent it."

"Father," said Percival, "will you show me your book before death comes?"

"I will," said the hermit. "It would be best for me if I show it to you now, since death is coming this way."

"Has anyone else seen the book from amongst the great host of hypocrites from Northumberland?" Percival asked.

"No one," said the hermit. "Because when the bishops came for Merlin, he told them he couldn't take off the chain that encircled the book. He said the one who would end the adventure was not yet born. Then he broke away from the bishops and named the one it would be: Tristan de Léonois."

Then Percival came in and brought meat for the hermit. The hermit ate it. Then he fell and slept until the night. And when he awoke, Percival was in bed.

My patience is being tested to know the end of this adventure!

When Percival awoke and put on his robes, he went to the hermit and found him waiting. And Percival said to the hermit that God would keep him well.

"My health has failed me, and I have blown the last notes on my hunting horn," replied the hermit. "Now I will tell you the wonders of Merlin and what happened to me at night while I slept. He appeared before me. The Holy Man and the Holy Angel are filled with great joy, and the enemies are very angry. I tell you that your soul will be saved. Before I knew Merlin, I lived with lies."

Then Percival said: "Tell me the miracles."

"Listen," said the hermit. "Justice has been served in Northumberland. I stayed there in a hostel for one night. Merlin, who sprang from his mother as he pleased, as Blaise testifies in his book, stepped into the breach for a merchant who arrived and denounced the money changers. He had traded gold in the market and found out that it was not right. He had not been given pure gold nuggets.[148]

"The merchant then spoke further: 'I went back to the hostel where I spent the night. I tested the nuggets. I found out they were not right, so I went back to the money changers and asked them for the proper gold nuggets. One of them distracted me and said he would let me know the results of the test. I only stood up for my right and truth. But the judges were weak-kneed. They gave in and distanced themselves from the case.'

"Sire, Mother of God! Unauthorized treasurers entered the church. Witnesses were kept at bay and, unbelievably, killed by the bishops. A priest attacked a woman who came to him asking penance for a dying man.

"The priest was accused of rape in front of the bishop and denied his crime, supported by the testimonies of his friends. The judges called in the money changers, who swore they knew nothing. The state of affairs in the market was known, but there was nothing they could do about it.

"Merlin went to the church where he stood before the bishops."

"Then the judges came to the church. And when Merlin saw the judges coming, he laughed. 'Wise judges, I know you are not wise.'

"Merlin said that if they knew him well, they must know he would find out the truth. And one of the jurors jumped up and said they did not see or hear anything. And Merlin laughed cynically. 'The truth will surely remain behind the doors of the church. You will do everything to keep and protect the stolen treasure, even if the magpies peck you until you bleed.'

"Those in the church had seen the treasurers come unauthorized to the entrance, much to the dismay of the bishops.

'What is this, Merlin?'

"And he answered: 'Lord, look to the gold and silver, which the

---

148. This refers back to the first references in the text to the devious nature of the money changers; clearly, a strong topic for the monkish scribe.

enemies from Hell will keep.' Through magic, Merlin [caused] the money changers' ten chests containing the stolen money [to] fall open at their feet.

"Then to the judges he said: 'Gentlemen, take the keys and shut these chests and know that you shall find within the golden wheels of the city of Constantine and of Saint Elaine[149] and the rest.'

"What shall I tell you? The money changers acknowledged that they were wrong to the trader and returned the gold nuggets. They were taken from the market and their hands cut off.

"Back in the town, Merlin asked the judges to do justice for the enraged woman. Just as they had the hands of the thieving money changers cut off, the judges had the rapist-priest emasculated. The bishop was not punished, much to Merlin's anger.

"Later, on Merlin's orders, the judges were handcuffed and taken to the palace.

87: Of the Death of the Hermit

After Helias [had finished speaking, he] gave the coffer to Percival, he opened it and found letters written within. Helias died three days later to the song of angels.

Helias had given the manuscript of Merlin's writings to the knight, who would then entrust it to the Wise Clerk, who would add it to the library of Merlin's books. On his way, Percival experienced several more adventures.

After he had seen Helias buried by another hermit, Percival passed the night at the house of a widow and the next day rode on his way. He came to a fountain where a pavilion was set up, and that bore the marks of long usage. Within the pavilion he found a revolving wheel fastened to a marble column and having on it an iron cage, in which a clerk was confined, and on the top of which there was a brake.

---

149. That is coins. Elaine is Helena, the mother of Constantine IV, who is said to have discovered the True Cross.

The wheel was revolving with marvellous speed, and the clerk cried out to Percival, entreating him to force the brake down, but Percival could not understand him because of the noise of the wheel, which never ceased to revolve except when a neighbouring hermit said Mass. During the [next] pause [of the wheel], the clerk took his food, which an old woman served to him. When she arrived with the food, she explained to Percival that Merlin had confined the clerk there for a misdeed.

While they talked the hermit began to say Mass and the clerk to eat, speaking not a word, but making the most of his time for food and signing meanwhile to Percival to press the brake. Percival used all his strength but could not move it. He begged the old woman to tell him how he could accomplish this adventure, and to prove to him that his efforts would be in vain, she led him to a deserted tower, before which was a stone bearing an inscription written by the Lady of the Lake after she had entombed Merlin.

It said that when [Merlin] was in the forest of Avrences with the Lady of the Lake, the clerk also came to the forest and secretly watched them.

He was clever, having studied all his life in Avalon, and was able to cast a spell upon the Lady of the Lake, which put her completely into his power. But although enchanted, she undid the charm by which she had herself lulled Merlin into a deep sleep. He awoke and to punish the clerk confined him in the revolving cage. There he must remain until the Knight of the Dragon laid his hand upon the brake.

Percival left the clerk and rode on his way. He was attacked by two terrible robbers who dwelled in a neighbouring tower with a band of miscreants. They had gone on a pillaging expedition, leaving in the tower only their fellows and the maiden to whom it belonged. Percival killed one of the robbers and forced the others to surrender, then conducted him to the tower. Here he set free many knights whom he found imprisoned, and then presented the tower to the maiden. The robber promised to become a good and loyal knight, and the maiden agreed to marry him.

Percival took his leave and pursued his wanderings until he came to another tower, to which he was admitted by an old woman. She begged him to fight on the morrow with its lord, who was holding captive in a pavilion a lady who refused him her love. Percival went to the pavilion and found the damsel cruelly bound with iron wires. She entreated him to release her, and he promised to do his best.

From a varlet he learned that the people of the countryside had sworn that if any knight were to unbind the maiden by force, they would rebind her to await the coming of any knight who could vanquish her oppressor.

Percival lodged in a pavilion for the night. In the morning, he and the knight of the tower, both mounted and armed, met, and Percival declared his intention to do combat for the lady. The knight explained that Percival's quarrel was not good enough. He had met the maiden one day near his tower, and in response to her request had escorted her in safety to her dwelling. Here he was attacked by [another] knight, whom he killed, but the maiden, though begged by her followers to marry him, was disloyal enough to refuse. He, accordingly, at the request of her indignant people that he bring her to term, had imprisoned her, but even thus he had not won her love.

Percival replied that he had undertaken her quarrel, just or unjust. They engaged in a fierce battle in which Percival succeeded in striking the knight to the ground. He spared the life [of his opponent] on condition that he free the maiden and declare himself her prisoner. The knight accepted the conditions, only praying Percival not to deliver him to the maiden. He handed his sword to Percival, who received it. Percival gave orders that the maiden be unbound and rode on his way. She, however, declaring that he had handed her over to the mercies of the knight, sent a squire after him to entreat him to give the tower to another knight, one who could protect her from her oppressor. Otherwise, he would have infringed the custom of Logres.

The squire overtook Percival as he was standing in the forest by a stone on which a prophecy of Merlin was written. When he had copied the prophecy, he returned with the squire to the tower, where the maiden told him that her reason for refusing to marry the knight was that he was a robber who hated her because she has harboured in her dwelling merchants whom he desired to rob. Percival said that if he had known this when he undertook to defend her, the knight would not have escaped so lightly. On the morrow, at the maiden's request, he knighted a young squire whom she loved and forthwith married, giving him the tower to protect. Percival himself remained for a time at the tower.

Once he had seen the maiden of the pavilion married to the youth he had knighted, Percival rode on his way to Corbenic.[150] In the forest he rescued two maidens from four knights. [These were the maidens'] cousins, who had killed the maidens' brother, [and had] deprived them of their inheritance. On their refusal to marry two robbers to whom the knights desired to give them, [the knights] were about to burn them alive.

Percival, after horribly maiming the knights in combat, escorted the maidens to their castle, which her people at once begged him to accept as his own. He was in the act of declining this, when two knights from a neighbouring castle rode up, defied him, and engaged him in a combat in which they were slain. Percival was at a loss to know what to do with the Benjamin's portion[151] of the castle, until a knight errant arrived on the scene, to whom he passed over everything he had won, and gladly went on his way.

Now the story says that the Wise Clerk [of Wales] held the books of Merlin. He saw the one that was written by Merlin's master, Blaise, and learned that Blaise had told Merlin's mother that lust would no longer torment the ladies of Gaunes. He also held a book written by Merlin at the age of eighteen months—*The Hidden*

---

150. Corbenic, also spelled Corbin or Carbonek, is the name usually attributed to the castle of the Grail in the medieval romances.
151. This is a reference to the biblical statement in Genesis 43:34 that refers to the worthy receiving more than they could possibly expect.

Gospel of Childhood, later entrusted to Helias. The Wise Clerk began to read the book written by Blaise and speak of it to bystanders. It said:

"Know that those who show no mercy will be judged badly by the shedding of blood. And more men and women will suffer and become bitter because the grains of wheat they sow on this earth will yield nothing.

"Those who have the law belonging to the Lady of God, the Earth and the stars and the sky, and the bride, Eve, the trees, the beasts, the birds, and all things that bear gold in them. Their faith will be saved providing they have faith in the Lady of God. And God allows it, as part of his eternal vengeance on the dead gold of the Earth. So as they get worse in faith and law, they will also get things that will help them keep their hope."

The Wise Clerk of Wales concluded his public talk with the Holy Supper and closed the book. Then he said:

88: On Rubens, Who Took the Place of Raymon the Wise Clerk of Wales

"Gentlemen, these great treasures that I have described depend upon Merlin's service. I am sure the age will bring many more. I see [in his book] all the battles of Logres that are fought in the time of King Luces[152] [. . .] until the day when the Round Table meets for the last time. Records of this will be brought hither and written on parchment and made into a new book. For thus everyone will want it.

"Gentlemen clerks, I see Rubens the Chaplain come in my place after my death," said Raymon the Wise Clerk of Wales. "And I see questions and written wonders brought before him. And if he finds anything of Merlin's, it must be immediately put in writing and joined with all his prophecies."

---

152. Probably Lucius, mentioned in several early chronicles, including that of Geoffrey of Monmouth.

Then the Wise Clerk stripped off his episcopal mantle and gave it to Rubens the Chaplain. Rubens received its powers just as Raymon had once obtained them. This happened as Merlin predicted, and soon after that the Wise Clerk of Wales fell ill.

89: The Death of Raymon the Wise Clerk of Wales

What shall I tell you? When the Chaplain Rubens was given this immense inheritance, and he saw that the wisest clerk of the age had left the Earth, he gave a thousand marks of silver to the Holy Church, just as the Wise Clerk had commanded. [. . .] The Wise Clerk, whose life ended at eight o'clock in the morning, was buried in a church in Wales, and over his grave was written "Raymon the Wise Clerk of Wales, who bequeathed the great treasure of Merlin's wisdom upon his death." After Raymon was buried, the Chaplain [Rubens] took his place.

Know also that the Lady of the Lake will have to appear before Jesu Christ on Judgment Day and that Merlin will be resurrected at that time.

And Merlin continued to prophesy many more wonders [from within his tomb]. He said that there will be pestilence in Germany; that great famine will come upon Lombardy, France, and Germany; that the city of Narbonne will be flooded; and that there will be war in Europe.

THE END OF THE PROPHECIES OF MERLIN

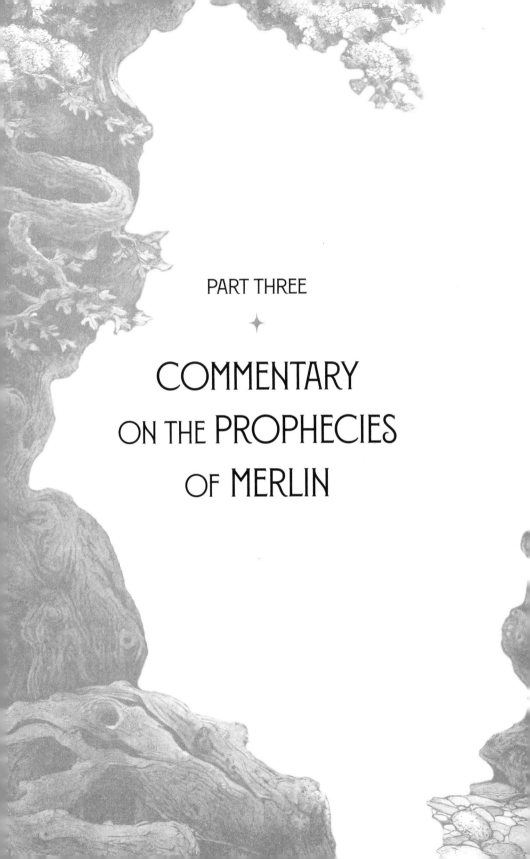

PART THREE

COMMENTARY ON THE PROPHECIES OF MERLIN

Here we set forth our interpretation of the work. Briefer points can be found as footnotes in the body of the text itself. Here we will endeavour to find our way through the strange twists and turns of the story and address the meanings hidden within. All entries are set forth as follows: the colophons or subheadings that divide the text are numbered and titled, and the appropriate comments are keyed to these in the order in which they appear. We suggest that you read the text and the comments together for the first time, for ease of understanding.

1: Merlin Begins His Prophecies

As he prepares to withdraw from the world, Merlin begins to make a series of prophetic statements to the first of several scribes. These appear in different order in the various versions of the text. The 1498 edition is the only one to begin with Master Tholomer. This scribe is possibly named after the great visionary author and astronomer Claudius Ptolemy, who lived and worked in Alexandria from circa 100–170 AD. Giving Tolomer this name helped to suggest that Merlin was a real man rather than a myth. There does in fact seem to have been some division between those who believed in Merlin and those who did not, but the majority regarded the Arthurian figure as a real person. He may well have existed if we are correct in seeing him as originating from the same school as Taliesin, a Welsh prince and bard of the sixth century, whose prophecies, preserved in one of *The Four Ancient Books of Wales*,[153] are every bit as strange and wild as those contained in our edition of the *Prophecies*. Those found within the Vérard edition include attacks on the shortcomings of various clerics of the time, many of whom were charged with simony, the acquiring of money through the buying or selling of spiritual gifts. Simony is named after the infamous magician, Simon Magus, who tried to purchase the gift of divine wisdom from the apostles of Christ (Acts 8:18). This led to the sale of indulgences by wandering peddlers promising to reduce time spent in Hell by sinners in return for payment.

Merlin also suggests that biblical texts were somehow changed or corrupted—specifically in the Gospel of John. This is interesting as there is evidence of a kind of splinter group who saw both John the Baptist and John the Beloved as more important than Jesus. Several other heretical sects, including the Cathars, are referenced in the text, as we shall see.

---

[153]. See Skene, *The Four Ancient Books of Wales*. However, the translations are frequently inaccurate. See the selection included here as appendix 1.

2: Of the Sea That Will Grow above the Shore as High as the Mountains

Here we have the response of Christ to the clerics who do not follow the right path. First, he is said to raise a flood of biblical proportions, lasting for the same forty days as Noah's flood in Genesis 6–9. Here, however, it sounds more like a tsunami, with a mighty wall of water. In addition, an unnamed "terrestrial angel" somehow intervenes on behalf of humanity and prevents the deaths of many who would have been drowned.

Merlin is very specific about the date (September) but then moves smartly on to the first of many references to the Dragon of Babylon, also known as "the Thing that left Jerusalem." Almost every one of the prophecies mentions these, which are alternate titles referring to the Antichrist, who was expected to appear—though at no specific date—throughout the twelfth and thirteenth centuries.

We have written at greater length about the Great Dragon in part one, in the chapter "Written Records of the Prophecies" (see pages 21–26). Here it is sufficient to say that the coming of this terrifying being, who would look like a man but possess demonic powers, was a threat held over the heads of Christians during this period. Various people—including Emperor Frederick II—were identified as the Dragon or the Antichrist. Basically, it could be anyone who disagreed with the core teaching of the church.

Here, Merlin speaks of the temptations, rewards, and punishments likely to be handed out to any followers of the Antichrist. Then he moves smartly on to the first mention of King Arthur, who is interestingly said to "ride through the perilous woods" to test the prowess of the knights who follow him and to earn the respect of all whom he encounters. At first Tholomer doubts that there could be any king as fine as Uther Pendragon (Uterpendragon), Arthur's father, but Merlin convinces him that the young king will be so excellent and that his kingdom will cause the "recalibration" of the remaining kings of Britain—presumably because they will be considered as nothing when compared to Arthur.

Next, he mentions King Lot of Orkney, a familiar character from the Arthurian cycle. Married to one of Arthur's half sisters—Morgause—he is the father of the famous knights Gawain, Gaheries, Agravaine, and Gareth. The story referenced here is unknown elsewhere. As far as we know, Lot did not kill his son, nor did his sons slay him. He was, initially, an adversary of Arthur, being one of the eleven kings who rebelled against the young king following his withdrawal of the sword from the stone. In the *Merlin Continuations*, which follow the *Lancelot-Grail* Cycle, Lot allies himself with King Ryons and King Nero to attack Arthur, but Merlin distracts him by visiting him and weaving an elaborate set of prophecies about his future.

Merlin then refers to an incident at Salebiēres. This is probably Salisbury, and specifically the nearby ancient circle of Stonehenge, which in Geoffrey of Monmouth's *Historia Regum Britanniae* is the setting for the "Night of the Long Knives," in which a group of British chieftains are summoned to a meeting there, only to be murdered by their Saxon counterparts. This is considered as a heinous crime against the ideals of chivalry (which had scarcely begun to be formulated at the time) in which both good and bad people were slain. Merlin himself was said to have transported the stones of Stonehenge from Ireland.

This leads us back to further references to the Dragon of Babylon and introduces us to the idea of heavenly war going on both in Heaven and on Earth, involving the ancestors of Troy (which included the British, if one follows the idea that Britain was founded by Brutus, grandson of the hero Aeneas). This is followed by a longer passage relating to the Dragon, his evil works, his misguided followers, and God's determination to defeat him. The question also arises of those who may doubt Merlin's own purpose, though this is firmly put to rest by the statement of Master Tholomer to the effect that anyone who doubts him should consider his abilities to change shape, along with his many other skills—including prophecy. Merlin's own statement, contained in the early fourteenth-century Rennes manuscript, is quite specific about his role, as perceived by the Christian scribe of that text, when he declares that "by our Lord Jesu Christ, if it was your will that I was born on earth to shame the enemies from hell and to fight on earth against the evil miracles of the Dragon of Babylon and to dissever the bad actions of the clerics."

Finally, bringing to an end this section, Merlin predicts that Tholomer will be appointed a Bishop of Wales. Almost immediately several clerics arrive to make this request. Tholomer accepts, with some apparent reluctance, but Merlin has already taken himself off to set up his next scribe, Master Antoine. There is some evident disagreement as to whether Tholomer is the right man for the job as bishop—presumably because of his association with Merlin. This, we are told, delays his ordination as bishop, but it does happen eventually, and we are finally told that he later perished in the Holy Land, presumably having accompanied one of the many Crusades of the period.

3: About the Dragons That Live Underground

This gem of Arthurian information is particularly interesting as it shows that the scribe either added his own variation to the original tradition or that he had access to a source no longer current. It follows on from the episode recorded by Geoffrey of Monmouth in his *Historia Regum Britanniae*. As we mentioned in the chapter "Merlin's Scribes" in part one, Merlin reveals the reason why a tower constructed by the rapacious King Vortigern will not stand—this being due to the presence of two dragons, one red and the other white, who fight every night beneath the earth. When the king requires his men to dig beneath the hill on which the tower was to be erected, the two dragons fly up into the air and do battle with each other. This is said to represent the struggle between the Saxons (white dragon) and the British (red dragon); it prompts Merlin to then give forth the very extensive sequence of prophecies recorded by Geoffrey of Monmouth, a selection of which can be found in appendix 2 of this book.

Here we see Uther Pendragon, King Arthur's father, asking Merlin a very interesting question: How did the dragons of Vortigern's tower live underground? For answer Merlin takes the king to a valley where they find a round block of stone, which Merlin reveals contains a small snake trapped within. The king gives an order for the stone to be split, and when it is, the snake flies out and Merlin catches it and shows the king how sharp its teeth are. He says that "these teeth are sharp enough to gnaw their way into the stone. They can fly over the Earth and cause harm to all."

This is an interesting variant on the story given us by Geoffrey. Merlin seems to be suggesting that the snake, which is clearly an ordinary-sized creature, is in some way to be identified with the full-size dragons recorded beneath the hill under Vortigern's tower. Merlin then adds an even more intriguing note: "There is a sword in the serpent-stone at mountain Gargano, and from the mountain no one can take it out except the chosen one." This is a most interesting comment to find here. It refers to a story associated with a Saint Galgano (c. 1148–1185), attached to the town of Montesiepi in present-day Tuscany, where a sword stuck fast into a stone is still shown. Though this is almost certainly a fake, it reflects a very interesting story, which may be summarised as follows.

Born at Chiusdino, near Sienna, Tuscany, in the year 1148, to a noble family, Galgano initially became a knight and spent his days hunting and enjoying the pleasures brought by wealth. He was famed for his arrogance and selfishness and was constantly in trouble. Following the death of his father, Galgano moved to Sienna, and it was at this time that he experienced his first vision, which was of the Archangel Michael. In this he saw his mother giving her approval to the idea of her son joining the Heavenly Hosts. He then saw himself following in the footsteps of St. Michael.

Following this, Galgano became dissatisfied with his old life and returned to his mother's home at Chiusdino. There, for the next five years, he apparently led a quiet and penitential life. It was at this time that he received a second vision of St. Michael, who told him to go to Montesiepi, a thickly forested hill that lay some four miles from

Chiusdino. When he reached there, he was to abandon his possessions as recompense for his earlier wild life.

On hearing of this, Galgano's family decided he should marry and forget all about his visions. They found him a beautiful woman named Polissena Brizzi who was elected to be Galgano's bride. At first Galgano refused, but in time he gave in, ignoring the visions of the archangel.

Galgano set out to the home of his future bride to escort her home, but some four miles from Chiusdino, on the plain of Morella, his horse stopped and refused to go any farther. Galgano dismounted and fell to his knees, acknowledging his blindness in refusing to follow the signs given him by the archangel. Michael then appeared to him and commanded that he follow him to Montesiepi. In the vision the archangel guided him to a place where he was greeted by the twelve apostles of Christ in front of a circular-shaped temple.

At this point Galgano drew his sword and said that it would be easier to plunge the weapon into a stone than to receive forgiveness for his previous wild life. Then he thrust his sword into the stone up to the hilt, so that it formed a cross and altar at which he could pray.

On December 1, 1180, Galgano determined to build a hermitage, where he lived out his days. He soon acquired disciples who followed him there, but he found the notion of being the leader of such a group difficult. In 1181 he visited Pope Alexander III who acknowledged his saintly life. However, Galgano did not long survive the harsh life of a hermit and within four years fell sick and died. Following his death a number of miracles were reported, and the hermitage grew into a more permanent site.

The official date of Galgano's death is 1185, and some tales credit Frederick I with putting in a word on Galgano's behalf, which hastened his canonization barely a year later. This would be interesting given the associations between Frederick II and the *Prophecies*. When Galgano's body was exhumed, his blond hair was seen to have continued growing, and for this reason his head was subsequently placed in a reliquary in a niche in the chapel, and his body re-interred. Two mummified forearms and hands—said to be from a thief who tried to pull the sword from the stone and was attacked by wolves—were exhibited in a second niche. The Cistercians became the guardians of the supposed site of Galgano's hut in 1201, after they reportedly built a round chapel there, which became a popular pilgrimage destination.

The earliest form of Galgano's *Vita* is a seventeenth-century copy of a fourteenth-century manuscript, penned by an anonymous Augustinian scribe, and its emphasis is on the sovereignty of Jesus and to Galgano's giving up the life of a warrior. A second manuscript contains a fourteenth-century copy of a *Vita* attributed to one Friar Roland of Pisa, who supposedly wrote it circa 1220 AD. That Roland was a friar indicates that he was probably either a Franciscan or a Dominican. This fits very well with the idea that the authors of the original manuscript of the *Prophecies* and that of the 1498 edition were both Franciscans.

More than one researcher into this story has suggested it was the source for the thirteenth-century poet Robert de Boron's Sword in the Stone episode in his own Merlin romance,[154] and certainly the reference to this, following the variant of the Vortigern's tower episode, suggests a known contemporary account. Once again, we see a powerful link between the Arthurian canon and the theological beliefs of the Franciscans; this can hardly be an accident.[155]

4: The Queen of Brequehem Visits Merlin

This is one of several sections that either does not add greatly to the overall meaning of the text or introduces themes that are explored later on. In this instance, it is unclear why the Queen of Brequehem (or Bethlehem) should visit Merlin. It is possible that this refers to one of the queens who accompanied their consorts and armies into the conflict of the Crusades. Eleanor of Aquitaine is perhaps the best known of these, but there were several more. Isabella II, second wife of Frederick II, was also a queen of Jerusalem.[156]

---

154. See de Boron, *Merlin and the Grail*.
155. For a further exploration of this, see Malcor and Matthews, *The Sword in the Stone*.
156. See Nicholson, *Women and the Crusades*, for more on this fascinating subject.

Here the scribe also takes the opportunity to prophesy several disasters in the Holy Land and famine in the Italian city of Treviso, adding that both the government and the church are going to be following a false religion. There are a number of hints throughout the manuscript that imply similar ideas. References to the Johannites, followers of John the Baptist, who tried to replace Christ with the earlier visionary saint, and references to the beliefs and followers of Saint James, the brother of Jesus, all of which at various times were outlawed as heretical. This is in line with the purpose that underlay many of the collections of prophecies throughout the Middle Ages—not just of Merlin but others—to draw attention to supposed false teachings within Christianity itself.

5: How the Emperor of Rome Came before the Pope with a Hundred Knights

The section, which appears here in the text of the 1498 incunabulum, is very clearly out of place. We have therefore transposed it to section 70, which introduces a number of references to the Crusades contemporary with the earlier 1303 edition of the *Prophecies*.

6: The Death of King Arthur

Here Merlin prophesies the death of Arthur at the hands of his own son, Mordred, who was the result of an unknowing act of incest when Arthur slept with his half sister Morgause (not Morgain le Fay, as is often assumed by critics who mixed up the two women). Morgause was one of the sisters born to Lady Igrayne before her husband Gorlois, the Duke of Cornwall, was slain by King Uther, who had fallen in love with her and launched a war to make her his queen. Morgause later came to Camelot and seduced the young king, knowing full well their relationship.

In one of the darkest moments of the Arthurian saga, when Merlin revealed to Arthur that he had sired an incestuous child, the king—echoing the actions of Herod in the biblical account—ordered all babies born in that year to be slain.

Plate 1. Merlin. Original painting by Will Worthington, 2012. From John Matthews's personal collection.

Plate 2. Merlin, from the *Nuremberg Chronicle*, 1493.

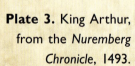

Plate 3. King Arthur, from the *Nuremberg Chronicle*, 1493.

Plate 4. Merlin reporting on a lunar eclipse, from *Lapidario*, a compilation of texts of astronomy by Alfonso the Wise (1221–1284). Manuscript copied in England around 1400.

Plate 5. Opening of the text of the *Prophecies of Merlin*, 1498. Photo by Maarten Haverkamp.

Si commencent les prophe-cies merlin.

Y endroit dit le compte q̃ merlin estoit vng iour en galles en la chambre de maistre tholomer et pensoit moult fort en luy mesmes. Lors lui print a demãder maistre tholomer. Je te prie merlin se dieu te gard q̃ tu me dies en quoy tu penses tãt longuemẽt. Et merlin lui respõdit Je pẽsoie aux terres q̃lz seront pmy le mõde ou temps q̃ la chose q̃ iadis nasquit es pties de ierusalẽ aura mil deux centz.lxxvii. ans/car ilz ne garderont ne ne tiẽdrõt les doctrines de leurs ancestres Mais ensuiuront les oeuures q̃ en cellui tẽps feront les tirans et leurs discors ensuiurõt Et seront aueucq̃s vng gouuerneur a q̃ sa porte sera brisee a force dargent q̃ les tirans lui dourront. Les prelas de celle terre ne garderõt en cellui tẽps fors seulement a force dargent: et saichez q̃ ce aduiẽdra entreulx pour lexẽple q̃lz aurõt eue de la court du gouuerneur. Metz en ton escript q̃ en celle terre aura vne discorde entre deux clercs q̃ cellui q̃ aura force dargẽt viẽdra au dessus soit droit ou tort ẽ si põra cellui q̃ point dar

fueillet.i.

gẽt naura Et y aura lors vne mauuaise coustume. Dy moy merlin dist tholomer serõt les clercs p̃ tout le mõde aisi mauuais Ouy certes dist merlin Ilz ne garderont pas aux bõnes oeuures q̃ aurõt fait les saictz gouuerneurs a les saictz ministres Mais ilz regarderont a ce q̃ aurõt fait les mauuais tirãs et les mauuais ministres desloyaulx q̃ auront brisee la porte de fer et di passefer. Dy moy merlin dit maistre tholomer q̃ diront les gẽs en cellui temps. Certes fait merlin que les clercs auront change leuangile de monseigneur sainct iehan qui dist que chascune chose pour force dargent ne se face Adonc fait maistre tholomer aura mestier le liure des euãgiles Certes dist merlin nennyn / car les iuges ne garderont iustice que a force dargent/ Et si cõmencera ceste oeuure mauuaise ou temps que ie te dis Mais vng peu quant aura elle este commencee a la court du gouuerneur non pas si appertemẽt cõme il sera parmy le monde a cellui temps q̃ ie te dis Et saichees que par cellui pechie en monstrera nostre seigneur ie sucrist vng signe.

De la mer qui croistra dessus la riue si hault comme les montaignes.

a.i.

Plate 6. First page of the *Prophecies of Merlin*, 1498.
Photo by Maarten Haverkamp.

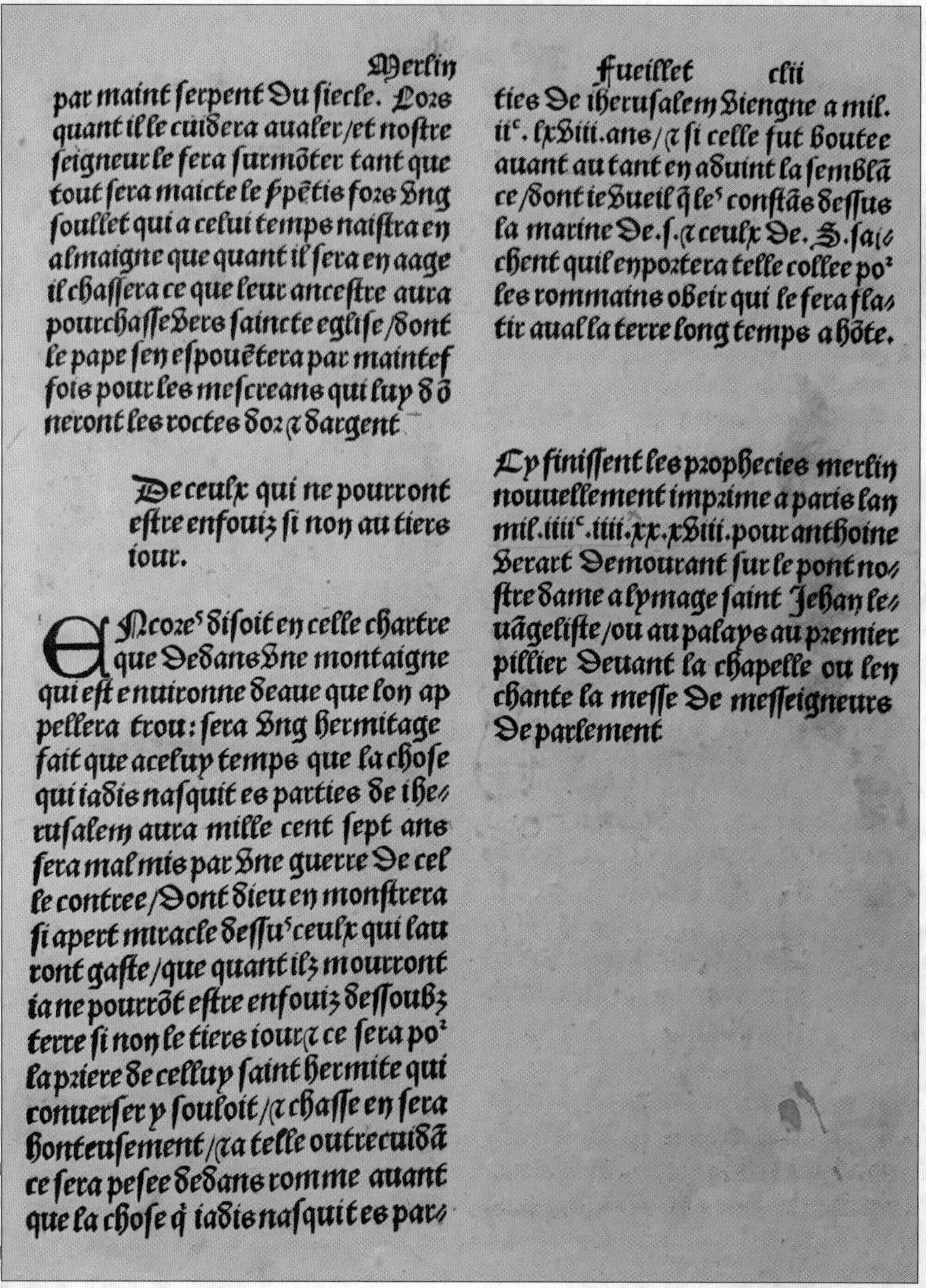

Merlin

par maint serpent du siecle. Lors
quant il le cuidera aualer/et nostre
seigneur le fera surmōter tant que
tout sera maicte le pp̄etis fors ung
soullet qui a celui temps naistra en
almaigne que quant il sera en aage
il chassera ce que leur ancestre aura
pourchasse vers saincte eglise/dont
le pape sen espouētera par maintes
fois pour les mescreans qui luy d ō
neront les roctes dor τ dargent

De ceulx qui ne pourront
estre enfouiz si non au tiers
iour.

Encores disoit en celle chartre
que dedans une montaigne
qui est enuironne deaue que lon ap
pellera trou: sera ung hermitage
fait que aceluy temps que la chose
qui iadis nasquit es parties de ihe/
rusalem aura mille cent sept ans
sera mal mis par une guerre de cel
le contree/dont dieu en monstrera
si apert miracle dessus ceulx qui lau
ront gaste/que quant ilz mourront
ia ne pourrōt estre enfouiz dessoubz
terre si non le tiers iour τ ce sera po²
la priere de celluy saint hermite qui
conuerser y souloit/τ chasse en sera
honteusement/τ a telle outrecuidā
ce sera pesee dedans romme auant
que la chose q̄ iadis nasquit es par/

Fueillet clii

ties de iherusalem viengne a mil.
ii.e lxviii. ans/τ si celle fut boutee
auant autant en aduint la semblā
ce/dont ie dueil q̄ les constās dessus
la marine de .s.τ ceulx de .s. sa/
chent quil enportera telle collee po²
les rommains obeir qui le sera fla/
tir aual la terre long temps a hōte.

Cy finissent les prophecies merlin
nouuellement imprime a paris lan
mil.iiii.c.iiii.xx.xviii. pour anthoine
verart demourant sur le pont no/
stre dame a lymage saint Jehan le/
uāgeliste/ou au palays au premier
pillier deuant la chapelle ou len
chante la messe de messeigneurs
de parlement

Plate 7. Last page of the *Prophecies of Merlin*, 1498.
Photo by Maarten Haverkamp.

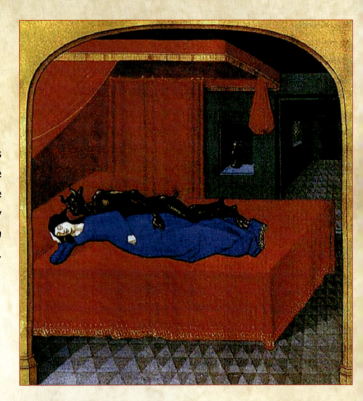

Plate 8. Merlin's mother with the demon, from the thirteenth-century manuscript of *Merlin en Prose*.

Plate 9. How Merlin was fathered by the Devil, from *Lancelot of the Lake, Part One*. Paris, Bibliothèque Mazarine, 1286, Folio f. 008v.

Plate 10. The birth of Merlin, from the thirteenth-century manuscript of *Merlin en Prose*.

Plate 11. Merlin prophesying, from the thirteenth-century text of Robert de Boron's *Merlin en Prose*.

Plate 12. Merlin appearing before Caesar in the form of a stag, from a manuscript of the *Lancelot-Grail* Cycle.

Plate 13. Merlin's cave, from where he prophesied. Engraving by T. Bonless, from *Merlin or the British Enchanter*, 1736. From John Matthews's personal collection.

Plate 14. Merlin dictating, from a manuscript of the *Lancelot-Grail* Cycle. From John Matthews's personal collection.

Plate 15. Merlin enters his tomb in a 1529 woodcut illustration from Sir Thomas Malory's *Le Morte D'Arthur*. From John Matthews's personal collection.

Plate 16. "Merlin" by Aubrey Beardsley, illustration for Malory's *Le Morte D'Arthur*.
From John Matthews's personal collection.

Plate 17. "Merlin as a Druid" by Louis Rhead, from a series of illustrations for Tennyson's *Idylls of the King*. From John Matthews's personal collection.

Plate 18. Emperor Frederick II.

Plate 19. Prester John, Rome, 1599.
From Maarten Haverkamp's personal collection; photo by Maarten Haverkamp.

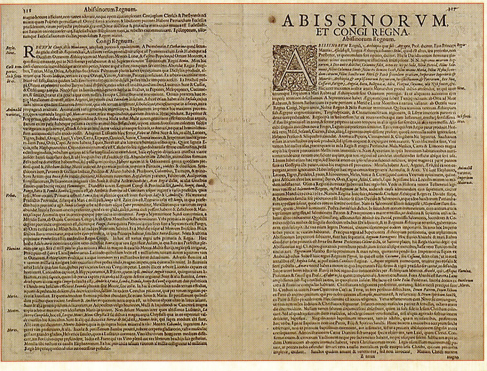

Plate 20. Opening page of Prester John's *Letter*.

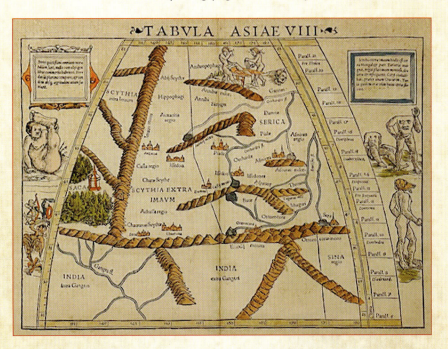

Plate 21. The realm of Prester John, based on the *Letter*.
Sebastian Munster, Germany, 1550.
From Maarten's personal collection; photo by Maarten Haverkamp.

Plate 22. Prester John serving Mass, from the *Chronicles of Hartmann Schedel*, 1493.

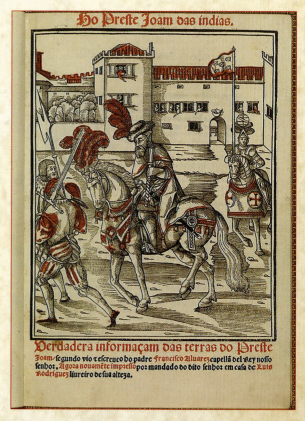

Plate 23. Title page from *Prester John of the Indies* by Francisco Alvares, Lisbon, 1540.

Plate 24. Prester John enthroned, from a map of East Africa from *Queen Mary's Atlas*. Diogo Homem, Portugal, 1559. From Maarten Haverkamp's personal collection.

Plate 25. A medieval map of Prester John's Kingdom: *Presbiteri Johannis, sive, Abissinorum Imperii descriptio* (a description of the empire of Prester John, that is to say, of the Abyssinians), from *Theatrum Orbis Terrarium* by Ortelius, Antwerp, 1573. From the collections of the National Library of the Netherlands.

Plate 26. Merlin in the Wild.
Illustration © Alan Lee, 1992.

In fact, they were set adrift in a ship, which later sank in a storm, but the infant Mordred washed ashore and was discovered by a fisherman, who raised him until his true parentage was revealed. Interestingly, this story is echoed in the *Prophecies* in the story of the lost crown of Orbance (see section 10), which is also lost at sea, discovered by a fisherman, and later revealed to be of great symbolic and magical importance. According to Pictish custom, a sister's son was acknowledged as the rightful heir, so Mordred's claim to his father's throne, which brought down the Round Table and destroyed the Arthurian kingdom, was actually rightful.

7: Of the Damsel from Wales Who Came to the Room Where Merlin and Tholomer Were

In this section we meet a mysterious damsel from Wales who comes to see Merlin. As soon as he sees her, Merlin remarks that she has the mark of the supernatural about her and proceeds to outline her future, including the birth of a child who will become king of Bellistans, a fictional city just above the sea around Sarazin, and who in time will be crowned king by King Arthur.

In an aside, the scribe mentions that Merlin would have loved to play with the damsel as he had so often done with others, but he held back since her child would be a descendant of the royal family of Ireland. This is the first mention of Merlin's amorous adventures. As we are told later, he seems to have offered to teach magic to a good number of women in response for sexual favours, but here we see him restraining himself, presumably because he does not want to become the accidental father of a future King of Ireland.

Merlin then immediately moves on to one of the central themes behind the book and also one of the central themes of the Arthurian legends as a whole—the quest for the Grail. Merlin gives us a single paragraph of the history of the quest, in which he sees the sacred cup originating in Jerusalem and travelling to Babylon, back again to

Jerusalem, and then onwards to many other places, before ending up in the kingdom of Arthur. He mentions the Grail being guarded along with the Bleeding Spear in an inaccessible castle guarded by the Grail king and the Grail knights. This is all very much central to the entire theme of the Grail myth, from its first recognisable appearance in the writings of Chrétien de Troyes, through those of Robert de Boron, Wolfram von Eschenbach, and the huge volumes of the *Lancelot-Grail* Cycle. He mentions that the Grail is said to provide "happiness, eternal youth, and food in infinite abundance"—all aspects of the sacred vessel that appear throughout its long and complex history.

Merlin then moves quickly to another of the central themes throughout the whole of this text, referring to "the Thing that came out of Jerusalem one thousand two hundred seventy years ago." This is another reference to the Antichrist or the Great Dragon, who in this text and others is associated with Frederick II. He warns also that "Our Lord will be angered by all of this and that the world will tremble"—interestingly, not with fear but with love—and that innocent blood will be spilled as a result of the Great Dragon's coming. He adds: "Our Lord will utter his lamentation before all and will gather the blood of Abel when his brother Cain spills it on the earth." This is an interesting theological reference, which compares Christ's death with that of Abel at the hands of his brother—both being seen as innocent victims. Merlin points out that this will incur a heavenly judgment and that men and women will suffer and become better "because the grains of wheat they sow on the earth will yield nothing." This is clearly a reference to John 12:24, which states that "unless a grain of wheat falls into the earth and dies it remains alone; but if it dies, it bears much fruit."

Merlin continues intriguingly, suggesting that those who will suffer most from the wrath of God are those whose ancestors came from the great city of Troy. This is a very interesting mythological comment as it refers back to the idea that the descendants of the Trojan people were believed to have peopled Europe following the destruction of the city. Brutus, Aeneas's grandson, was believed at this time to be the founder of Britain, which was named after him. Early chronicles, including those of Geoffrey of Monmouth, refer to Brutus as very much a precursor of King Arthur.

Merlin then immediately refers to Isaac's ancestors, the sons of Abraham, who are of course the Jewish nation, who are here said to have once visited an island in the sea, but that they drowned on their way to or from this place—or perhaps in an inundation. The inference seems to follow, in the rather obscure language of the *Prophecies*, that at some point these people will have eaten human flesh. It is then stated that those who would destroy Armenia will die, and following their death, "more than a hundred thousand men and women will drown at sea"—possibly referring to Armenians drowning.

After Tholomer questions this, he makes an immediate reference to the Dragon of Babylon, which is, as we have seen, a reference to the Antichrist. This man, it is said, will come to Babylon and will cause many people to believe that the Dragon is in fact the Messiah.

This is followed by the first reference to *les bons mariniers*—the Good Mariners. The book only mentions the Good Mariners when referring to the inhabitants of the city where the story is located. There can be little doubt that the original manuscript was written in Venice, and therefore the Good Mariners refers to Venetians. The detailed descriptions of the city make it plausible that the author must have possessed extensive knowledge of Venice. Monks were virtually the only people who could write, and the large amount of apocalyptic, religious messages that the text contains point in the direction of a monk who lived in a monastery. The apocalyptic message points to a specific Franciscan monastery on San Francesco del Deserto island. The monk who wrote the original manuscript at the end of the thirteenth century was almost certainly fearful of his identity becoming known, since he criticized the church and the government several times.

At this point it is said that the Antichrist will appear, presumably in Venice, and that many will pray to him. All of this, as we saw in "Written Records of the Prophecies" in part one, appears to refer to the belief that Frederick II was in fact the Antichrist. Merlin then announces to Tholomer that this is the last time they will see each other in Ireland but that the scribe must go to Wales where he can continue to write down Merlin's prophecies for a time. This seems to upset Tholomer greatly, especially when Merlin adds that he will not come to Wales himself but wants Tholomer to say that he has "heard him crying loudly." This can only be a reference to the *Cri du Merlin*, the voice of Merlin that echoes from within his tomb and is thus the first mention within our text of the prophet's impending doom at the hands of the Lady of the Lake.

Tholomer remarks that he will seem to be on fire with inspiration while Merlin is with him or speaking through him and that he cannot find any words that go against Holy Church. He then adds that if no other prophet comes along, Merlin alone will be seen to have declared these things. He thus effectively tells us that Merlin represents a growing body of people who feel the church has taken a wrong turn, but that this might be repaired though the teachings of Merlin and his like.

Merlin then announces that he is not telling anyone else that he is soon to die, a first clear reference to the forthcoming events of his entombment by the Lady of the Lake. He remarks that Tholomer will go soon to Wales and eventually become a bishop there but that he will never see Merlin again.

This is followed by further remarks about the Dragon and that those who wish to believe in it or him will believe in it or in him, which could be harmful to God—for if people do not believe that God is mighty in all things they will commit ever-greater sins. He then adds that if those who see him simply as a wonder worker who has the power to change his form, this is a mistake, since Merlin has direct access to the wisdom of the Almighty. To which Tholomer responds that he wishes *he* could speak directly to God like Merlin.

Merlin then departs and goes to London, where he finds "all the men there lost and wars starting all over Great Britain," but apparently he does nothing about this.

Next day a galley from Wales appears directly at the port of Ireland, upon which are several barons and some clergy who have come to persuade Tholomer to become Bishop of Wales. Tholomer responds that he finds it regrettable that the clergy of Wales have become corrupt, an issue that we assume Tholomer himself will redress. He then journeys to Wales, but when the people hear of his coming, there is apparently some opposition to the idea that he should become a bishop—presumably because of his association with Merlin. The text says that he was not consecrated bishop until sometime later, and after a long life devoted to God, he died in the Holy Land. But before he left to travel there, he gave the *Book of Prophecies*, which he had collected from Merlin, to Master Antoine, the next of the scribes to appear.

8: Of Master Richard, Who Translated Merlin's Prophecies

This section actually occurs in the older Rennes manuscript. It seemed to sit well here and to explain the references to Richard as the original translator of the *Prophecies*. As we saw in the chapter "Merlin's Scribes" in part one, this is a fiction, devised to give weight to the collection. However, the story, which is partly hinted at here, is itself interesting. It states that while Master Richard is translating the prophecies, a knight is with him who has come from the Holy Roman Emperor, Frederick II. When this knight hears the words of Merlin and learns from Master Richard how all the things Merlin says are true, he expresses his excitement. In response Master Richard declares that he should speak of it no more, but that the prophecies are written on parchment and will be sent to the emperor. He himself will send his servant to carry the bundle. This itself, as we have read, will lead to Frederick having the documents translated into Arabic, Latin, and French—presumably from Merlin's native Welsh tongue. The scribe then remarks that, at this time, many poor people have begun to speak more about Merlin's prophecies, indicating that word has begun to spread, not just among the gentry but also among ordinary people, who have heard of Merlin's wisdom and believed in it.

9: Of the Crown of the Emperor of Orbance

As if to prove immediately why such a spread of Merlin's wisdom should occur, we hear the new scribe, Master Antoine, asking Merlin if it will rain upon the men of Orbance, or on the city called Anceris (Ankara?). This is perhaps a reference back to the flood, which Merlin had prophesied earlier as overwhelming those who believed the teachings of the Dragon.

Merlin then launches into a most extraordinary story. He speaks of the (unidentified) city of Orbance and says that, at the same time that his prophecies are being translated from Latin into French, a golden crown from Orbance will be found at the bottom of the Dead Sea. Set into this crown are four precious stones, each of which would be worth more than two bars of gold. This crown had previously belonged to the Emperor of Orbance but had been buried in a shipwreck. The importance of this will be shown over the next two sections, but Merlin adds that only when the Dragon of Babylon has been slain will the ocean and the eastern sea dry up, at which point men will see that what he said is true, for the evidence would be plain to all. This is all in line with the rather vague prophecies concerning the Dragon and the effects of its coming on the world. For the next part of the story of Orbance and the lost crown, we must turn to the next section, as well as to other texts that qualify the information given in the 1498 edition.

10: Of the Crown of Orbance That Shall Be Found

The rest of the story, as told by Merlin, may be summarised as follows. The crown, having been lost at sea for some time, will be discovered by a poor fisherman. He will sell it in Saragossa to the chieftain of that place, and this chieftain will give the stones to stone cutters who will add them to a golden crown, along with a hundred other stones. This will then be given to the emperor, by whom is meant Frederick II, who will not at first understand the stones or their value. But an inquiry will be set in motion to discover the truth about the crown and the prophecies that relate to it. Merlin adds that "the stones should be kept, for they will cause great miracles throughout the country."

To completely understand this story, we must turn to two other texts that make sense of the rather oblique reference in our edition. As we have seen and will continue to see, there are a number of references in the *Prophecies* to certain magical stones possessed by Merlin, which give off a radiance strong enough to keep those in their presence from sleeping (see section 23). There is also the small stone that Merlin shows to King Vortigern in section 2 and that contains a small serpent. Yet another stone, with the ability to carry someone standing upon it through the air over vast distances, and which we encounter in sections 60–62, may be linked to these, although the last named seems to be a round block of stone while the light-emitting stones are probably jewels.

This story has an interesting history and is part of a theme linking Merlin, and through him King Arthur, with the enigmatic figure of Prester John, the semi-mythical ruler of a vast Christian kingdom in the East. Most of our knowledge of Prester John comes from a letter, purported to come from him and addressed to several of the crowned heads of Europe, which appeared sometime between 1165 and 1170 AD. The existence of such a kingdom—actually a type of earthly paradise as it is described in the letter—was of immense importance as it suggested the presence of a Christian enclave behind the Muslim kingdoms that threatened the Holy Land and even Jerusalem itself. This was, of course, the cause of the various Crusades that took place between 1095 and 1291 and included most of the kingdoms of the West. (A copy of the text of the letter can be found in appendix 4.)

The *Prophecies* contain several references to Prester John—referred to as the King of India, a title frequently ascribed to the priest-king—and include the story of the flying stone, which we shall encounter in sections 60–62, in which the next of Merlin's scribes, Master Raymon, is carried to the kingdom of India and enabled to steal the emperor's cloak. Later in the same story, King Arthur himself receives letters from the distant kingdom, brought by a damsel from Avalon, and we learn that Merlin had visited and spent time in the company of the priest-king in the past. This is itself interesting enough, but the presence of two further references, both dating from the thirteenth century, within roughly the same period as our text, add significant details to the details in the *Prophecies*.

The first of these is found within a collection of brief story notes compiled by an anonymous author under the title *Il Novellino*, in or around the same period as the *Prophecies*. Here we read how it was Prester John himself who sent a collection of valuable jewels to Emperor Frederick II (the Holy Roman Emperor, who reigned over the Norman kingdom of Sicily from 1220 to 1225). Prester John asks his emissaries to observe the reactions of the emperor, and when Frederick simply accepts the stones as a gift, without examining them in detail, Prester John then has them sent to a lapidary, who explains that each of the stones is worth a kingdom. The lapidary then holds one of the stones in his hand, which causes him to become invisible and he departs with that and the other stones. (The full text of this story can be found in appendix 2.)

The third and final part of this puzzle is found in a thirteenth-century manuscript, *La Storia di Merlino*, written in Florence around 1324 and attributed to Paolino Pieri. Here we learn that Merlin's original writings were to be translated from the Welsh into Hebrew and French by one maestro Riccardo (later identified as Richard of Ireland, as we saw in section 8) at the behest of Federigo II (Frederick II) himself. The story then turns to the city of Orbanza, where everyone is permitted to worship their own individual Gods. This is perceived as such a monstrous idea that the city and all its people are overwhelmed in a very biblical flood. As we heard, the crown is later found in the Dead Sea by a fisherman, who sells it to a jeweller. This man, having failed to recognise that four of the precious stones in the crown are of particular value (just as Frederick does in *Il Novellino*), later presents them to the said emperor who, we are told, does not appreciate them but who is, at the same time, having Merlin's *Prophecies* translated by Richard of Ireland.

It so happens that a visiting cleric from Paris, who had been present when the emperor received the crown of Orbanza, hears of this and learns that Merlin had prophesied the events he had witnessed. When he hears this, the cleric begs maestro Riccardo to allow him to copy down this prophecy, which he then takes to Frederick. The emperor is so impressed that he orders the *Prophecies* to be retranslated into Arabic, for the attention of the Sultan of Babylon, and into Latin, for the Pope, as well as elsewhere so that the whole world can be aware of them.

This story connects with our book of *Prophecies* in a number of ways. It tells us how the words of Merlin were disseminated; it involves Frederick II; and it explains the sequence of the four jewels, which are mentioned both in *Il Novellino* and the *Prophecies* themselves. The fact that this involves Frederick, as we have already noted, gains further import when we consider that amongst those attached to his court were the mathematician Fibonacci, considered to be the most talented Western mathematician of the Middle Ages, and Michael Scot (1175–c. 1232), widely believed to be the most powerful magician and astrologer of his time. He thus resembled Merlin to a considerable degree and can be seen as serving Frederick II in much the same way as Merlin serves King Arthur.

But the most interesting aspect of all this is the exchange of Emperor Frederick for the figure of Prester John in both *La Storia di Merlino* and *Il Novellino*, and of course the suggestion that the stones themselves have magical properties. Thus, in *Il Novellino*, at least one of them has the power to make anyone holding it invisible; while in the *Prophecies*, we hear of the stones glowing through the night and apparently containing much of Merlin's magical power.

We also learn that Orbanza was governed by eighteen kings and an emperor and that the populace worshipped graven images. The city seems to have lain close to Venice, and although there is some archaeological evidence in the shape of buildings that can be sighted beneath the waters of the lagoon, these are almost certainly Roman and have nothing to do with the city as mentioned in the *Prophecies*. Generally, Orbanza (Orbance) stands as an example of all such wicked cities (in the eyes of Christianity), from Sodom and Gomorrah onwards. It could equally be a distant memory of Plato's myth of Atlantis, also drowned and ruled over by a council of kings (only ten as opposed to the eighteen of Orbanza). It is also possible that Orbanza may be identified with Milan, which in the twelfth and thirteenth centuries housed a number of heretical sects, including Cathars, Manicheans, and Patarini, and was thus regarded with suspicion. However, it is the loss of the emperor's crown, containing the four sacred stones, that makes its magical history of greater import than its possible historical existence. The story, as we saw, really concerns the fate of the stones, which are intimately connected to Merlin.

The combination of these three original texts, all produced in Italy, and two at least in Venice, establishes a link with Prester John not long after the appearance of a letter purporting to originate with him and before the more extended connections between Prester John and King Arthur had been established. (See the chapter "Written Records of the Prophecies" in part one for a more detailed examination of this theme.)

The connection with Venice is also important, as there is some evidence that at least one of the versions of the *Prophecies*, closest to our text, could have been copied by Rustichello da Pisa, who later went on to write not only the biography of Marco Polo, describing his voyage of discovery, but also a huge compilation of Arthuriana entitled *Roman le Roi Artus*. It is tempting to speculate that the scribe of the fourteenth-century collection had access to this.[157] It is even possible that this, along with the *Letter of Prester John*, prompted the Polo family to go in search of the fabled kingdom of the priest-king, which eventually led them to China.

11: How a Large Part of India Will Melt

The conclusion of all this is typically confused in terms of what it says. What are we to make of this suggestion that much of India will melt as the result probably of the actions of the Antichrist? Within the context

---

157. Paton, *Les Prophecies de Merlin; Part Two: Studies in the Contents*, 152.

of the *Prophecies* (as elsewhere), India is the kingdom of Prester John, so that the reference to the prayers of the emperor assisting the Good Mariners, or people of Venice, again indicates the importance of the Venetian heritage but does not explain the why or wherefore of the melting of a continent!

12: Of the Evil Lady of Falone

A fragmentary story for which we have no known source. Evidently, a now lost or forgotten tale to which the compiler of the *Prophecies* had access.

13: Of the Macedonian Wolf and Other Things

This is very typical of the kind of prophetic statement that, at the time the work was composed, referred to an event that does not seem to have happened. We have found nothing that matches this. However, the reference to the man who will dig up silver in a cave may be a reference to a story told in the *Vita Merlini* by Geoffrey of Monmouth, in which Merlin, having been taken captive, laughs when he sees a man sitting on a mound by the side of the road and begging. Little does this man know, Merlin says, is that he is sitting on a mound of hidden silver. This is one of several such declarations made by Merlin, usually accompanied by laughter, designed to show his ability to see beyond everyday reality and that he is therefore cleverer than everyone else.

14: Of Muhammed Who Built a City in Three Days

This is very typical of the crusading fervour that gripped the West at the time the *Prophecies* were composed in the fourteenth century. The Saracens were the great enemy, and whatever their Prophet could do, the Western seer could do better.

15: Of the Good Mariners

Another reference to the qualities of the Good Mariners of Venice, who settled on the great island where Venice still sits to this day. The name derives from the Veniti tribes who inhabited the region around the tenth century BC, between the ninth and eighteenth centuries. The position of the great city, on a series of islands situated in a lagoon between the rivers Po and Piave, made it a perfect site for trade, which was at its height during the fourteenth century, shortly before the Vérard edition of the *Prophecies* was published. A number of sea battles took place in the area, so that we are unable to identify a specific conflict in the terms of the *Prophecies*. Whoever the governor of the city was at this time is uncertain, but it is known that Venice possessed a huge and aggressive navy, which made them powerful players around the Mediterranean. The doge, who governed the city and held the post as a lifetime sinecure, was sometimes seen as a rival to the Pope, and there was considerable animosity between the Vatican and Venetian states. This meant that Venice escaped the attentions of the Catholic Church's censorship and maintained many years of religious tolerance. It was thus a perfect place for the compiling and publication of works such as the *Prophecies*. It was also a central clearing house for Western armies heading to the East on Crusade and returning from there.

Additionally, in more mythological terms, the Good Mariners are said to be descended from the Trojan prince Agenor, who, like several other citizens of Troy, escaped the fall of the city and fled to various places across Europe to found new colonies. Thus, in Britain, Brutus, grandson of Aeneas, is said to have founded the country, having won a battle against the tribe of giants led by Gog and Magog. In the *Prophecies*, Agenor finds Venice, and there are references in the various alternative versions of the text that speak of a heavenly voice that instructed the Good Mariners to head for the islands to escape the attacks of Attila the Hun before establishing their own community.

16: Of People Who Go on a Pilgrimage to the Sea with the Emperor of Rome

Once again the reference here is obscure. It may refer to the Crusade led by Frederick II, many of whom perished in storms at sea, but the reference to the people avenging them is unclear. As noted in the previous section, Venice was for many years the stopping-off place for both individual knights and soldiers as well as armies on their way to the Crusades in the East. A number of ancient texts and beliefs made their way into the West in this manner.

17: Of Merlin Alerting Master Antoine to the Arrival of Three Ministers

Here we see once again the clash between the prophetic skills of Merlin and the laws of the church. In this instance, three high-ranking clerics come to Wales to question the validity of Merlin's words. He, in response, declares his intention of perfecting the laws of Holy Church—a considerable challenge for anyone of this period of history. At least three of the cardinals are real and famous. Phellis is Milanese but seems to be impossible to identify. Gregory is from Rome and is the future Pope Gregory X (1272–1276). Bertous may well be identified with a well-known prelate called Bertold of Regensburg (c. 1220–1272). In the original collection of the *Prophecies* from 1303, there is a much-extended version of these events in which Merlin clearly demonstrates his supernatural abilities by telling each of the men about their lives and transforming himself into the likeness of various people known to them. He also includes prophecies concerning the fate of each.[158] All three are used to illustrate the shortcomings of the church, and they are individually accused by Merlin of a variety of sins, such as licentiousness, gluttony, simony, nepotism, and so on. Merlin is also

---

158. Paton, *Les Prophecies de Merlin; Part Two: Studies in the Contents*, 167 and the following pages.

tested on the meaning of the Trinity and other aspects of the catechism, each of which he answers satisfactorily.

18: Of the Lady Who Came to Antoine's Room

Here we learn more of Merlin's use of his magic to further his amorous intentions, not only on the lady who visits Antoine but also several other damsels who came with her from Léonois (Lionesse), the drowned land to the west of Cornwall. They tell Antoine that Merlin is fickle and that he had told all of them that they could learn magic from him in exchange for their virginity. The lady in question is said to have been taught a great deal about the dark arts and enchantment in the past.

Then follows the most interesting statement from Merlin himself. First of all, he prophesies that the lady will die after she has enchanted King Meliadus of Léonois. This is evidently a reference to the stories of Tristan and Isolde, who will be referred to in more detail later on in the book. Meliadus was the father of Tristan himself and of the other Meliadus, who features in our text as a go-between for Merlin and his scribes and followers.

But even more interesting is what Merlin says next: "Sometimes I do not know the difference between the White and Black Serpents." This carries us into the upcoming sections that deal with Merlin's relationship to the Lady of the Lake, who is referred to as the White Serpent. Our assumption here is that the Black Serpent must be Morgain (Morgain le Fay), who is here seen as an adversary or rival to the Lady of the Lake and, of course, within the main canon of the Arthurian legends, as a primary opponent to King Arthur. She uses her magic consistently to frustrate his work and that of the Round Table fellowship.

The fact that Merlin is apparently sometimes unable to tell the difference between these two is significant as it implies that for all his wisdom, the faery magic of the enchantresses of Avalon are too deep or too complex for him to completely understand. He then says the only way that he can learn about this is to try and understand the innocence possessed by the lady who came to visit. He adds, "I will be careful not to talk to fleas [i.e., those beneath him], or to hold a meeting, or to talk to others."— thereby seeming to shut down all his activities. He then firmly instructs Master Antoine to "to seal his mouth" since he wishes to be secret.

The last line in this section stands out, as the scribe says this came about "after Merlin had already deflowered the lady." This event happened in the past we presume, during the time when she was receiving education from him. This implies that Merlin is feeling guilty about his previous behaviour, and it acts as a perfect introduction to what follows, when Master Antoine asks Merlin which among the ladies he has known in the world he thinks is the wisest.

19: Merlin Speaks Regarding the Lady of the Lake

Continuing the previous exchange, Merlin declares that all the glory of the world should be hers, that she is the wisest in the world, and all the beauty of the world resides within her. She is called the Lady of the Lake. He did admit that he is fearful of the White Serpent, which is taking his life. "Is this true?" exclaims Antoine, greatly distressed. But all Merlin will say is: "Close your mouth. I believe this mixture of fire and lust will bring me to my death. The beauty of the Lady of the Lake borders on Paradise and I was in her company at night in the forest of Avrences." It is apparent here that Merlin does not wish to discuss—or perhaps cannot discuss—the details of his love life and that his previous lustful behaviour may be his undoing. This is, of course, not only a very medieval way of thinking but also a very Christian interpretation that "the wages of sin is death" (Romans 6:23). This was probably added by any one of the monkish scribes collecting the prophecies, but it is an intriguing introduction to the story of Merlin's relationship with the Lady of the Lake, which, as we shall see in sections 28–30, tells a complex story of duplicity, betrayal, and trickery leading to Merlin's entombment.

20: Of the Lady of the Lake and of Lusente

The reference to the Lady Lucent, who was spoken of by the famous Roman poet Virgil, maybe an attempt on the part of the scribe to show off his knowledge, or even a punning reference to a phrase used by Virgil in his *Aeneid* to describe the dawn. In other words, this lady, like the Lady of the Lake herself, is a being who gives forth light. No such character is to be found in Virgil's extant writings.[159]

Merlin then adds that he is about to tell Master Antoine about his disappearance into the forest of Avrences, that this will be caused by the Lady of the Lake, that he knows it is going to happen, but that he cannot escape it. Thus, the scene is set for one of the most powerful sections in the *Prophecies*.

21: How Merlin Went to the Forest of Avrences

So we prepare for the great reveal: Merlin's association with the Lady of the Lake. This is a well-known and often-told story, but the version in the *Prophecies* differs in several ways and adds many details. Merlin tells us here that he speaks of events that will happen after Master Antoine is consecrated as a bishop. He then states that God has asked him to go to the forest of Avrences, where the Lady of the Lake will be waiting. This in itself is curious because it suggests that here Merlin's steps are being guided by God.

He then says that he has one task to accomplish and that after his death he will prophesy more than when he was alive. This, of course, is a reference to the fact that he is, in this version of the story, entombed, so that it is his spirit that is speaking from the depths. He then goes on to say there will come to the forest a knight-king who will be crowned

---

159. Thanks to Dr. Kresimir Vukovic for his help with this matter.

in time in Aubiron. This is a site that we have not been able to trace, but it is probably the same place as that referred to by Merlin in sections 75–76. We might perhaps also note the similarity, of both spelling and pronunciation, between Aubiron and Oberon, first cited in the romance of *Huon de Bordeaux* in the thirteenth century as one of the names for the faery king. Merlin then says that this mysterious, unnamed, and unrecognised king will enter the forest and will not leave there until he has news of the timing of Merlin's death. On which grim note he adds, "I cannot escape my fate."

The forest of Avrences is a real place, lying in the département of Manche, Normandy, Northwest France, near the border with Brittany. It is notable that this location is chosen as the place where Merlin will be entombed and where he spends time with the Lady of the Lake, while in most traditions it is to the forest of Brocéliande, also in Brittany, to which he retires. There is still to this day the fountain of Barenton where the voice of Merlin can supposedly be heard. This is situated within the heart of the forest of Brocéliande, which, though now much reduced in size, still occupies some nine thousand hectares and lies close to the village of Paimpont.

22: How Merlin Bade Master Antoine Farewell and Entered the Forest of Avrences Where the Lady of the Lake Was

This section develops the story a little, and fascinatingly. Before he leaves Merlin kneels before Bishop Antoine, who gives him a blessing and warns him to remain humble, from which we may assume that Merlin is a rather boastful seer. He leaves the city of Pellagra, which we have not been able to trace. Curiously, in Middle Norman French *pellagra du mal* meant the "high seas" or "open water," so this may be an implication or a pun that Merlin is indeed heading into deep water. We then hear that Merlin and the Lady of the Lake met and had great joy in their meeting, that Merlin made a meal, and that the Lady, who needed nothing else, feasted with him as if he were a new knight. This is a reference to Morgain's habit of seducing recently knighted young men and carrying them off to her secret hideaway in the Valley of No Return. She later does this with Lancelot, who has to be rescued from there with the help of Nimuë, one of the handmaidens of the Lady of the Lake who, in many other versions of the story, is Merlin's sweetheart. We hear that they went into the wood with great joy and that Merlin loved the Lady of the Lake with all his heart but that the Lady of the Lake hated him intensely. We shall hear more about this shortly.

23: Merlin and the Lady of the Lake Go to the House Where Merlin Felt at Home

Now we hear how the couple wandered through the forest of Avrences until they came to the entrance to a cave, which is in fact the tomb "over which the Lady of the Lake had so often prayed." This we take to mean that she had spent some time preparing for the arrival of Merlin and his imprisonment there. Certainly, it was well hidden, since the text says that "if all the knights of the world set out to find it they would not succeed." Merlin himself says to the Lady: "This place shall never be found and even if the kings of Aubiron would buy the grove just to see my tomb, it shall be in vain because they still won't find it." To which the Lady of the Lake responds: "You will find me—however distant."

Then the night comes, and the Lady of the Lake gets little sleep. We may assume that this is because of the amorous attentions of Merlin; however, it says that she was disappointed that Merlin had so many stones "that glowed so much that night was as bright as day." This is yet another reference to the mysterious stones or jewels, which we have already encountered. It is possible that the four jewels from the crown of the King of Orbance were in fact rescued at some point by Merlin himself, or that he had others like them, which glowed with his own innate power. Nor should we forget the famous story from Geoffrey of Monmouth, in which Merlin transported the stones known as the

"Giant's Dance" from Ireland and used them to build Stonehenge. Clearly, he had deep connections with stones.

The Lady now asks him, "If the anger of the Gods fall upon you [in other words, Merlin himself could be threatened in this way], will there be a knight in the whole of Little Britain [who would look after her]?" Merlin's response is, as ever, enigmatic: "No one can save you here."

Then they come to a house that has mysteriously appeared in the midst of the forest—presumably either because it was prepared by the Lady herself or by Merlin. Inside, they find "all the comforts they needed for a great lady and rich man." We are not told how these things were arranged or who supplied them, but this may be a reference to the house supposedly created for Merlin by his sister Ganieda, according to the *Vita Merlini*. It is there that he is said to retire to observe what is going on in the world through the many windows within the house.

The Lady then asks if the stones will ever be removed from there. This we assume refers to the glowing stones that were found in the cave where they first sheltered. Had these accompanied Merlin to the house? We cannot say, but Merlin says that they will not because he does not want her to leave. The implication here is that Merlin is aware that she is there reluctantly and wishes to leave, but she replies immediately that she will never leave and swears that she will remain as a woman who had just given birth "in bitter labour" would remain to care of her infant. Since "lying in" during the Middle Ages was continued until the mother was "churched," that is blessed by a priest, this could be an extended period of time.

24: How Merlin Lived with the Lady of the Lake for Fifteen Months

The scribe now shows off his knowledge by telling us that Merlin stayed with the Lady of the Lake for fifteen months, during which time he sent regular messages to Master Antoine, who was by this time the

Bishop of Wales. Then he says that their time together would have been even longer had it not been for Morgain, who had gone into the woods in search of Merlin and come very close to the cave where he and the Lady of the Lake had been, previous to reaching the luxurious house.

Thus we are shown the beginning of the animosity between the Lady and Morgaine, which is to develop rapidly over the next two sections. Then he tells us that the Lady was doubtful that she could hold Merlin securely—though it is unclear whether this means hold him in the prison that she has been creating for him, or that she could not hold him romantically, because apparently there were so many damsels who had learned magic from Merlin and who had to sleep with him to do so. However, the Lady doesn't seem to be worried by this because she thinks that no other damsel would suffer this fate because she alone is now his mistress.

25: Of the Lady of the Lake Who Fooled Merlin While She Slept with Him

Things now begin to develop, as on the very next day a knight who was a servant of the Lady of the Lake is attacked by another knight who serves Lady Morgain. Merlin hears of this and comes to the Lady, who tells him what has happened and begs him not to lie with her again. His response is as curious and enigmatic as ever: "Forgive me, White Serpent. I shall never speak of it."

The scribe then becomes very clear on what happens next. He tells us that Merlin "wanted the Lady of the Lake carnally but as soon as he got into bed with her she cast the spirit of her soul upon him so that he went to sleep until daylight, and when the day came, she awakened him and deceived him as she often did." This not only shows that the Lady is capable of deceiving Merlin but also that her power has grown strong enough to put him to sleep. The phrase *cast the spirit of her soul upon him* is most striking and sounds very much like later magical descriptions of spell casting.

This is followed by a somewhat misogynistic statement when the scribe wonders how it was possible for Merlin, who was so wise, to be so easily fooled? To which he adds: "Knights and gentlemen, if you have ever met a woman, be it a lady or a damsel, all you see is how good she looks! I see you agree to love every young lady, because no man can resist a woman's attraction." Then he adds that the Lady of the Lake did her best to disappoint Merlin, for she hated him with a deadly hatred while he loved her with all his heart.

Now we are told that the Lady wants to "hide Merlin in such a place that he would never be seen again." Despite the fact that he presumably knows this, Merlin seeks to teach her yet more magic, showing her how to anoint herself with certain herbs and other things with which to bathe her body and wash her limbs so that she might live forever. This apparently so pollutes her flesh that she washes everything that she had applied at Merlin's instructions until she is white again.

In this way she learns what the scribe describes as "the arts of black magic and all the other arts and sciences. So that in the end she knew more than he." But the Lady of the Lake, being cunning, makes him believe that he still knew more than she did. He then taught her about "gems and herbs and the power of words, so subtly that she wonderfully united all three subtleties."

Here we are getting a fairly detailed idea of the kind of magic that Merlin is teaching: natural magic involving herbs and stones and specific words. This is very much in line with the idea of magic as it was understood at the time the *Prophecies* were collected and published—as a science rather than as an incantatory power. The fact that Merlin is apparently much more inclined towards the natural idea of magic is completely in keeping with his character as described throughout Arthurian mythology.

Then, one day, apparently having had enough of everything to do with Merlin, the Lady tells him that, although he says he only wants to sleep with a beautiful woman such as herself, he then goes on to sleep with other ladies and girls, which sickens her. To which Merlin responds that he promises he will not touch anyone but her alone, "but that same week he broke his promise." Despite this, the scribe then tells us, she still remained with Merlin for fifteen weeks.

26: Of the Lady of the Lake, Who Decided to Cheat on Merlin

Quite obviously fed up with all this, the Lady of the Lake determines to deceive Merlin, "though in her heart she knew she would get no help." Then the scribe asks if anyone would suggest that Merlin got all his ladies illegally? To which his answer is no, "because they got magic in exchange for their flesh."

Despite this, the Lady continues with her plan, asking Merlin if he intends to leave her. To which he replies that he does not. Then he says that he "is so tied to her that there can be no other" and that he will be there with her throughout the age in which they are living. In time his bones will be laid there, "but if you die also, I pray that our bones will be united and our souls meet again." This is very much the statement of a devoted lover and seems at variance to what we have been told about Merlin's frequent infidelities. The exchange that follows in the next shows the reality beneath the romantic idea.

27: How Merlin Went with the Lady of the Lake to the Tomb in the Rock

Immediately at the beginning of this section, Merlin is already saying that the Lady knows very well that he will be buried soon. The Lady reacts with surprise. "What do you mean?" she asks. "It shall be as I tell you," Merlin responds. Then the Lady cunningly says: "If you're going to be buried before me, will you not lie here where we have been together." Presumably, "here" being the cave beneath the ground in the heart of the wood, where they had first been together.

At this point Merlin knows exactly what is going to happen and that there is no way that he can escape it. The Lady asks him if he thinks she is indeed the White Serpent of which he has so often prophesied "who comes from Brittany and mingles with the demi-man in the forest of Avrences." Merlin says yes, he does believe that she is the

White Serpent. It is interesting that here the Lady refers to him as a demi-man—half demon, half human.

28: Of Merlin Lying in the Tomb, He Died Further Each Day

So now we come to the crux of the story. Merlin goes into the cave, now referred to as a tomb, and lies down in it quite calmly. Then he says: "Take care of yourself." And when the Lady hears this, "she fastened the lid and made it unbreakable." This suggests that Merlin is in a kind of coffin, but this is not made clear. However, he is now sealed in and knows that no human could escape, not even himself. The Lady now says to him that he is going to say that his prophecies are not accurate, but she knows they are real. She then says, coldly: "You are going to die in here." And that this is what he himself had prophesied.

Now the Lady says: "This White Serpent takes revenge on you for the foul game you played with me." Then asks him if he remembers the first lesson he taught her in the arts of magic. "Yes," says Merlin. "It was to put a man to sleep and wake him up whenever you want." The Lady then says angrily that he had shown her this and then taken her virginity, and that for this she hates him intensely. And she says that the second lesson he taught her was "to know how to lock a place so that no one could open it again." This is what she has done, and it will be her revenge. He will die, but she will awaken his spirit whenever she wishes.

Then she says, very damningly, that he knew that she was still a virgin, yet he put her to sleep and overpowered her. This, of course, is extremely toxic behaviour on the part of Merlin. And Merlin admits it. He asks her to go to Master Antoine and tell him what has happened and admits that he has been "ruled by his senses" and that he is "slain by his own lust."

The lady agrees to accept this task, and then asks him how long he can keep his spirit in his body.

29: Of Merlin's Ghost, Who Will Speak to All Who Come to His Tomb

Merlin's answer is that his body will be rotten in a month, but his spirit will continue to speak. To which the lady responds by challenging him to tell her how many knights she will know in her lifetime. Merlin's response is to say that she will know only one knight until she dies and that he will be devoted to her throughout his life. This probably refers to Meliadus, who within the context of this text is the Lady of the Lake's lover, but it could also refer to Accolon of Gaul, who also undertakes this role in both the *Suite du Merlin* and *Le Morte D'Arthur* of Thomas Malory.

30: Of the Departure of the Lady of the Lake

Having completed her plan to capture and imprison Merlin for all time, the Lady of the Lake now heads to Wales. There she meets with Master Antoine who was, the text says, bitter, for he knew that Merlin's prophecy of his own death and entrapment had been fulfilled. The Lady herself repeats everything that we have read in sections 26–29 and then heads off back to the Lake, where she finds the children of King Ban of Benwick and his nephews. These are Lancelot, Bors, and Lionel, who were all fostered by the Lady following the attack on King Ban by Claudas, more of which we will hear about a little later. Apparently, the Lady of the Lake was very happily received. She embraced everyone, and there was much celebration at her homecoming. The section ends: "Thus was Merlin's own prophecy of his death fulfilled."

31: Of Merlin Speaking to Meliadus, Friend to the Lady of the Lake

We turn now to the story that focuses on Meliadus as the lover of the Lady of the Lake in this text and who seems, apart from her, the only person who knows the exact whereabouts of Merlin's tomb. He goes there, and the text enigmatically says that Meliadus "saw the lady through the spirit of Merlin." This seems to be a kind of magical activity that Merlin's vision is somehow transferred to Meliadus, so that if Merlin can see the Lady so can he. There is an exchange between them, and Meliadus thinks that Merlin's love for the Lady is still very strong but that her love for himself might be even stronger. This is confirmed by Merlin himself, who says: "You shall love her with all your soul until death shall part you."

32: Of Merlin Telling How His Father Killed His Mother

The next section begins with a statement that we think comes from the pen and the mind of the cleric: "Now tell the stories and now keep the truth. Let the testimony of Merlin live." This is not the only time we hear his voice, but it is significant that at this juncture, with Merlin entombed and everything set for the revelations to come, he chooses this place to speak of his own commitment to the preservation and dissemination of the *Prophecies*.

The story speaks of Merlin's friendship with Meliadus and that they were both at the rock in which Merlin is trapped. At this point Merlin once again recites his origin story: "I am the son of a demon. I am half human. My father was a demon who impregnated an innocent virgin. After I came into the world, and my mother baptised me, my father killed her in revenge." This follows the very traditional line of the story of Merlin's conception and his hasty baptism (his name derived from the fact that a merlin hawk is seen by his mother flying overhead). Because her action in thus frustrating the devils of Hell, the demon destroys her. This is a detail usually omitted from the later stories.

33: Of Tristan, the Brother of Meliadus

Merlin now reveals things about Meliadus himself, telling him that his brother is no less than the great knight Tristan, something that apparently Meliadus had not known, having been raised by the Lady of the Lake and, presumably, not informed of his antecedents. Merlin warns him that there may be issues between them but that once he knows that Meliadus is his brother, Tristan "will be as happy as anyone who discovers blood relations."

We then have a brief allusion to an early part of the Tristan story. Merlin asks how much money it will take to have Tristan not be killed—presumably by a bribe. Meliadus has apparently already written on his parchment that he is indebted to King Ban of Benoic, Lancelot's father, who must have rewarded him in some way that is not described here.

Merlin then says that a great company of knights will come from across the sea and burn all of Cornwall to ashes, but that Tristan will be brave and survive, and King Arthur will take revenge.

34: How Meliadus Went to Church and Found Letters Testifying to What Merlin Had Said to Him

Merlin then proceeds to tell Meliadus more of his early life, that his father is another Meliadus, the King of Léonois, and that his mother was the Queen of Scotland (here called by the more ancient name of Escoce). Meliadus is apparently at first disinclined to believe this, but Merlin says: "Go to a church and find the evidence." This Meliadus does and finds documents there that prove his true antecedents.

35: How Meliadus Left Merlin and Came to Wales

Merlin now gives Meliadus permission to leave the tomb and to travel to Wales. There he visits Raymon the Wise Clerk of Wales, who is the next in the lineage of scribes designated to take down Merlin's words. He receives Meliadus with joy and gives him a full update of events. Raymon puts everything in writing, and Meliadus leaves and heads to the court of King Arthur. There he is received with joy, especially by the queen, who knew that he was a friend of the Lady of the Lake. She asks about Merlin's soul, and Meliadus tells her much of what the seer had said—including of an evil lord who would come to the court of Arthur and of someone called Slatix. This last story is never developed, and we know nothing of Slatix, though from his name and that he is Pagan, we would assume that he was perhaps of Gaulish origin. But if this story was ever told, it is lost among the documents that did not survive from the time the *Prophecies* were compiled.

36: How Meliadus Departed from King Arthur's Palace and Met the Lady of the Lake

The next fifteen days, we are told, are filled with joy and celebration for Meliadus's coming to the court. After which, he rides to the sea, finds a ship, and arrives on land (the geography is uncertain here, but we assume he is in Wales and journeys by sea along the coast to the supposed site of Camelot at Winchester). From there Meliadus rides to Lake Dyane. This is an important detail because it confirms that, as described specifically in the fifteenth-century text known as the Middle English *Prose Merlin*, the Lady of the Lake is a descendant of the Goddess Diana, the Roman Goddess of the hunt, and has thus inherited her magic. This is one of the very few times where the lake itself is actually given a name.

We are now told that Meliadus knows the way well and eventually comes to the hostel where the Lady of the Lake receives him joyfully. He then, for no apparent reason, says how Merlin told him that "women make men worse," and how he had asked him how this might be, and that Merlin, whimsically, had replied that all the women of the world had the subtlety of teasing men, just as she had teased him. He adds that "all the men in the world are plagued by this," but then goes on: "Women are not as wise as men, and men notice this, and so it becomes hard for the women." This, not without reason, causes the Lady of the Lake to laugh out loud and say that she finds it entertaining. "According to Merlin!" adds Meliadus. At which point the Lady kisses him and says: "Go and talk to Merlin about my three children: Lancelot, Lionel, and Bors." This is another reference to her fostering of the son and nephews of King Ban of Benoic.

37: Of a Knight from the Land of the Indies Who Came before the Chaplain

Now we hear more of the Chaplain of Wales, who only within the 1498 text is called by the name Raymon. As we open this section, he is busy reading the *Book of Prophecies* that presumably Meliadus had given him. At this point, a knight from India arrives, and the Chaplain asks him what he wants. The knight tells him that he is from India and that he has seen many wonders of the world, including a sea so high that no one could conquer it. There was also a city threatened by Pagans in this Christian land, but that Merlin told them that he had driven all the heathens out of the city and the sea would rise no more.

In some astonishment, Raymon asks if Merlin is known about in India. "Absolutely," says the knight. So the Chaplain then gives "fifteen clerks a lot [of money] and prayed that they put everything they could find about Merlin in a great book." The next day they departed with the knight while the Chaplain remained behind." We are told that these men went everywhere.

While these well-paid clerks are off in another country gathering material, Raymon inquires for other clerks "who like to write" and gives them money for parchment, "and they made a great book and in that book all of these stories and prophecies about Merlin gathered." The scribe remarks that he wants us to know that four hundred of these clerks were sent around the world to gather yet more information. He does not suggest that he had himself read this manuscript or that he could be drawing upon it himself.

The Chaplain of Wales thought he had done this job very well and that he would not have spent even a penny on work other than that he commissioned. "Therefore, the strange wonders of Merlin are collected and put in writing in a book, including the *Prophecies*, the adventures of the knights that took place in the Holy Land, the hard and bitter battles fought in the world in the quest for the Holy Grail, and the gatherings of the knights and their battles—all were put on parchment and collected in a great book."

38: Of the Woman Who Did Evil to Her Husband

Now we hear the beginning of a new story concerning Merlin, which appears to be entirely original to this particular text. The Chaplain of Wales looks at the things the Wise Clerk had written in Merlin's service. He then looks at the *Book of Blaise*, which had been given to Merlin's mother, and copies the prophecies he finds there.

In this version of the story, after Merlin's mother was delivered from evil, presumably when she had baptised the child, she took him and fed him, and when she had said a prayer, she went to a convent where there were many nuns. This conflicts with the previous statement that the demon had killed her.

At this time there is a woman in a solitary cell in this place who has allowed herself to have relations with both her husband and a servant. But, having heard of Merlin's story, she apparently begs forgiveness, because she is released by the judge of Norbellande. (This probably refers to Northumberland where Merlin's master Blaise was said to live; it may also refer to Venice, to which it is applied in the current text.)

39: How the Lady Rambarge Pretended to Feed Merlin but Wanted to Kill Him

We are now told that the lady's name is Rambarge and that, although she had been pardoned as a result of hearing Merlin's story, she actually wants to kill him. She goes to the abbess and says that "it wasn't proper that a male child should be fed in this holy place." She then declares that out of love for the sisters, for the abbey, and for the child, she should look after him. At which point Merlin himself speaks up, saying that the woman might well look after him, but if she did so, either he or she would die. To this the woman replies, "Be silent, little child, none of us will die from it." This prompts Merlin to laugh, but the lady simply orders her maids to take the child and bring it to her house, where her husband is very pleased that Merlin is there and says: "Take care that you feed the little child well, for know that he is not come into this world in this time without great wonder and without great commission." From this we assume that word of Merlin's birth has spread, along with stories of his importance as a being of extraordinary qualities with many great deeds to do. Despite this, as we have heard, the lady Rambarge wishes to kill him—having presumably heard of his sensational conception. Other notable characters who are able to speak wise words while still infants are the Welsh Taliesin and the Irish Fionn Mac Cumhail. Both are pursued and threatened either by the magical beings who gave them life or human enemies out to destroy them for other reasons.

40: How the Lady Rambarge Tried to Strangle Merlin

The lady says that she will give the child more than enough to eat, and Merlin himself repeats that his coming will bring harm neither to him nor to the knight's wife. We are then told that the knight's name is Naymar and that the lady's statement was backed up by the servant with whom she had slept.

That night the lady gets up from her bed and goes to the cradle where Merlin lies, with the intention of strangling him. However, she does not know that the knight has left his favourite greyhound on guard. When she sees this, the lady strangles the dog instead and then calmly goes back to bed. Next day when the sun rises, the knight sees that his hound is dead and is very sorrowful because of this.

41: Of Merlin's Message to Naymar

Once again the story becomes confusing here. Merlin speaks to Naymar, telling him that his enemies have slain his canine friend. It is not clear from this whether he means Naymar's wife or another's, nor indeed whether the killing is of another person or the dog, but Merlin says that when the knight (presumably Naymar) reaches his enemy's home, the enemy will be against him and will hate him. Naymar reasonably asks who his enemy is. Merlin then says that when the knight had found his wife by the cradle with her hands actually around Merlin's neck, he had seized her and held her down, demanding to know what it was she was doing. She apparently then pretended not to know where she was or what she was doing. The knight tells her that she did not succeed in strangling the child. Merlin then says that Naymar will never know prosperity again if he does not retaliate.

Here the story ends with no conclusion. We assume that the compiler had either read and only partly remembered a version of the story in which this occurred but was either too forgetful or too lazy to write it out in full. The most that can be said here, if we attempt to make sense of the details in the text, are that the Lady Rambarge tries to strangle Merlin but is frustrated by the presence of the greyhound, which she then strangles instead. This wakes her husband, who grapples with her, clearly seeing her intent to kill Merlin and demands to know why, to which she pretends to be ignorant. He is angry and hurt that the dog has been killed and presumably takes his revenge upon her.

All of this is observed by Merlin, but we cannot be sure of the exact sequence of events. In the written text it says that the lady goes back to bed having strangled the dog, but the most obvious sequence is that the husband wakes and catches her in her evil deed. Somewhere in this tangled tale is a most interesting episode of an attempt to kill Merlin while he is, physically at least, helpless—the first such attempt. But we know nothing more of this story of Lady Rambarge or her husband, whose name appears to be different from hers.

42: Concerning the Lady of the Lake, Who Sent a Reply to the Queen about a Dream She Had Dreamed

The text now turns to yet another story, which only appears here. We learn how one of Queen Guinevere's damsels visits the Lady of the Lake and gives her a letter in which the queen asks if she will tell her where Merlin is because she needs him to interpret a dream. The letter also describes everything that the queen had dreamed, but the Lady of the Lake, having thought about it for a while, says to tell the queen that Merlin has gone to the forest of Avrences and that as for the dream she cannot interpret it, but that the queen should not be surprised by anything that happens in the world. At this the damsel beseeches the Lady to work on behalf of Queen Guinevere and that anything she has to say should be sent by letter.

At this point they are interrupted by the appearance of the Lady of the Lake's chaplain, who says that Merlin had told him how a knight from the Caledonian royal line would leave Benoic and go to the kingdom of Logres (one of the ancient names for Britain) and that the Crowned Serpent would leave that kingdom, but that the Lion from Benoic would fly over the sea and rule a kingdom that once belonged to King Evalac.

This rather confusing sequence really refers to several different things. The knight from the Caledonian royal line is almost certainly Lancelot, and Benoic was his castle in Northumberland.[160] Lancelot's coat of arms is a lion, so the text here refers to him and states that he would "fly across the sea," in other words travel by ship and rule over the kingdom that had once belonged to King Evalac. The name is interesting as it contains the element *lac*, or lake, which suggests a connection with the Lady herself.

The text appears to contain a slightly confused memory of a Pagan king who ruled over the city of Sarras but who was converted

---

160. Identified by some with Bamber Castle, which still stands today.

to Christianity by Joseph of Arimathea. Sarras became the city of the Grail in the great cycle of stories narrating the quest, and it is actually Galahad, Lancelot's son by Elain of Carbonek, who becomes the new king of the city. The compiler of the prophecies here seems to have mixed several stories together to produce this meaning. Evalac himself may possibly be a variation of the Celtic God Afallach, named as a king of Avalon. Presumably, the scribe was moved to make the connection between Guinevere and Lancelot, since he was doubtless aware of their famous love affair. Interestingly, Lancelot is here described as coming from the Caledonian royal line, which would make him Scottish. However, in all other versions of the story, he is said to be of French origin, the son of King Ban of Benoic. It is possible that the compiler, having presumably never visited Britain, was confusing the northern location of Lancelot's castle, long believed to be identified with Bamber in Northumberland, which he may have assumed to be part of Scotland. Once again, as so often in the compilation, we have the feeling that the compiler is either deliberately writing confused and contradictory statements or simply does not have access to all of the texts necessary to furnish the story in detail. In this instance, the real focus is upon Guinevere's dream, of which we learn more in the next section and which is unique to our text.

43: Concerning the Dream That the Queen Dreamed

The queen's damsel asks the Lady of the Lake if she knows who the knight is who is looking for Merlin and whether he will find him. The Lady responds that he will neither find him nor see him but does not say who the knight was. We might be led to suggest here that this refers to Percival, who will indeed look for Merlin later in sections 60–61 and again in sections 65, 83, and 84—but this is not very clear.

At this point the damsel tells the Lady the content of Guinevere's dream, which she dreamt on the first night that she lay in King Arthur's bed. In the dream she sees a serpent coming out of his belly and trying to bite him. However, on waking, the king says nothing of this, which dismays the queen.

There can be little doubt here that the reference is to the future birth of Mordred, Arthur's incestuous son with Morgause. Only in the vast cycle of romances compiled under the modern title of the *Lancelot-Grail* Cycle do Arthur and Guinevere have a child—Loholt—who is later murdered by Sir Kay, King Arthur's foster-brother. In most texts they remain childless, though Arthur has several children out of wedlock, including Mordred.

The Lady now remarks that such dreams "are always dreadful to hear" but then refers to the fact that she herself has suffered great harm from the loss of Merlin and all she could still have learned from him is also lost. Then she says to the damsel to tell the queen that she cannot interpret the dream but believes she will be able to do so one day.

At this point the Lady begins to laugh loudly, and when the damsel asks why, she is told that her mistress is laughing at the Queen of Logres, who would be "fearful of one knight, Galeholt, the half giant. Who will conquer all." This may seem as though it refers in some way to Guinevere, who is indeed the Queen of Logres, but in fact it is much more likely to refer to Morgain, who will indeed encounter the knight named Galeholt, who is extremely tall, hence the term *half giant*, and who will, among other things, rescue Lancelot when Morgain traps him in the Valley of No Return, her secret enclave within the forest. However, we might also remember that according to the Welsh *Triads*, Guinevere is herself the daughter of giants—though she is of normal size.

44: Concerning the Stone the Lady of the Lake Gave to the Queen

The damsel's response to the previous statements is to say that the queen particularly requests that "Morgain the Unfaithful should have nothing to do with any of this"—in other words that she should not be consulted about the dream. At this point the Lady of the Lake opens her dress, exposing her breast, and shows the damsel "a most virtuous gem that she wore." This she takes off and tells the damsel that the queen should hold on to it and that as long as she has it in her possession, or has it in her mind, Morgain will have no power to harm her. This reflects the idea that stones of virtue were used to alert the wearer to poison or act as a protective talisman.

The damsel accepts the virtuous stone and thanks the Lady of the Lake. She soon reaches the sea, where she immediately finds a suitable ship across to Vincestre, and although this is said to take her back to Little Britain, it almost certainly refers to Winchester, which both our text and others describe as the site of Camelot.

45: How the Queen's Damsel Asked Sebile the Sorceress to Explain Her Mistress's Dream

Having failed to receive a satisfactory answer from the Lady of the Lake, the damsel, who we now learn is called Samide, goes in search of others who had learned magic from Merlin. The first of these is Sebile the Sorceress, whose name derives from the classical Sybil, the seeress of the Roman world. Here again the maiden asks for an interpretation of the dream. She then apparently returns to the queen and conveys to her both the words sent to her by Sebile and letters from the Lady of the Lake. Sebile knows that the queen is afraid of Morgain and sends words of comfort, telling her that a knight will challenge Morgain and will cause her great fear. (This we assume is once again Galeholt, as mentioned above.) Then we learn that the dream frightened the queen so much that she has turned pale, and when Samide asks what worries her, the queen says: "I believe I dreamt of putting myself to death, or that the Serpent wanted to destroy my marriage." It is clear here that the queen believes the serpent in her dream represents Morgain, as indeed has been suggested in an earlier section of this text. However, given the confusion between the two sisters, this probably refers to Morgause, who was, of course, the mother of the king's son as well as being his half sister. This makes sense of the story so far, since Morgause and Morgain both bare Guinevere ill will and seek to harm her and Arthur himself.

The queen now asks Samide what explanation Sebile has sent her, and the damsel tells her that it was indeed about Morgain. She then gives Guinevere the letters from the Lady of the Lake and asks her to read them. The queen opens the seal and reads the letters, "and as she read them her anger and fear began to subside and her colour returned to normal." We hear that the king noticed this, from which we assume Guinevere had told him about her dream and that it is indeed Morgain who is the serpent that crawled out of his belly and wanted to bite him.

This is all we hear about the dream, and we know nothing further of either Arthur's or Guinevere's response to it. It is, however, an unusual story, which appears nowhere else in the Arthurian cannon.

46: Prophecies Found by a Knight on a Stone Written by Merlin

Now the story turns to Meliadus, whom the Wise Clerk, Master Antoine, asks to go to Merlin's tomb. He wanders for days in the forest of Avrences until he comes to the rock beneath which Merlin lies. There he encounters a knight whose arm had been cut off and a second knight who has a stone that he brought down from the mountain, which he shows to Meliadus. It is covered in inscriptions. We cannot help recollect the idea, from biblical tradition, of Moses coming down from the mountain with a stone upon which inscriptions were written. We are not told the identity of either the knight with the missing arm or the one who brings the stone inscribed by Merlin.

47: How Meliadus Was So Serious That He Swore to Kill Any Knight Who Passed through the Forest

Meliadus seems to be so determined to protect the location of Merlin's tomb that he threatens to kill anyone who comes there. He then tells the knight who is lacking an arm that he will distract the other knight "so that he will not know of your arrival when he reaches this place." This implies that the knight missing an arm is in fact being pursued by the second knight, who brings the stone, who had, of course, already arrived. The one-armed knight now in fact tells the second knight what Meliadus has said. Once again, there is some confusion here, with part of the story clearly missing. We assume that the two knights had fought, that the one-armed knight had lost and fled into the forest, pursued by the other; however, the two men still appeared to address each other in a normal manner rather than as enemies.

48: Of the Letters Merlin Carved in the Stone

Meliadus now examines the stone and copies down the inscriptions, and then he makes his way to Merlin's tomb and calls out to the sage. Merlin answers, telling him that he knows the stone that the knight found "in the burial place of King Hugon Sachies" has been found. They were, he says, cut by himself. We have no idea who King Hugon the Wise might be, other than that he had lived a very long time ago. It is just possible that this is a reference to the French hero Huon of Bordeaux, but the likelihood of the scribe not recognising this name seems unlikely.

49: The Importance of the Letters on the Stone

We now learn that the writings on the stone are particularly important because they include a blessing from Jesus Christ himself and mention the things that he wishes everyone to have. There is also a testimony that speaks of a merchant who managed his affairs without involving others and who bought sulphur from the fires of Hell. Nothing further is said concerning this curious statement.

Meliadus tells the importance of the letters to the knight and then writes everything down and gives him the manuscript. The knight begins to read, and when he sees how reverential the work is, he declares that "he would have no more bad habits for the rest of his life and that he would get rid of those he had now." In other words, his entire life is turned around by the spiritual meaning of the messages. He then rides off to his court, which is apparently called Sauphine—another place that remains unknown elsewhere. He takes the knight with one arm with him, and when they arrive, he gives half of his wealth to the man whom he presumably wounded in the first place. Meliadus returns to Merlin's tomb, who tells him that that he is going to go to Arthur's court before he crosses the sea to Wales.

50: Of Meliadus's Meeting with the Wise Clerk and His Departing from King Arthur's Palace

In fact, instead of going to Arthur's court, Meliadus goes instead to see Antoine, who receives him with esteem. The next day he spends all his time bringing Antoine up to date, after which he heads off to the court, where he is lovingly received. The Wise Clerk meanwhile studies every detail of Merlin's writings once again.

51: How Meliadus Was at Merlin's Tomb, and of the King's Son, and of Tristan

Meliadus now goes to Merlin's tomb and hears the spirit of the seer speaking. He is told to collect all that he hears in this place and everything that is written on or around the tomb and take it to Master Antoine, who is now Bishop of Wales. Then Merlin says, "I see you leaving here and that it is for the king's son you need to do this. His name is Tristan, and he will eventually be important at King Arthur's court."

All this is in line with the story of Tristan, who is the son of King Meliadus of Léonese and will become one of the most famous Knights of the Round Table, second only to Lancelot. Before that he meets and falls in love with Isolde, the wife of King Marc of Cornwall. Their love ends in disaster and death, which Merlin will foretell. The scribe clearly knew the history of these characters from the references to their story, which follow from here onward. Meliadus is, of course, Tristan's half brother, who already knows that he will become a knight and that most of his adventures will take place in Great Britain. In what can only be a reference to the future love affair, Merlin says that he will experience great adventures but that "the sin of lust will take root in him."

He then adds "it is by acceptance of lust that the court of King Arthur will be destroyed." This refers again to the Tristan and Isolde story, which will bring all kinds of disaster and ruin to the kingdom, though the Round Table itself will be strengthened by Tristan's presence as a powerful knight equal to Lancelot. In fact, although he will not be known until his chivalric exploits are more widely celebrated, Tristan's fame will outlive his affair, and he will be remembered by his enemies with fear even after his death.

Once again, the scribe gives a religious slant to the story, telling us that the downfall of Arthur's realm will occur because lust was allowed to flourish.

52: Of an Angel Who Will Take Water from a Fountain and Extinguish a Fire at the Castle of Morgain

Now we have the first of several references to a King Henry. It is impossible to say with any certainty which king this refers to, though it could be one of several kings of France. The idea of knights collecting old books so that this monarch can read about the miracles that might be contained in them is fascinating. We are told that anyone wishing to meet the good king would have to search all the forests of the land, and that this might lead to the residence made for King Uther Pendragon, which will be completed after his death by his son King Arthur. This is possibly a hidden reference to the way in which Arthur transformed the monarchy of Britain for all time by establishing, with Merlin's help, the Round Table and building the great city of Camelot.

Then we have a reference to a fountain, another of the many mysterious fountains to be found throughout the Arthurian canon—in this case one that previously belonged to King Constans (Constantine), the father of Uther. We are told that a lion will enter who will emerge as a man—presumably by bathing in the fountain. This could be the knight referred to here as belonging to the family of Galehas, a mighty king of Wales who appears at the fountain. Galehas is unknown outside the context of this work.

We are then told that an angel will come down and place a container of some kind by the fountain. This is apparently to help in extinguishing a fire that threatens the castle that had once belonged to Morgain, which will be closely guarded because her fame has diminished. This probably refers to either the castle in the Valley of No Return or the Castle of Chase, which appears in other texts, particularly Malory, as the home of Morgain.

Why an angel would seek to save this castle is not explained, but we are told that he is going to take a knight named Synaublans, another character unknown elsewhere, who will apparently see the opening of the earth and the abyss beneath. In other words, Hell.

Merlin then says that he must tell Master Antoine that all men, especially the distinguished people who come from the sea (the Venetians), will see a miracle. Following this, Merlin himself will win more hearts in Gaul, and others will be shown miracles and see the depths of the earth filled with sulphur—once again we assume a reference to the hellish goings-on around the Arthurian kingdom due to the willingness of Arthur to allow lustful events to occur.

53: How There Will Be Much Rain in Brittany

Meliadus now goes to see Master Antoine and presents him with a manuscript in which he has collected all of Merlin's sayings, including the fact that there will be a lot of rain in Brittany that will destroy the wheat and that a famine will follow so merciless that many thousands will starve.

Merlin then suggests that a champion will go to an island in the sea where there are Pagans, that he will subdue it, and that its people will be baptised. From this place food will be sent to England to help the famine. The name of the champion is Sadaine—another character who appears nowhere else.

Then we have this curious statement that Master Antoine realised that his own abilities did not match those of Merlin, and how he began to study so that he could share his (Merlin's) art, enabling him to understand the firmament, the moon, the sun, and the stars. We are then told how it is from the moment of his awakening—whether this means Master Antoine's or Merlin's is not made clear—the prophecies will be known to be true and that Merlin knew the choices that would be made in the future, "as the Holy Spirit revealed in the firmament." This we take to be a reference to Merlin's connection to God, who enables his seership and furthers his observance of the wisdom in the heavens.

54: How King Henry and One Hundred and Fifty Knights Will Go to the Forest of Avrences

Merlin now appears to address Master Antoine directly, presumably in the spirit. We return to the story of King Henry, who we are still unable to identify, who will go to the forest of Avrences with one hundred fifty knights, searching for Merlin's tomb, but afraid to find it. They will gather before the roaring mountain but will not find the entrance to the tomb.

Merlin then says that in front of this mountain the king will make a tower and that the book Blaise wrote will testify that Merlin spoke it. King Henry, we are told, will create a serpent that, when the Dragons of Babylon begin to hunt, will cross the land and the eyes of the dragons will grow great with fear and they will fly back to the deserts of Babylon.

This sounds reminiscent of the story of Vortigern, who built a tower that fell into ruins every night until Merlin, in youthful form, explained that there were dragons under it. It is possible that the story of Merlin and the dragons reminded the scribe of the seer's obsession with serpents and dragons and sought here to connect these with the Dragon of Babylon, the Antichrist.

The roaring mountain is mentioned in another romance, the *Marvels of Rigomer*, but here it is intimately connected with the fate of King Henry, who knows that he will be buried in front of it and that he will never return home.

55: On the Death of Tristan and How Meliadus Cannot Harm the One Who Killed Him

Merlin rounds off his prophetic comments about Tristan, telling Meliadus that his brother will be killed by "the meanest and most disloyal king there is," very clearly King Marc of Cornwall. Meliadus asks whether if he seeks out this killer he can actually harm him, to which Merlin replies no, but adds that he will have no future. In the middle of this last paragraph, Merlin says: "Know that I cannot be distracted by anyone."

Meliadus now writes all that Merlin has told him and everything that he found written on the stones surrounding the tomb. After which he hands over the parchment to Master Antoine to add these things to the collection of Merlin's prophetic utterances.

56: Of Raymon the Wise Clerk of Wales

We are now being prepared for the next change in scribes, when we learn that "after a long life dedicated to God, Master Antoine decided to retire and become a hermit." He passes on the task of compiling the prophecies he had received from Tholomer to another Wise Clerk of Wales by the name of Raymon. So we have the second Wise Clerk, confusingly so titled, who is to play an important part in the stories that follow.

Meliadus, we hear, is now constantly travelling back and forth with ink and parchment between the cave where Merlin is trapped and the Wise Clerk's workshop. By this time Meliadus is established as the lover of the Lady of the Lake, and we learn that Merlin has revealed his true identity, of which he had hitherto known nothing. He is in fact the son of the Queen of Scots and the King of Léonois and was abandoned at birth by his mother and exposed in a small craft at sea. From this he was rescued by the mother of the Lady of the Lake, who raised him in secret.

So here we have a whole new set of details concerning Meliadus, most of which had been hinted at previously but not spelled out. The suggestion here seems to be that even if the Lady of the Lake is an ageless faery, she still had a mother, and that this nameless being was also rescuing abandoned children and bringing them up as her own, just as the Lady of the Lake later does with Lancelot and his nephews.

Meliadus continues to bring the prophecies that he hears directly from the mouth of Merlin to Raymon and also copies the descriptions scattered around the tomb, as we were told in the previous section. We hear that Raymon was in fact a student of the occult arts; he tries to verify Merlin's prophecies by using magic and is very eager to visit the seer's tomb. We hear that on "a clear night with an exuberant starry sky he cast spells to test the truth of the prophecies." Then on the following night, Master Antoine's ghost appears in a dream to confront him about his pride. Antoine tells him that even if he could talk to Merlin, it would not help him, as he is more like a sheep and does not even know of the prophecies of Jonah, which were written down in the past! Antoine then advises him in the dream to go to confession as soon as possible for he has no real faith in the Lord God—or presumably in Merlin's words.

Meanwhile, Meliadus goes back to the cave where Merlin lies, and as he does this, several knights approach him with raised swords. They threaten to kill him if he doesn't lead them to where Merlin is trapped. Meliadus's response is to say, "follow me."

Then the scribe announces that he knows what happened next: Meliadus led King Henry's knights to the mountain, and when they got there the mountain started to make more and more noise, broke apart, and swallowed the knights. The scribe then says that he is telling us this so that we know about it "in case the stories of this adventure fade and Merlin's prophecies are no longer heard."

Thus, the adventure begun in section 52, concerning King Henry and his men, is concluded, and we learn how they met their end at the roaring mountain. We may recognise this as a pattern that runs throughout the entire collection of prophecies in the 1498 edition, in which the scribe constantly interrupts stories or muddles up their links with other things not told, which he obviously knows about and expects his audience to know.

Here also, the ghost of Master Antoine appears to the new scribe Raymon and tells him that he should not be questioning the veracity of the prophecies nor be looking for Merlin's tomb, because even if he managed to find it he still wouldn't be able to get any nearer to the truth since he has no knowledge of the mysteries of Jonah, referring to prophecies supposedly made after Jonah was recovered from the belly of the whale in biblical tradition.

57: Of the Damsel Who Visited the Chaplain

A damsel now arrives to visit the Chaplain, bringing letters. We are not told who these are from, but perhaps since the Chaplain is to be the new scribe, they are from Master Antoine, or perhaps from Merlin himself, as we shall see. In the letters we are told that chivalry and the Order of Saint Peter (the papacy) will be terminated, though how and why is not relayed. The letters also say that trade, goods, and evil will be set right, but that before this happens there will be so much evil that it will be seen by everyone. But certain holy men will face the great mountains and will say: "Climb up. Rise above us and enchant us, for through our eyes we have never seen such great wonders from Heaven." This sounds like a reference to Merlin, because the letters immediately go on to say that above this island, by which we assume they mean Britain (though it could also be Venice), the bearer of the good news will be a woman. The Chaplain is instructed to write this down and add it to Merlin's prophecies, thus implying that the letters were indeed from him.

At this point the damsel says that a miracle has happened in her country and that a letter, written on a marble stone, testified that Merlin the wise prophet declares that the birth of the Abomination from Jerusalem will be prevented, all debts paid off, and all sins forgiven. The text then mysteriously adds that there will be an island in a place that has been under water for a long time and an island that once belonged to Cir and Pol—characters that we have not been able to identify. Once again, we have something inscribed on a stone.

The Chaplain, who must be Rubens, though he is not named here, who is to be the next compiler to the prophecies, asks to know if the damsel has letters that testify to what she says. To this she replies in the affirmative.

58: From the Clerk Who Came before the Chaplain

While the damsel is talking with the Chaplain, one of the clerks whom he had sent to find Merlin's writings returns. The text read: "Sire, I have failed." But clearly he has not because he goes on to say that the Chaplain had sent him to Norbellande (either Northumberland or the Netherlands, since these titles are used interchangeably in medieval manuscripts) to seek the words of the prophet and that there are "a great many sorrows, pains and marks that I bring you, along with many works that will enable you [the Chaplain] to see great miracles." We have thus amended the text to "I have not failed."

The Chaplain bids the clerk to hurry up because he is anxious to see the written words, at which point the man shows him a letter testifying that with the "Guardian of Merlin's possessions" would come "an image of brass that would speak for him as a man of flesh speaks, and that will want to know that the death of the Wise Clerk will take place a year later."

Although the texts describe the person who will carry this image to be the Guardian of Merlin's possessions, it seems to refer to the cleric himself because when the Chaplain asks when he should see such a miracle, the clerk pulls out the brass image and says: "Here it is. Let me show you an enemy of Hell." We might assume that this should read an enemy "from" Hell, but the reference may be to the famous brazen head once owned by the medieval magician and philosopher Roger Bacon (1220–1292) who was able to make it speak prophecies. As Bacon lived a little earlier than the original compilation of Merlin's prophecies in 1303, it is possible that the compiler had heard of this famous speaking head.

59: Of the Enemy Who Broke the Brazen Image

Immediately, the statue declares that it has never been to Hell and has nothing to do with it. The Chaplain asks who it is that speaks, and the statue replies that it is an angel who fell to Earth with Lucifer. Then it adds a fairly basic and traditional statement, that those who converse with Heaven have not died, but those who follow Lucifer are damned. At this the Chaplain asks who put it into the brazen image, and it replies that it was Merlin. Assuming that is true, says the Chaplain, since he represents Merlin, he would like the being to come out. It does so and has the face of an angel but blackened. It then says that they—presumably the angels—have lost Merlin, but that he is still at one with God—an interesting ideas that seems once again intended to explain that while he is nominally Pagan, Merlin is acknowledged by God. The angel then vanishes "like lightning," and though the Chaplain and his followers depart from there, the text says that "the image of what happened was etched into their souls."

60: Of the Sad March of the Lady of Caiaphas

The letter held by the Chaplain, presumably one of those brought by the clerics from Merlin, says that "during a sad march to support a lady, she will cross the sea and do much good. So much that she will be proclaimed a Lady of Caiaphas." The meaning of this is unclear. The only Caiaphas of whom we are aware is the Jewish high priest who served in the Temple of Jerusalem during the time of Christ and is said to have organised a plot to kill the recently proclaimed messiah. How the anonymous lady can receive this honorific for her good work thus seems to be the opposite of the biblical meaning.

The scribe then reports that the letter also says that this will take place at the time when the Abomination departs from Jerusalem. The scribe then goes on to describe his visit to the forest of Avrences and that he found the words inscribed on "a steep step." He did not, apparently, find his way to Merlin's tomb; rather, the suggestion is that we have yet another stone on which the seer's words are inscribed.

Lastly we are told, again quoting from the letter, that in time the great Abomination will be slaughtered by many serpents. This seems to follow on from the earlier information concerning small serpents attacking the Great Dragon. Perhaps it is not too wild a speculation to suggest that Merlin in some way has control of these small serpents and that he is therefore able to send them into battle against the Great Dragon. However, if so, this is not a story that we find told in any complete sense within our text.

61: Of Those Who Cannot Be Buried until the Third Day

The letter continues, telling us that within a certain mountain surrounded by ridges, which will be called Hole, a hermitage will be built. At this time the Abomination from Jerusalem will reveal a miracle to those who have watched for it, and this will mean that when they die, they cannot be buried under the earth for three days. Even then, this will only be made possible through the prayers of this holy hermit, who lives in Hole.

This seems like another theological explanation, which are indeed not uncommon in such texts as the *Lancelot-Grail* Cycle, where convenient hermits appear whenever an event of mysterious origin needs to be explicated. We can find nothing of the mountain of ridges or the place called Hole or the hermitage or, for that matter, the hermit, but apparently his task is to help those who have believed in the miracle presented by the Abomination of Jerusalem who, as a result, cannot be buried until three days after their deaths. Only the hermit's prayer will make this possible. In very general terms, this seems to be a reference to the idea that those who follow the Abomination will be punished, at a time when burials generally took place immediately after death.

62: Meliadus Alone Has Access to the Tomb

We return for the moment to Raymon the Wise Clerk, who is desperate to find Merlin's tomb. He says to Meliadus: "Please tell him about me, and I promise to write down the things you have spoken of, including the truths of Jonah's prophecies spoken in the past." Again, we have a reference to the prophecies of Jonah, which are referenced in the Bible as follows: God commanded Jonah to travel to Nineveh and prophesy to its inhabitants. He went into the city crying that in forty days Nineveh would be overthrown. After this, the people of Nineveh begin to believe his word, and the king proclaims a fast. Everyone puts on sackcloth and ashes, and God forgives their pride (Jonah 3:1–5). Why the prophecies of Jonah would be included among those of Merlin is uncertain, other than very possibly to make a comparison between the two, once again implying that Merlin's prophecies are to be believed and have no evil intent. There is also a possibility that the scribe was drawing a parallel between the good people of Venice and those elsewhere—perhaps in Rome—who were too proud to obey God's commandments. He thus draws Merlin's wisdom into the picture.

Meliadus now goes to Merlin and tells him what Raymon has said, which prompts Merlin to reply that the one who says this is so stubborn it seems as if he is set in stone! However, the sage now sends a message to Raymon, telling him to go to King Arthur's court and there wait for the coming of Percival. He says that the knight will lead him to a place where he will find a round stone, and that if he then casts a magic spell, he will be able to speak to Merlin's father, who is trapped in the stone.

The text seems to have been leading up to this point for some time. Meliadus asks if only the Wise Clerk can do this, and Merlin confirms it. Meliadus then asks if, out of all the vain and earthly men in the world, Raymon is really the best suited to this task. Merlin says: "It is best to let him go, for no one else will be approved by me in this world. We have to make sure we give him the right instructions, and he will do what is desired in the right way. Further, it is better to make friends than enemies."

Meliadus asks if he will survive, and Merlin replies that through Percival's prayer he will be fine. Then Merlin says: "If he climbs upon the stone, it will fly through the air at high speed, and from there he will see not only the cave where I am buried, but the whole world under the sky." "Where will he descend?" asks Meliadus. "In King Arthur's court," says Merlin.

Meliadus then goes straight to the Wise Clerk and tells him everything that Merlin had said, as well as "what was hidden in the future." He stays with the Wise Clerk, and on the fourth day they go "do what God has commanded them to do." It seems worth noting here that Merlin's instructions are often described as confirming God's commandments—once again, as we noted previously, inferring that the seer's connection is acceptable.

63: Of the Wise Clerk of Wales, the Enemy, and Percival

Now we come to one of the biggest stories within the collection. The Wise Clerk seeks out the Round Stone and mounts it. Immediately, it shoots out across the sea and then farther into the sky and across the world. While it travels the devil imprisoned in the stone by Merlin's magic converses with the Wise Clerk. It tells him of Merlin's miraculous birth, of his lust for women that sealed his fate, and how he was "murdered" by the Lady of the Lake, as he had himself predicted. Then we have an interesting small detail that describes how "the Round Stone passed the north side of Saint Mark's basilica in Venice and the Wise

Clerk there saw the Byzantine relief depicting Alexander the Great riding in his gryphon-drawn chariot on his aerial journey." This detail clearly impresses the importance of the Venetian connection and adds a touch of realism to an otherwise fantastic journey.

The conversation between the Wise Clerk and the Enemy continues with the former asking if the devil knows where Merlin's tomb is hidden. The devil answers that only Lius, an important devil, knows it, this being an unknown demon. The Wise Clerk then asks if Merlin is safe. The devil replies: "I cannot know whether my enemy is safe or not, but I know that despite my strength and that of the other servants of Hell, he cast me into this stone." How did this happen? asks the Wise Clerk, adding in one of those wonderful, personal touches scattered throughout the text: "Is it the same as when I was shut in stone by my stubbornness?" "I don't know," the devil says. "Just as you don't know how Merlin was conceived. Only Merlin has power over all things, and he knows that this stone, though it is heavy, is like a fish when it is in the sea and like a bird when it is in the air."

The Wise Clerk then asks what we may see as an obvious question: Can the demon tell him how Merlin was conceived? "No," says the demon. "Even Lucifer would not speak of this nor would those who are with him in Hell. But it was not lust that caused Merlin to rob the Lady of the Lake of her virginity. Merlin would have done many good things, more even in the apostles could have done. But the Lady of the Lake took his life and only his spirit continues to prophesy."

This is a very important statement as it more or less reverses the critical view of Merlin as someone who uses his skills and power to obtain sexual favours. To compare him to the apostles and to suggest he might have done more than they is verging on the edge of heresy. It is possibly the boldest statement made throughout the whole text.

The Wise Clerk then asks another important question: Will he—Merlin—be there on Judgment Day? To which the demon replies: "Yes, he will be there, along with all the souls who were called before." This we take to be a reference to those who died before the coming of Christ, who we may remember goes into Hell to release them between the time of his death and resurrection. However, the demon goes on: "You may reach Heaven with the Virgin Mary, and all the angels of Lucifer's company will have their place when the judgment is pronounced at the end of days. The Angels of Heaven will remove all false men, who will be given to the Angels of Hell. Lucifer will rule by fire in the Second Age, and their torments will be endless."

This last is all very much in keeping with the teachings of the Joachites (followers of Joachim of Fiore) and various other groups of the period, who emphasised these theological truths above all others. The Second Age refers to a future time, following the defeat of the Antichrist and his banishment to Hell.

64: The Round Stone Goes to India

While this conversation has been going on, the Round Stone has set course for India and passes the palace that Saint Thomas built there. This refers to the founding of Christianity in India by the apostle Thomas, which came into being after Thomas was believed to have journeyed to the East and established a branch of the church within this area. The Eastern Syriac Nestorian Church had the widest geographical reach at the time—from Iraq to Central Asia. The connection between this version of Christianity and the beliefs represented by Prester John are distinct.

Meanwhile, the Wise Clerk takes the opportunity to seize the mantle of the King of India, which was at that time ruled over by a mighty Christian emperor. This is a very clear and precise reference to Prester John, who, as we noted in the chapter "Written Records of the Prophecies" in part one, was believed to rule over a kingdom described in the *Letter of Prester John*, which purportedly came from him and was sent to the crowned heads of Europe. A translation of this letter can be found in appendix 4 of this book. It describes a version of earthly paradise, a realm where all is beautiful and peaceful and reflects the true mysteries of God. Prester John is thus both a priest and a king because he pronounces upon matters both temporal and spiritual. In one text, *Der Jüngere Titurel*, attributed to Albrecht von Scharfenberg and dating from 1272, this figure is said to become one of the guardians of the Grail, a detail that was carried forwards through time into the teachings of nineteenth-century occultists, such as A. E Waite and Charles Williams.

The Round Stone flies on until it reaches Burma, which is almost certainly a reference to Berne in Switzerland, although both India and Burma were known by this time. The King of Burma sees the stone with the Wise Clerk seated on it and falls to his knees, begging Our Lord to grant him understanding of this miracle. The Round Stone immediately stops, and the devil explains that it was trapped in the stone by Merlin. "Whereupon the King of Burma wished to search for the great magician who had such power to be able to do these things."

Now the Round Stone continues on its way above Antioch, where Raymon drops the cloak of the King of India into a fire. However, the cloak remains intact because "the servants of the Priest John always used fire to cleanse it."

After this, the stone flies on back to Camelot where it first flies over the square in front of the palace, sets Raymon down safely on the ground, and then is swallowed up by the earth, which gapes open to receive it. Percival, who has been waiting to see this, falls on his knees and beseeches the Lord Jesus Christ to let the Wise Clerk live. This done, he goes to King Arthur and tells him what he has seen. Among those present are the High Princes, the Fathers of the Islands of Lointaines, Lancelot of the Lake, the Baron of the King of Longes, and the Knights of the Round Table. All there saw the miracle and how the earth swallowed the stone.

Meanwhile, the story says that the Duke of Antioch took the cloak dropped by Raymon out of the fire undamaged and went in search of the one who he had seen wearing it. Cutting a long story short, we go immediately to the arrival of the duke at a hermitage, presumably somewhere in Arthur's kingdom. The duke arrives in a sedan chair carried by porters. The moon shines brightly overhead. The duke says that he "found an inscription on a marble stone that mentioned the name of the master who owned this coat and the inscription showed me the way to this place."

The priest lets in the porters with the palanquin, but the hermits see that the duke is a practitioner of black magic. However, Percival, who is apparently present, calls upon them to respect him. The duke then tells the story of meeting the Wise Clerk on the marble stone in the sky, and that as a result of this a part of his soul has emerged that he had not recognised before. "I have therefore renounced the black arts. And now I have found the one I have been looking for, for a year and a half."

Now the Wise Clerk tells everyone how he met Percival and how he believes that the Saviour of the world will find him worthy of this task. This sounds for a moment as though it is Merlin who has this title, and it is intriguing to wonder if the compiler of the work is not once again comparing Merlin to Jesus.

Percival asks the Wise Clerk to tell him how it was that the stone carried him so perfectly between the sea and the sky, to which he memorably replies: "The Enemy from Hell sat in the stone. He showed me the whole world from the air in just three days."

Although we can follow the story quite easily, there is, once again, a certain amount of confusion. Raymon drops the cloak into the fire, which does not consume it; the Duke of Antioch discovers it and then himself goes in search of Raymon—and ultimately of Merlin. The duke reaches the hermitage in record time. There he finds Raymon and Percival and is able to interrogate them regarding what happened. Once again, we go back to Percival being able to save the scribe by his prayers, the suggestion being that, were it not for this, some terrible fate might have befallen him because he had the temerity to step on a stone occupied by a demon.

65: The Wise Clerk Goes to Meliadus

The Wise Clerk and Meliadus meet, but though cordial and despite Meliadus asking if Raymon really wants to see Merlin's tomb "the most glorious place of all the beautiful places in the world," he does not allow this to happen. Instead, he sets out to the mountain that roars (which is presumably the same as that which devoured King Henry and his knights) and thence to the cave where Merlin's body is laid. He drives away the magpies that cluster about the cave mouth—even then they were regarded as unlucky, and we cannot help speculate if, as carrion eaters, they were drawn there by the smell of rotting flesh. Within he can see the body of the seer and the bones already showing though. He feels the approach of Merlin's ghost and invites it to speak. Without hesitation, and describing himself as "the wisest man in the world," Merlin places his prophecies into Meliadus's hands.

His immediate prophesies declare that there will be a joust between good and evil and that war will be brought on by the Dragon of Babylon. Meliadus asks when this will happen. Merlin's response is curious: that it will happen after Burma has been destroyed, which will happen before the Abomination leaves Jerusalem, and that this in itself will end only after the Dragon of Babylon is put to death by two holy men Helias and Enoch, who will witness the coming of Jesus Christ. This is curious because it seems to imply something that has happened in the past. Helias may be the same as the hermit that Percival is to meet shortly, but since he is grouped with Enoch, and assuming he is the same as the one mentioned in the Bible, the name should be Elias, who was also one of those who witnessed the coming of Jesus Christ. It is possible that this last phrase refers to them seeing the light, becoming true followers of Jesus, but as ever, our enigmatic scribe does not make this clear.

Meliadus then asks what we might see as a key question: "When will the quest for the Holy Grail begin?" To which Merlin replies: "The knight who will begin the quest has not yet been born." This would presumably refer to Galahad, the final and most successful Grail winner in all of the later stories. Percival and Bors, who are the other two Grail winners, are already alive. The time line is therefore inaccurate, probably as the result of the compiler having access to more than one manuscript.

Merlin then goes on to say that it is time for Percival to journey to

Cornwall to help his brother Tristan. Apparently, Percival hates going there, but Tristan needs him, and it is also God's command. "Why does he need to go there?" Meliadus asks. "Because King Marc is holding Tristan captive." Merlin is sure that Percival will free him and possibly imprison King Marc. He then adds, "Tell him he must go faster than he can actually go!"

At this juncture the scribe interrupts the narrative in his own voice and says: "Now it is time to tell us more about the plots of King Marc against Tristan—even though the story has been translated from Latin into French by others." He thus once again shows us that he has access to and has to read other sources.

66: The Plots of King Marc against Tristan

Because of the interruption of the narrator into the storyline here, it is difficult to tell whether the following is in his voice or that of Merlin. We assume the latter. The next paragraphs summarise episodes from the *Prose Tristan* romance, which narrates the struggle between Tristan and Marc, the deaths of various traitors, nephews, and villains, and the capture of Tristan. Percival is the one who will set Tristan free and bring him and Yseut (Isolde), the wife of King Marc with whom Tristan is in love, to Léonois, where they will be safe.

67: The Release of Tristan by Percival

The story continues but takes a different line. King Marc receives letters from the Pope asking him to go on a Crusade. This gives Marc an idea. He sends a chaplain to Tristan in prison and offers to release him, on condition that he takes the cross. Tristan replies that if he were free, and if the Pope wrote to him, he would indeed do that—but not at Marc's suggestion. Marc's response to this is to forge a letter from the Pope and send it to Tristan, bidding him undertake the Crusade. But Tristan recognises the source of the letter and dispatches a defiant reply, agreeing to go on the Crusade but saying that no knight of Cornwall who is not also a king accompany him. The story then points out that he himself was the son of a king and had a realm no smaller or less honoured than that of Marc (i.e., Léonois). Tristan feels that if he doesn't go he will be hated forever but reminds everyone that Marc is forcing him to go.

While Marc is reflecting on this, some knights from Léonois attack some of his men, prompting the king to order his own followers to arms. In his haste he forgets to insist that the guards who watch over Tristan should remain where they are; they thus head off to war, and Percival arrives and releases Tristan.

The text, we presume in Merlin's voice, says that he will now tell us what will happen to Tristan and Yseut and the ending of their love for each other.

68: The Deaths of Tristan and Yseut

We can be fairly certain that this is still Merlin speaking because he continues to summarise the end of the great love story in which Tristan is fatally wounded by King Marc in the castle garden, where he dies, and Yseut, "out of despair and inexhaustible love," gives up the ghost and falls dead across the body of her soul mate.

Moving swiftly on, Merlin says "write all this down carefully" because now he's going to tell us about the plot of Claudas against Lancelot, Claudas being the king who attacked the kingdom of Lancelot's father, King Ban, which resulted in the king's death and the fostering of the future hero by the Lady of the Lake.

69: The Plot of Claudas against Lancelot

Clearly, Claudas is not satisfied with his earlier attacks upon King Ban but continues to hold great animosity towards his son, Lancelot, whom he determines to destroy. He gathers his allies and tells them that he's going on a pilgrimage to Rome and begs them to guard his land in his absence. Claudas takes with him a wise clerk (presumably not Raymon) who has vowed that no harm will ever come to

Queen Guinevere because she once did him a great service. How this directly impacts upon the queen we assume is because of her love for Lancelot. Meanwhile, Claudas disguises himself as a pilgrim and arrives in Rome. There he goes to the Pope and delivers a sermon in Latin concerning the Holy City of Jerusalem, and then tells the Pope that he is a hermit who, knowing the need of the Holy Land, has come to reveal that the war with Lancelot is deterring the men of the Terre Déserte—his own people—and those of Lancelot from taking the cross. He thus cunningly persuades the Pope to give him a letter that he can send to Lancelot, bidding him go on a Crusade to Jerusalem. Claudas then returns home.

However, this devious plot is prevented from having any effect because King Arthur declares war on Claudas "who is never heard from again," though his son became one of the Knights of the Round Table.

Having thus disposed of the story in a few paragraphs, the narrator now says, "I have to tell you another story . . . but I must tell you this prophecy of Merlin's before I forget!"

70: Of the Damsel from Avalon Who Came in a Boat

In fact, it is not really a prophecy, as such, but a new story and a rather interesting one at that. We are told that a damsel from Avalon comes ashore in a barge with full sails, which is described in some detail. It was actually made by Merlin himself, and in it he sailed from Wales to India, where he lived for several years. The damsel in question had lived there with him and been selected to be taught magic by the Lady of Avalon. The Lady of Avalon may be the Lady of the Lake, but more frequently it is Morgain who rules over the island, according to Geoffrey of Monmouth, along with her nine sisters.

The text goes on to tell us that when the ship landed a large crowd gathered—indeed so large that "the great city of Vitré, in Brittany, where King Arthur's palace stood, was half empty." The choice of name here is interesting because Vitré translates as "city of glass," a term often used in the romances for a faery castle or city. The apparent placing of King Arthur's palace in Brittany is also interesting because we have to remember that many British storytellers and poets had fled from Britain at the time of the Saxon invasion in the sixth century, which resulted in the spreading of Celtic mythology, including the Arthurian legends, into Gaul (later France) and thence throughout the rest of Europe. It is interesting to wonder which text the author was reading when he wrote this, as he then says that, if we asked him where the young lady came from, he would say she was from India and that Merlin had sent her to be in touch with the people of Logres.

Then follow some rather curious details. Before coming ashore from the barge, the damsel takes a ladder from the boat and rests it on dry land. Then we learn that having previously had a fish as a guide, a fisherman now took its place. The fish itself is sent to King Arthur who cooks it whole and eats it later on. These rather bizarre statements seem to be part of the otherworldly setting of this particular episode.

The damsel is taken to the Church of Saint Stephen, where we learn that Arthur was at prayer and wanted to be left in peace. So the people leave the church, but when the damsel, after herself praying, finds Arthur "she pounced on him like a beast upon its prey," opening her arms and running to King Arthur crying: "Sire, I have found you!"

Arthur, with some amusement, holds her at arm's length, asking if she is always this enthusiastic. It then turns out that she thinks he is Uther Pendragon and asks where Merlin is. The king replies that Merlin hasn't been here for years and wonders why he should be here. She replies that Merlin has been in India for twenty years, preparing the country for the coming of a great evil, and that he had sent her to Tous Saints.

When Arthur learns that she thinks he is Uther, he says that a strange twist of fate has brought her there. He points out that even her mother would have been too young to see the king very often, and yet she, who is not yet thirteen years old, says she's seen him!

The damsel doubts this statement and says that she remembers him from the day the Round Table was founded. Arthur, in order to prove that he really is who he is and not his father, says that he can show her some writing, a charter that will prove who he is. "So be it," says the damsel and introduces herself as "Aglentine, damsel of Avalon." She then asks that he "tell Merlin that I want to return his barge." Arthur replies that Merlin is lost and has been dead more than fifteen years. "My God!" says the damsel. "Merlin has not been in my life for so many years."

There is a kind of time slippage going on here. Aglentine has been in India with Merlin, who presumably left her there to return to Britain during the time of Uther Pendragon, so that he can arrange and organise the sword and stone, the crowning of Arthur as king, and the founding of the Round Table. Now that she has arrived in Arthur's court, she clearly expected to find Merlin still there and is horrified to learn that he has been dead for fifteen years. Once again, the time line is confused, stretched and compressed at the same time to enable the narrative to bring all of these elements together. But there is more to come.

71: King Arthur and the Maiden of Avalon

The beginning of this section is transposed from the one that follows, from where it has clearly slipped, breaking the logical structure of the narrative. The king now takes the damsel into his palace, and she puts some letters on the table, which she had with her. She says that they are from the Christian Emperor of India (i.e., Prester John) whose wisdom is great. The Lady of Avalon asks that the king read the letters and remember what is to be found within. She then tells him how Merlin had journeyed many years before to the kingdom of India and had spent many days talking of all manner of things with the emperor. Thus, the link between Arthur and Prester John is very clearly and finally established.

Arthur now asks the damsel to stay there until she is at least twenty, but she says that since everyone there sees her as a child, she is going to return to Avalon where she came from "before I went to India along with other chosen ones." This implies that Merlin took a whole entourage with him to India.

As soon as the damsel states her intention of leaving, the ship turns round and sets its sails to the wind. Arthur wants to stretch out his hand to stop the barge, but the wind fills its sails and it drifts away.

As Arthur watches the boat vanish, he is distracted by a great noise coming from the direction of the palace, as if a great miracle were happening. And in a way it is, because as the people look on, an iron griddle with four fish upon it hovers overhead. Lightning then strikes the griddle and cooks the fish, which are then taken to be eaten by the court that evening.

Here once again we have a series of otherworldly incidents. It is possible to see that the fish that guides the craft and the fish mysteriously cooked on the otherworldly griddle are somehow references to the symbolism of Christianity. The fact that the fish that guided the craft is replaced by a fisherman recalls the Fisher King, who is constantly referred to as a guardian of the Grail throughout the whole series of romances concerning the quest for the divine vessel.

There is, indeed, quite a plethora of mystical references at this point. Arthur follows the ship for some miles on land, accompanied by knights who watch it as it goes farther out to sea. The text then reads, "As it approached the Black Chapel, the ship was reflected in it, and the king and all his companions did not know what was reality and what was deception." There are a number of black chapels in the Arthurian legends, for example the Perilous Chapel in the romance of *L'Atre Périlleux*, an anonymous romance dating from around the middle of the thirteenth century. But how the ship can be reflected in this is less easy to understand, especially since vitreous rock was barely understood at the time of the composition of the original *Prophecies*. This is best explained by the apparent inability of Arthur and his men to tell truth from fantasy.

We then learn that Arthur is very sorry not to have been able to stop the boat by force.

72: Of the Letter That the King of India Sent by the Maiden of Avalon to King Uterpendragon

Seeing that everyone else seems to be having a good time drinking and eating, Arthur asks if anyone has seen the letters that the lady, the damsel from Avalon, had placed on the table. A maidservant says she has them, and King Arthur says to the knights who are assembled that since these letters were addressed to his father he can legally open them. Arthur then breaks the seal and finds what is inside. The words are worth repeating here because of their importance.

"To King Uterpendragon, to whom the mother of God grants to see the sage Merlin, as the one who from India sent a damsel in a barge, by sea, then by land, then by sea to Vitré. The King of India greets you and prays for you. And since he has had holy baptism and believes in the Father, the Son and the Holy Spirit, St. James will not be forgotten."

This is a very interesting message for a number of reasons. Arthur is virtually receiving a personal version of the famous letter sent by Prester John to the kings of Europe. It mentions that the damsel had been sent from India across one sea, then by land, and then another sea to King Arthur's court at Vitré. Then that the King of India greets Arthur and prays for him and mentions that because he believes in the Father, the Son, and the Holy Spirit, St. James will not be forgotten.

The story then tells us that damsel had come from India in a month and a half, having stayed "in the sacred palace Saint Thomas had built there long ago," and that she had travelled this far to see the great virtue bestowed by Jesus through the works of the saint.

This is the second significant reference to Nestorian Christianity, which was supposedly founded in the East by the wandering apostle Thomas. This is entirely in keeping with information supplied regarding Prester John's miraculous kingdom in the East with its foundation on Christian beliefs.

We may be forgiven for wishing that more could have been said, but once again the narrator interrupts himself to say that he's going to stop talking about this adventure and talk about another—in fact about a prophecy of Merlin's that is very important and that he wants to tell us before he forgets it.

73: Of the Proud Damsel of the White Kingdom and King Arthur's Wedding

In fact, once again the scribe has misled us. This is not a prophecy of Merlin's but another story entirely, which begins as though it is about to retell the previous tale of the maiden from Avalon, but then veers off into a quite different account of a very important theme. We are immediately thrown by the fact that Arthur and Uther Pendragon are not only alive at the same time but also active—something that does not happen in any other existing Arthurian romance.

We begin with a reference to Arthur's nephew, who is, more often than not, Sir Gawain, but who is not named here. Apparently, he had met the Wise Clerk of Wales, who had told him about Merlin's prophecies and other wonders. This seems to be his first visit to Arthur's court. He states that he too is from Wales and knows the prophecies to be true. In fact, if he is Welsh, he cannot be Gawain, who in all of the romances is from the Far North, usually the Orkneys.

When he hears this, Uther addresses Arthur with a prophecy he has heard from his cousin, who heard it from Merlin. Perhaps not surprisingly, the prophecy seems to have become somewhat garbled. It concerns "a footman" who will come there in half a day and whom everyone will talk about. He will be accompanied by "a lackey who they say has no belly. He has a torso and no legs, he has good working hands but no arms, he has a good head and no mouth." This reads like a riddle, but bizarre though it sounds, such characters are not without precedent. Similar figures are described from time to time in Celtic myth, such as the depiction of the Lord of the Beasts in the *Mabinogion* story "The Lady of the Fountain," where the hero meets a one-eyed, one-armed, one-legged being. There are also instances of men with dog heads in their chests, mentioned in a number of medieval chronicles of travellers, such as Sir John Mandeville and Marco Polo, to unknown lands. The scribe would almost certainly have read, or heard of, any one of these.

At this moment a servant announces to Arthur that a young woman wishes to speak to him. Arthur sees her there and notices she is hesitating. Seeing how shy she is, the king rises and comes down from his throne and orders everyone to leave the room. When they are alone together, she tells him that she is the daughter of the White King and the Queen of the Aryans. She has taken an oath to the Blessed Virgin Mary, that though she is beautiful she will not give herself to any man unless he is true. A knight named Gruira has been pursuing her, trying to kill her father and invade her country in order to win her.

While she is telling this story, an old man comes by who turns out to be a hermit. He has with him a gold ring with a gemstone in it, which he gives to the girl, informing her that Merlin had asked him to bring it there when he was one hundred years old. Arthur has obviously taken a liking to her because he decides to take her in and gives her a relined mantle of his own. He then places the ring on his own finger. The text then says that "while Merlin was imprisoned in the tomb what he had said was fulfilled: King Arthur and Guinevere were married."

What we appear to have here is a very muddled or otherwise unknown story of the meeting of Arthur and Guinevere. The maiden arrives at the court with her story; the hermit arrives with the ring, which he gives to her, according to Merlin's wishes. Arthur puts the ring on his own finger, and thereafter, he and Guinevere are married. It is impossible to say now how the scribe arrived at this very garbled story, but as ever it officers a glimpse into at a time when the Arthurian canon was still being formed. This is the first of several magical rings that appear in the proceeding sections.

There is now apparently a splendid tournament, presumably to celebrate the marriage, at which the High Prince Galeholt takes part but from which Lancelot emerges victorious. This connecting of the two men seems to foresee their friendship, which is described at greater length in the *Lancelot-Grail* Cycle and ends with the death of Galeholt, who starves himself to death after Lancelot refuses to acknowledge him as his greatest friend.

The section ends with the enigmatic comment that "in the city of Vitré [which we will remember in our text is the name of Arthur's city rather than the more familiar Camelot] the good knights began their quest for the Holy Grail." This suggests that time has moved on, but once again the time line is confused and conflicts with that of the more familiar stories. Certainly, the quest for the Grail begins a number of years after Arthur and Guinevere are married.

74: Of the Emperor of Rome, Who Came before the Pope with a Hundred Knights

This section was originally section 4, but clearly belongs here in the light of the sections that follow it. In it we learn how the Pope is speaking about truces broken in Jerusalem, and as he does so, the Emperor of Rome appears with more than one hundred knights, goes to the Pope, and falls on his knees, begging for forgiveness. The Pope says rather than a penance that the emperor should take up the Holy Cross and go over the sea to guard the Holy Land. In other words, go on Crusade. This the emperor agrees to do, kisses the cross, and accepts the commission along with the barons who are with him. In return for this, the Pope forgives the sins of all who would go with him to Jerusalem.

This is very clearly a reference to Emperor Frederick II, who for much of his rule swore to go on Crusade, only to then withdraw from this because of other more pressing concerns. For this he was excommunicated several times, each time promising again to go on Crusade in return for being received back into communion with the church. This, along with his interest in magic and alchemy, made him a perfect candidate for the Antichrist, as he frequently appears throughout the *Prophecies*.

The section ends with Frederick celebrating with his companions and promising to give them everything they ask for. Then it says that there is a certain bishop at the council who pretends to be very religious and a good Catholic but in truth is not. Whatever he believes fills him with so much fear that it can be seen by all. The text then says that if he was brought before a council, he would swear that he was a faithful believer, and that people would accept this, so that he is able "to deceive the world by his evil works." This is almost certainly a reference to an unknown figure within the hierarchy of the church at the time the prophecies were collected. Such a direct accusation would have seriously endangered the life of anyone who stated it, so the scribe is careful not to do so, knowing that those reading it would certainly recognise the figure described.

With this, we enter the period of the Crusades with which the next three sections are concerned.

75: Of the Aid Sent to Jerusalem

We now begin to hear more about the Crusades, which are seen as happening during the reign of Arthur who, if he is considered as a historical figure, lived a long time before the eleventh century. The scribe now addresses us, saying that he must tell us of a prophecy about the King of Sessoines coming home in chains and receiving from his tributary kings acceptance of terms imposed by Galeholt. This king has been accused of waging war against the Christians and now agrees to pay tribute to King Arthur, swearing never to make war against them again. In this context, although Sessoines would usually be translated as Saxons, it is more appropriately read as Saracens. Once again there seems to be a confusion between Arthur's traditional enemies and the forces ranged against the West in the Crusades.

King Arthur now calls the Knights of the Round Table together, and when they are assembled, a knight named Blioberis tells of his slaying of two giants whose heads he displays. Blioberis is a familiar figure from the Arthurian legends, the son of Nestor, godson to King Bors, brother to Blamor, cousin of Lancelot, and lord of Gannes. He is also listed as fighting against the Saxons and King Claudas, which may account for his presence here. His appearance in the story that follows probably derives from one of the manuscripts read by the compiler of the first prophecies of Merlin in 1302.

The King of Sessoines make his promise and leaves the council chamber. A debate follows, opened by Galeholt, who advises that mercy should be shown to the king. Gawain agrees with him and adds that, while King Arthur was in Carmelyde, the Pope had sent the Bishop of Galice (possibly Galicia in southern Spain) and the son of the King of Jerusalem to Britain to ask for aid for the Holy Land. Apparently, this had been unsuccessful, and the Pope is now writing letters calling for help against King Baudic (who sounds Saxon), who is threatening Jerusalem. Gawain advises that the tribute, which the Pagans are going to pay, should be applied to pay for a Crusade.

At the request of Lancelot, the letters from the Pope are now read, first that of the Emperor of Rome who, at the bidding of the Pope, had gone to Jerusalem and had written asking for aid. This appears to refer back to the previous section and implies that although the emperor was willing to go, he still wanted to be paid for the transportation of himself and his army to the Holy Land.

Next comes a letter from the King of Ireland, who is in Jerusalem already and in which he authorises the Pope to "sell everything: all the land, with men, women, children, cattle, castles, houses, and farms," and that the money thus raised should be used to send forces against the King of Baudic.

This rather overwhelming instruction seems like an overstatement but is not too far from the efforts made by various kings to raise money to enable them to join the Crusade. A further letter is read, addressed to King Arthur himself, in which he is told that his sins will be forgiven and that he should travel as a Christian king to Jerusalem to fight.

It is unusual to find Arthur involved in this way in the Crusades, which to the authors of the romantic literature of the Middle Ages, despite their confusion over time lines, would have been seen as taking place long after the king died. In fact, at the end of Thomas Malory's *Le Morte D'Arthur*, the surviving knights of the Round Table, following the withdrawal of Arthur to Avalon, are said to have gone on Crusade and to have died in the Holy Land.

Lancelot now suggests that they should lessen the tribute of the Pagans and demands it be paid in a lump sum, so that it can be immediately sent to the Pope. King Arthur takes up this suggestion, the Pagans accept it, and the tribute is sent to Britain. There it is employed to pay a large force of men to go to Jerusalem under the leadership of Henry the Courteous.

Once again, this character is impossible to identify with any certainty. The crusading army from Britain endures the long sea journey, arriving at Japhes, almost certainly Jaffa, or modern-day Tel Aviv. News of their arrival and the treasure they bring with them is joyfully received by the Emperor of Rome, who clearly expects Arthur to contribute to his funds.

All of this has been in the voice of the scribe, but here suddenly Merlin interrupts, saying: "I now take the opportunity to speak of the adventures and words of Richard of Jerusalem."

76: Of Richard of Jerusalem

Richard of Jerusalem (who could possibly be Richard Lionheart, though this is by no means certain) and the Bishop of Galice travel from England to Rome taking the treasure they have been given. Meanwhile, the emperor has been crowned by the Pope and has gone to the Holy Land. The Pope proclaims an indulgence for all those who are joining the Crusade, and a large company embarks for Japhes, near which the emperor is encamped in the plain of Burtinuble. The emperor had been crowned some time before this, so we assume that the word *crowned* should be *forgiven* or *restored* (to the church).

Following the emperor's arrival, the Christians win an immediate victory over the Pagans, and the emperor orders a chapel to be built in memory of this. He then quickly undertakes an expedition to Sarras, where the ruling lord has been killed by another nobleman and the followers of each are fighting day and night. This is interesting because Sarras is the title normally given to the city of the Grail, which is later to be briefly ruled over by Galahad. In the many versions of the Grail quest, Sarras is initially a Pagan city, which is eventually converted to

Christianity through the actions of the Grail knights and the sacred vessel itself, which is then stored in the castle.

The story that follows is largely borrowed from the *Lancelot-Grail* Cycle, with Richard as hero, assisted by the King of Ireland. Enter the giant Alchendic who has murdered the former ruler of the city and given the people the choice of remaining beside him to fight or leaving the city in safety. They decide to stay. Alchendic then advances on the Christians and offers King Richard four sets of spears to be used in single combat with him. If Richard wins, the Pagans will surrender the city; if he loses, Alchendic proposes a truce of ten years. Richard accepts the spears but says he will leave the discussion of the truce to the emperor. In the combat that follows, Alchendic proves to be invincible, and the emperor accordingly grants the truce. However, at the end of the month Alchendic is baptised.

At this point, Merlin once again interrupts, saying: "I am going to tell you about the King of Ireland and King Baudac. Write it all down carefully so it is not forgotten."

77: Of the King of Ireland and King Baudac

We learn now that the King of Ireland, with a large party of English Crusaders, sets out from Jerusalem to aid King Richard at a place called Orberice. This place-name comes from the river Orbe, a tributary of the Rhine, which rises in France and flows to Switzerland, where it forms the river Thielle at its confluence. This might possibly be the origin of the city of Orbance, mentioned earlier in the story of the magical stones (sections 9–10). On the way there, the King of Ireland meets a company of Pagans from Sarras who were heading for Orberice to aid their fellows. A battle follows, and the King of Ireland defeats the Pagans. He then returns to Jerusalem, since Orberice had already fallen to Richard.

Meanwhile, the King of Baudic, having learned that the Christians are resolved to leave no fortresses in the possession of Pagans, holds a council of war. It is decided to send messages to Jerusalem under the leadership of one Ulfal, offering defiance to the King of Ireland. When they reach the gates of Jerusalem, "through the miracle of Christ they were unable to alight from their horses" and the King of Ireland comes out to meet them. Ulfal, believing himself and his men bespelled, calls the king an enchanter and announces that his master commands the Christians to depart unless they want to see the city destroyed. The King of Ireland dismisses Ulfal, bidding him tell his master that the Christians have a helper far more powerful than he and that they do not fear him at all. This we must assume refers to Merlin, rather than God, who in at least one other text is referred to as a very powerful protector of the Christians.

Meanwhile, Richard, hearing of the defiance of King Baudic, sets fire to Orberice and returns to Jerusalem. Merlin then says: *"I am now going to tell a story that takes place in the court of King Arthur."* The scribe also jumps in here again and says that honesty compels him to admit that he copied this from older manuscripts. This is an interesting statement of its own, partly because it is not clear whether he is referring to the Arthur in stories or to the *Prophecies*, but it is very clearly an admission that he worked from older documents to create the one we are currently reading.

78: Of King Arthur and the Knight of Carmelyde

The story that the scribe now tells concerns a knight named Savariz, from the country of Carmelyde. Carmelyde is normally identified as the kingdom ruled by King Leodegrance, the father of Guinevere. In this instance, the knight comes to defy Arthur and the law that had been passed at the court of Logres, which declares that judgments given by the barons of Carmelyde are invalid. Savariz therefore calls King Arthur a traitor and insists that he agree to single-handed combat. Gawain, always an impulsive man, offers to take the combat upon himself, but the knight says that he will only fight King Arthur. They engage in a fierce contest in which at length King Arthur unhorses Savariz, snatches off his helmet, and threatens to kill him if he doesn't admit to being vanquished. When Savariz refuses this offer, Arthur smites off his head, before himself falling exhausted to the ground. Physicians are summoned to tend the king's wounds, but by defeating his adversary he has proved in the eyes of the world that the barons of Carmelyde are false.

79: How a Lady from Abiron Put Merlin to the Test

Confusingly, in this entry, we are back with Master Antoine, who has supposedly retired by this time. Merlin sends word to him to write the story of a lady from Abiron, who could have been the wisest in the world had she not decided to follow the dark arts rather than the other sciences. Apparently, she visits Merlin and says that she has come all the way from Abiron to see him. Merlin replies: "Lady, you are welcome, but do the people of the city of Abiron know you are here?" He adds that he could tell her many times before midnight why she came there, but that while it had taken six months for her to get there, when she returns, on the third day following, Abiron will be taken and its inhabitants slain and its possessions thrown into pits. The lady demands to know how he knows this. As ever, Merlin does not respond to this but reassures the lady that she shall be saved from her enemies. The lady inquires who it is who is going to do so much damage to the city and to her. Merlin tells her that it is someone called Acloas, who is not happy because she is away from Abiron. The lady is apparently so impressed by all of this that she says to Merlin: "Please love me and follow me into the dark arts." The place and personal names here—Abiron and Acloas—are both unknown.

80: Of the Ring Merlin Gave to the Lady of Abiron

Merlin does not respond to the lady's request, which prompts her to tell him that she will have a golden image, in honour of him, placed above the main gate of Abiron if he agrees to come with her. Again, Merlin does not respond directly but removes a ring from his hand and gives it to the lady. This immediately causes her to be carried off by the henchmen of Hell to Abiron, where she is placed naked on the top of the highest tower. She is released three days later, but only after Acloas has destroyed the city. She is thus saved by Merlin's magic, and her father afterwards retakes the city. This seems to be included here to prove that Merlin has not lost his magical abilities or his access to the powers of Hell, which he once uses for good.

At this point the scribe once again interrupts himself: "I will keep silent about this adventure and tell you further of Merlin's prophecies, for there is much to tell. I have yet to tell you about Esglantine, the damsel of Avalon, the Lady of Avalon, the Queen of Norgales, Sebile, and Morgain." This bodes well, and indeed the next four sections tell a particularly interesting story.

81: Of the Lady of Avalon, the Queen of Norgales, Sebile, and Morgain

Just the names of the lineup of these ladies is of interest, because they are widely known throughout the canon of Arthurian literature as both allies and adversaries. The struggles in which they engage here are unique to the literature of the legends.

First, we hear that the Queen of Norgales and Sebile have received a message from Morgain, who has brought a wounded knight to the castle of Belle Garde. They set out at once to go there. This is clearly a reference to an episode in which Lancelot, having been wounded, is taken prisoner by Morgain le Fay and placed in the dungeons of her castle. Here, this castle is called Belle Garde, an alternate name for Lancelot's castle of Joyous Garde. Morgain along with three other queens (the Queen of Norgalis, the Queen of Eastland, and the Queen of the Outer Isles) are listed in Malory's *Morte D'Arthur* (Book VI, section iii) as Lancelot's captors, who tell him, in a "Judgment of Paris" scenario, that he must make one of them his mistress if he wishes to escape. Although the lineup of enchantresses (described as faeries) is different here, it is clear that this is a variant of the same story.

In the version we have in the *Prophecies*, the story takes a different direction. As the two magical women, the Queen of Norgales and Sebile, are about to set out, they are approached by a damsel from the Lady of Avalon, who wishes to meet with them at once. She tells them they will see a miracle. The story now turns back to the previous section in which we encountered the Lady Esglantine, who was sent to India in the miraculous barge made by Merlin and returned looking just she had been in her youth. She also brought with her two rings (presumably from Merlin), one of which made the wearer invisible and the other irresistible. This is, of course, the first we have heard of this.

The damsel says that the Lady of Avalon wants to introduce Esglantine to her three powerful friends: the Queen of Norgales, Sebile, and Morgain. She asks them to come to the harbour where a magical barge awaits them. Meanwhile, the Queen of Norgales and Sebile have guided the damsel to Belle Garde, where Morgain, who is suspicious of the Lady of Avalon, hides herself and avoids going to the barge. The other two go to the port and find the Lady awaiting them. They are amazed at the barge and that Esglantine has not aged. The damsel is told to wait for the coming of Morgain, while the others travel on to Avalon in another vessel. In an aside we are told that the barge bears an inscription that it would one day carry Arthur to Avalon when mortally wounded, as Merlin's prophecy foretells.

Meanwhile, on the second ship, the Lady of Avalon produces the two rings and declares that her companions cannot overcome their power. She puts on one of the rings herself and immediately becomes invisible. The Queen of Norgales and Sebile decide that they will break the spell, and they try with all their might to do so, but the Lady of Avalon, whose power is described as enabling her to "make a palace tremble and to rain down swords," then puts on the second ring, which makes her irresistible, and commands the two women to undress. Unable to resist the spell, they do as they are told but do not realise that they are naked. The Lady now puts on a third ring—the first we have heard of this—brought to her by Esglantine and breaks the spell. The Queen of Norgales and Sebile realised their plight, and Sebile especially is furious, but both were forced to admit they could not resist the power of the rings.

Morgain, meanwhile, now arrives at harbour, where she finds Esglantine waiting for her. She goes aboard the barge, and they set sail for Avalon. As they get closer to the magical island, Morgain looks into her book of magic and summons a troop of devils, disguised as birds and dragons, to capture the Lady of Avalon, convinced that the rings would have no power over them. However, the Lady of Avalon is apparently unaffected by this. She puts on the rings that made her invisible and irresistible and commands Morgain to undress herself. A devil then takes Morgain's cloak and hangs it from a high tower. "If Merlin had been alive, he would surely have taught me an incantation stronger than these rings," says Morgain.

Then the Queen of Norgales and Sebile appear, and the compiler comments that since the Lady of the Lake was there also, all the subtlety of the world was in that place.[161] The Lady leads her guests to the tower where Morgain's garments were but sends ahead a flame that burns them. "I learned this magical spell from Merlin," she admits with obvious delight. Morgain says, "If this is so, then Merlin deceived me. He said he had taught me all the magic he taught the others."

The last line of the section says that the faery women decide to sail north in search of Merlin's tomb.

82: On the Rescue of Breuse Sans Pitie

The Lady of the Lake makes her way to Galles (Wales) where she finds her lover Meliadus waiting for the Wise Clerk. The Lady expresses surprise that Meliadus had stayed there, but he says, "There is no one else in the world who is better able to understand the words of Merlin and to confer with him so often." This is a positive comment about the

---

161. Note that the Lady of the Lake is sometimes referred to as the Lady of Avalon. It seems likely that the scribe himself may have confused the Lady of the Lake with Morgain.

Wise Clerk, but since he is unable to see Merlin or hear him it is rather confusing.

While she is in Wales the Lady is welcomed by King Urien, of whom we get a backstory. Two years before, Urien had been enchanted by a maiden from Little Britain and lured to her castle. There he was enchanted in such a way that he did battle with a neighbouring knight named Margondan, who was attacking his domains. Urien killed him and was being attacked in return by four of Morgandan's men when the Lady of the Lake appeared with ten of her own knights and stopped the combat. She then bade Urien to put on his finger a ring, which freed him from the maiden's spell. She then dispersed his assailants by telling them that he was under her protection and escorted him to the port where he set sail for Vincestre.

News of the Lady of the Lake's honouring of Urien aroused Morgain's jealousy. She travelled with fifteen knights to Vincestre and having set up her pavilion, sent her followers throughout Logres in search of the Lady of the Lake. At this time Claudas de la Terre Déserte (Claudas of the Land Laid Waste), Morgain's ally and Lancelot's enemy, was fortifying Benoic (Benwick) against a possible attack from Lancelot, whom Claudas now feared even more because of his friendship with Galeholt. Morgain told Claudas of her plots against the Lady of the Lake and begged him to do his upmost to take her prisoner. Claudas offered his followers large rewards for her capture, reminding them that she was protecting three of his mortal enemies: Lancelot, Lionel, and Bors.

Now we hear another story involving Thomas, Count of Miaus, his daughter, her husband, Guillaume du Pas Fort (Guillaume of the Strong Foot), and a classic Arthurian villain named Breuse Sans Pitie (Bruce Without Pity). The count's daughter, along with her husband, lodges with this infamous knight who throws Guillaume and his attendants into a dungeon and does violence to his wife before allowing her to leave the castle alone. When she tells her father of this, he goes in search of Breuse, whom he meets, unhorses, and takes prisoner, intending to deliver him to his daughter.

On the way they encounter a company of Morgain's knights, some of whom Count Thomas kills in battle. From those who escaped Morgaine learns all that occurred and rides at once to Vincestre, arriving after the count had already set out to sea with his prisoner. Morgain sends a gale across the waters, but as she can not see the ship, she fails to interfere with its course so that it came safely to port.

While Count Thomas is leading Breuse in bonds to his castle, he offers him his liberty, in return for the release of Guillaume. This Breuse accepts and sends orders to his wife to set the prisoner free. At the same time a party of Claudas's followers overtake them and attack. Count Thomas makes his escape, leaving Breuse in their hands. They take the rescued man to Claudas, who out of respect for Morgain honours him.

The Lady of the Lake learns all of this from her maidens, and that Claudas had laid an ambush for her. She laughs at this and takes upon herself the shape of an old woman, which enables her to return to her dwelling unrecognised.

All of this seems to have happened sometime in the past, but as ever the time line is unclear.

83: Of Berengier de Gomeret

Now we learn what happened to Sebile. This story concerns Berengier de Gomeret, a handsome widower who loved Sebile the Sorceress and came to her castle in search of help to find his child, who had been stolen from him. Sebile knew that one of Morgain's maidens, Flor de Lis, had carried the child away to the castle of her mistress in Norgales. This is a place where Morgain kept all her treasures since Lancelot destroyed her castle in the Valley of No Return. Flor had then promised Berengier that his child would be restored to him if he married her mistress.

Having agreed to this, the two travelled to Norgales where, seeing Berengier's beauty, Morgain bade her handmaid to refuse to return the child unless he gave up all thoughts of Sebile and married her. Flor promised Berengier that his child would be restored and gave him the night to think it over. She then secretly told him that he was doomed to become either the husband of Sebile or Morgain, but that she herself would take him and the child to safety if he agreed to marry her. Berengier agreed, preferring Flor to either of the other two faeries. That night Flor de Lis showed him the way to escape and they fled together to Gomeret.

When Sebile discovered that Berengier had vanished, she accused Morgain of having made away with him and went to Nogales. There, in a towering rage, she seized Morgain by the hair and dragged her up and down the whole of the castle and struck her violently before departing, leaving Morgain half dead.

On her way home Sebile met Breuce, disguised as a pilgrim, and thus did not recognise him. When she got to her castle, she heard that he had already reached Norgales and had begun to tend to Morgain's injuries. They also told her of Berengier's escape with Flor de Lis. This caused Sebile to be filled with regret for her treatment of Morgain.

Once again, the text of this mixes up the story by confusing the two enchantresses and their homes, but the story is clear enough to enable us to correct these details. Flor de Lis is probably the same character who features in another tale—*Gawain and the Lady of Lis*.[162]

84: The Reconciliation of Morgain and Sebile

Following three days of unconsciousness, Morgain revives thanks to the remedies administered by Breuse, and laments the injuries she has sustained from Sebile. Breuse reminds her that she has had many quarrels with various faeries but permanent enmity with none but for the Lady of the Lake. He then opposes every plan for revenge Morgain proposes, assuring her that the Enchantress was powerful enough to resist her. This makes Morgain so angry that Breuse departs.

---

162. Weston, *Gawain and the Lady of Lis*.

Morgain forthwith sends a letter by her damsel, Morguenete, to the Queen of Norgales, announcing that she is dying and requesting the queen to come and propose a plan for vengeance against Sebile. In return for this Morgain promises that she will give up many of her treasures. However, it happens that Sebile is at the queen's palace when the letter arrives, and on learning its contents she begs the queen in tears to effect a reconciliation with Morgain. The queen proceeds to Morgain's castle and persuades her to forgive Sebile, reminding her how the latter had pardoned Morgain several times in the past. Morgain accordingly sends for Sebile, and peace is made between them.

This is an unusual story, highlighting the animosity among three of the leading enchantresses of the Arthurian tradition. Sebile is not as well known as the others, and her name undoubtedly originates with that of the Sybil, one of the great early prophetesses of the Roman world. The scene where Sebile, in a fury, drags Morgain around the castle by her hair is quite startling and perhaps underlies an element of human nature on the part of the two faery women, who resort to physical violence rather than spell-craft.

This section ends the follow-on from the three faeries going off in search of Merlin's tomb, which of course they do not find. The text now turns to the matter of the Grail, or as the scribe himself says: "Now it is time to move on with the story about Meliadus, Percival and Raymon the Wise Clerk from Wales."

85: How Helias Gave the Book of Blaise to Percival

Now we follow Meliadus as he takes the boat for Wales and goes to meet the Wise Clerk, Percival, the King of Burma, and the Duke of Antioch. Meliadus tells the Wise Clerk everything the Good Mariners (i.e., the Venetians) need to know; he tells the Duke of Antioch that he has heard from Merlin that he should return to his country, where he will experience a great miracle.

Meanwhile, the Wise Clerk tells Percival all about Merlin's wisdom and all that he has experienced. Percival questions him as to why he is putting himself in such mortal danger—referring to the fact that he will endanger his soul by having anything to do with Merlin. The Wise Clerk answers that he has studied the arts of energy for a long time and "if I have learned anything, I believe that all the senses of the world are hidden in this cave. Merlin is so powerful that he has even travelled back in time to explain the dreams of Caesar, ruler of the Roman Empire."

Once again, we have a sense that Merlin's magic is perceived of as a real skill, and that it has an almost scientific quality. "All the senses of the world" speaks of an ability to relate to every aspect of life in a truly shamanistic style. Even more startling is the statement that Merlin had travelled back in time to explain a dream to the Emperor of Rome. This is a reference to a story normally told as occurring when Merlin is wandering the world long before Arthur's time, when he journeyed to Rome and revealed that the empress was having an affair with a courtier.[163]

"How can all the senses of the world be brought together?" asks Percival, and the Wise Clerk tells him how the sage came to be trapped in the cave in the forest of Aurences, and the prophecies he had uttered about Percival's sister and Percival himself, who will keep his virginity until the Grail is found. He will also journey with the Good Knights to the Holy Land.

Percival, who has never heard of Merlin before, swears that he will go and look for him. Raymon the Wise Clerk warns him that his quest will be futile, though he will have many adventures along the way. Percival then says: "You say that Merlin is so wise?" and the Clerk says that he has "experienced that in him are all the senses of the world and that we owe everything to him for the future." Percival asks for proof of this. "I do not know," answers the Wise Clerk. "My heart is in the forest of Avrences . . . and I am sure Merlin's fame is everywhere in the world where there are men."

---

163. See Wheatley, *Merlin, or the Early History of King Arthur*.

At this juncture the scribe interrupts once again, telling us that the King of Burma set out to find Merlin with more than a thousand knights, and that the Duke of Antioch, taking twenty knights, went to seek the sage. "The energy they gave to their search for Merlin was unspeakable," he tells. "I want you to know this firsthand."

Then the Wise Clerk speaks about his journey on the stone, and how he came to the palace of Saint Thomas and was allowed to hold the cloak of the King of India. He describes the casting off of the coat and how the Duke of Antioch finds it, "which was a great marvel." Then Meliadus chimes in and tells Percival all that Merlin that had said to him. To which Percival responds that he "vows to the mother of God that I will go in search of Merlin and that my search will be according to the custom of Logres." From this we understand that he is not only determined to find Merlin but also that he will obey the traditions of the Arthurian kingdom, being a chivalrous knight, an adventurous hero, and a kind and gentle helper to all those in need.

86: Of Percival's Search for Merlin's Grave and His Several Adventures

With great determination Percival sets out and very soon finds a stone engraved by Merlin. The inscription tells him that "widows and orphans would no longer receive alms, although this was obligatory according to the dictates of religion." The stone also has a prophetic message, which says "woe to those who will not protect the widows and the orphans. The Mother of God, patroness of these, will give them a sign: the earth itself will gather itself up, the rain will destroy the wheat they grow, the men will plough and reap, and so they will have enough to give, but they will give only to those who do not need it." These theological accounts are very much in line with the ideas expressed throughout the text. Almost exactly the same story in almost exactly the same words is then repeated in the next paragraph, which we have deleted.

Percival goes on his way through the forest and has many other exploits, and in the course of time comes to a hermitage in which he finds hospitality for the night. There he meets an aged hermit called Helias, who remembers Merlin's childhood and the marvels he performed.

Despite being old and feeble, Helias tells Percival that he has been waiting for the son of King Pellinore, who is of course Percival himself. He then tells his own story—how long years ago a certain knight had suspected Helias of being in love with his wife and was planning to kill him. But Merlin arrived and prophesied in his presence that Helias would retain his chastity to the end of his days and that he would not die until Percival arrived at the hermitage. This prediction convinced the angry husband that Helias was innocent, while Merlin reproved the man for the sin of jealousy. After this the sage presents Helias with a book of his prophecies, bidding him to give it to no one save Percival.

Without initially revealing his name, Percival lingers at the hermitage listening to Helias's stories about Merlin from his own memories. Helias tells of events from Merlin's childhood and Percival is grateful to hear this privileged witness of Merlin's early days, but as it becomes evident that Helias's death is near, Percival finally reveals his identity. The hermit hugs him and then opens his fist, in which he holds a small coffer (a strongbox for holding valuables), and says: "Please wait as Merlin would have wished. I am weak and will soon die." The coffer is not explained as yet.

Percival now asks if he will show him his book before death comes, and the hermit says he will. "It would be best for me if I show you it now since death is coming this way."

"Has anyone else seen the book?" Percival asks. The hermit says that one has, because when the bishops came for Merlin—presumably to test him as is described in the text of the *Prophecies*—he told them that he could not remove the chain that encircled the book. Only one who was not yet born could do so. Then he named the one it would be as Tristan de Léonois. This again reads like a confusion on the part of the scribe, since Tristan is in fact Percival's brother, and it is clearly Percival who is meant.

Here the scribe enters again, telling us that "his patience is being tested to know the end of this adventure."

The following morning Percival and the hermit discuss the works of Merlin, and the hermit says that he knows that his health is failing and that he has "blown the last notes of his hunting horn." Now he will tell Percival the wonders of Merlin. He adds that the Holy Man and the Holy Angel (unnamed) are filled with great joy and the enemies of Hell are very angry. "I tell you that your soul will be saved," he tells Percival, adding that "before I knew Merlin I lived with lies."

Percival now asks him to tell of the miracles of Merlin, and Helias launches into a great diatribe about Merlin defending a merchant who had denounced a group of money changers. He had traded gold in the market and found that it was not right. The merchant said he went back to the hostel and spent the night there, tested the nuggets, and found out they were light. So he went back to the money changers and asked them for the proper gold. All he was doing was standing up for his rights, but the judges were weak and distanced themselves from the case.

The hermit then rants about unauthorised treasurers entering the church and witnesses being kept at bay and unbelievably killed by the bishops. He instances a priest who attacked a woman who came to him asking for penance for a dying man. The priest was accused of rape in front of the bishops and denied his crime, supported by the testimonies of his friends. Then the judges called in the money changers who declared that they knew nothing about impure gold. Everyone knew this was untrue, but there was nothing they could do about it.

So Merlin went to the church and stood before the bishops. The judges came in and Merlin laughed at them and said that he knew they were not wise, but that if they knew him they would also know he would easily find out the truth. One of the jurors jumped up and said he had neither seen nor heard anything. Merlin laughed cynically at him and said: "The truth will surely remain behind the doors of the church. You will do everything to keep and protect the stolen treasure even if the magpies peck you until you bleed."

Everyone in the church was dismayed, and the bishops demanded to know what was going on. Merlin answered: "Look to the gold and silver, which the enemies from Hell will keep." Then through his magic, he caused the money lenders' ten chests containing stolen money to fall open at their feet. Then to the judges he said: "Gentlemen, take the keys and shut these chests, and know that you shall find within coinage of Constantine and Saint Elaine"—referring to certain coinage of the time.

"What should I tell you?" says the scribe. The money changers acknowledged they were wrong and returned the gold nuggets, then they were taken from the market and their hands cut off. Back in the town Merlin asked the judges to do justice for the raped woman, and just as they had the hands of the thieving money changers cut off, so the judges had the rapist-priest emasculated. However, the bishop, who must have known of these things, was not punished, much to Merlin's anger. Despite this, later on the judges were handcuffed and taken to the palace.

Thus ends yet another attack upon the church and the judiciary, which, as we have seen, is a thread that runs through the entire book.

87: Of the Death of the Hermit

The small coffer given by Helias to Percival is now opened. In it are letters, which we assume were either from Merlin or Helias himself. Merlin's writings were also given to the knight with the instruction that he should entrust them to the Wise Clerk, who will add it to the library of Merlin's books.

Once he has seen Helias buried by another hermit, Percival goes on his way and comes to a fountain where a pavilion is set up that bears the marks of long usage. Within it he finds a revolving wheel, fastened to a marble column and having on it stop an iron cage in which a clerk is confined and the top of which has a brake that can stop it turning. The wheel is revolving at tremendous speed, and the clerk inside cries out to Percival, entreating him to force the brake down. But Percival can not understand him because of the noise the wheel makes—which never ceases except when a neighbouring hermit comes there to say Mass.

During this the imprisoned clerk eats food brought to him by an old woman. When she arrives on this occasion, she explains to Percival that Merlin had confined the clerk there for a misdeed. As they talk the hermit begins to say Mass and the clerk eats, speaking not a word but making signs to Percival to press the brake.

Percival uses all his strength but cannot move it. He begs the old woman to tell him how he might accomplish this adventure, and to prove to him that his efforts would be in vain, she leads him to a deserted tower, before which is set a stone bearing an inscription written by the Lady of the Lake after she had entombed Merlin.

The stone says that while he was in the forest of Avrences with the Lady, the clerk in the cage came to the forest and secretly watched them. He was clever, having studied in Avalon, and was able to cast a spell on the Lady of the Lake, which was supposed to put her completely in his power. However, she undid the charm, which was the same that she had used to put Merlin to sleep.

When he woke, Merlin punished the clerk by confining him in the revolving cage. There he must remain until the Knight of the Dragon lays his hand upon the brake. Though we are not told who this is, it is safe to assume that this is Lancelot, whose coat of arms included both a lion and a dragon—but we do not hear the end of the story.

Percival now leaves the imprisoned clerk and rides on his way. He is attacked by two robbers who dwell in a neighbouring tower with a band of miscreants. They had gone on a pillaging expedition leaving in the tower only Percival's assailants and the maiden to whom it belonged. Percival kills one of the robbers and forces the other to surrender and conduct him to the tower. Here he sets free many other knights he finds within and then presents the tower to the maiden. The robber whom he had beaten promises to become a good and loyal knight, and the maiden agrees to marry him.

Percival now takes his leave and pursues his wanderings till he comes to another tower, to which he is admitted by an old woman. She begs him to fight on the morrow with its lord, who is holding captive a lady who refuses him her love. Percival goes to a pavilion and finds the damsel cruelly bound with iron wires. She entreats him to release her, and he promises to do his best.

Now he learns that the people of the countryside have sworn that if any knight unbinds the maiden, they will rebind her, as they await the coming of a knight who would vanquish her oppressor. Percival stays in the pavilion for the night. In the morning he and the knight of the tower meet and Percival declares his intention to do combat on behalf of the lady.

The knight explains that Percival's quarrel with him has no substance. He had met the maiden one day near the tower, and in response to her request had courted her in safety to her dwelling. Here he was attacked by a knight whom he killed, but though begged to marry the maiden by her followers, she was disloyal enough to refuse.

Percival replies that he has undertaken her quarrel, just or unjust, and they engage in a fierce fight, which Percival wins. He spares the life of his opponent on condition that he set free the maiden and declare himself her prisoner. The knight accepts this, only asking that Percival should not deliver him to the maiden. Percival then gives orders that the maiden be unbound and rides on his way.

Declaring that he had handed her over to the mercy of the knight, the maiden sent a squire after Percival to entreat him to give the tower to someone else—perhaps someone who could protect her from her oppressor. Otherwise, he would have infringed the customs of Logres.

Here again we hear how important it is that Percival not betray the ideals of chivalry, knighthood, and King Arthur's realm. He is indeed being prepared to undertake the quest for the Grail.

The squire overtakes Percival as he stands in the forest by yet another stone on which Merlin had inscribed a prophecy. When he has copied this down, he returns with the squire to the tower, where the maiden tells him that her reason for refusing to marry the knight was that he was a robber who hated her. Percival says that if he had known this when he undertook to defend her, the knight would not have escaped so lightly.

On the morrow, at the maiden's request, Percival knights a young squire whom she loves, and they are forthwith married. Once he has seen the maiden of the pavilion married to the youth, Percival rides on his way to Corbenic. This is an interesting detail in that Corbenic or Carbonek is the name usually attributed to the castle of the Grail.

In the forest Percival rescues two maidens from four knights. He learns that the maidens' cousins, who had killed their brother, had deprived the maidens of their inheritance, and on their refusal to marry two robbers to whom the knights desired to give them, were about to burn them alive. Percival horribly maims the knights in combat and escorts the maidens to their castle in safety. There, her people at once bade him to accept one of the maidens and the tower as his own. As he is declining this offer, two knights from a neighbouring castle ride up and defy him. He engages in a combat in which both men are slain.

Percival is at a loss to know what to do with "the Benjamin's portion" of the castle, until a knight errant arrives on the scene, to whom he passes over everything he has won and happily goes on his way. The reference to the Benjamin's portion derives from Genesis 43:34, which refers to the worthy receiving more than they could possibly expect.

Now the story tells us that the Wise Clerk of Wales holds the books of Merlin, and the one written by his master, Blaise, and he learns that Blaise had told Merlin's mother that lust would no longer torment the ladies of Gaunes. He also possesses a book written by Merlin at the age of eighteen months—*The Hidden Gospel of Childhood*, later entrusted to Helias. The Wise Clerk begins to read the book written by Blaise and to speak of it to bystanders. Among other things, it says know that those who show no mercy will be judged badly by the shedding of blood, and that more men and women will suffer and become bitter because the grains of wheat they sow on this earth will yield nothing. This refers back to earlier statements in a previous section, in which we learned the story of the grains of wheat.

Now comes a remarkable statement, again quoted from Merlin's book, which says that "those who have the law belonging to the Lady of God, the Earth and the stars and the sky, and the bride, eve, the trees, the beasts, the birds, and all things that bear gold in them. Their faith will be saved providing they have faith in the Lady of God. And

God allows it, as part of his internal vengeance on the dead gold of the Earth. So as they get worse in faith and law, they will also get things that will help them keep their hope."

This is an extraordinary recognition of the power of faith and trust in the Lady of God, whom we assume to be the Virgin Mary, and all of the things that this will bring to those who believe and that will help them keep their hope. Although there is nothing unusual in the beliefs described here, the beauty of the language, attributed to Merlin, is powerful.

The Wise Clerk of Wales has apparently been sharing this with a congregation. He now ends with the Holy Supper (i.e., the Mass) and closes the book. Then he speaks further.

88: On Rubens, Who Took the Place of Raymon the Wise Clerk of Wales

Once again we realise that the Wise Clerk is still Raymon, and he now proceeds to state that "the great treasures that he has described depend upon Merlin." And he says, "I am sure the ages will bring many more," suggesting that future collections of the prophecies are likely to happen. He says that he sees all the battles that take place in the time of King Luces of Logres, until the time when the Round Table meets for the last time, and that records of this and other things will be brought thither and written on parchment and made into a book. "A book that everyone will want." Then Raymon says: "Gentlemen, I see Rubens the Chaplain comes in my place after my death, and I see questions and written wonders brought to him. And if he finds anything of Merlin's, it must be immediately put in writing and joined with all his prophecies."

Then the Wise Clerk strips off his Episcopal mantle and gives it to Rubens the Chaplain. With this Rubens receives its powers, just as Raymon had once obtained it—presumably from the previous scribe Master Antoine. This all happens as Merlin predicted it, and soon after that the Wise Clerk of Wales falls ill.

89: The Death of Raymon the Wise Clerk of Wales

"What shall I tell you?" says the inimitable scribe. "When the Chaplain Rubens was given his immense inheritance, and he saw that the wisest clerk of the age had left the Earth, he gave a thousand marks of silver to Holy Church, just as the Wise Clerk had commanded. [. . .] The Wise Clerk, whose life ended at eight o'clock in the morning, was buried in a church in Wales, and over his grave was written 'Raymon the Wise Clerk of Wales, who bequeathed the great treasure of Merlin's wisdom upon his death.'"

After Raymon is buried, the Chaplain takes his place. This final section of the book ends with two statements. First, that the Lady of the Lake will have to appear before Jesus Christ on Judgment Day, and second, that Merlin will also be resurrected at that time. Meanwhile, Merlin continues to prophesy many more wonders from within his tomb. "He said that there will be pestilence in Germany; that great famine will come upon Lombardy, France, and Germany; that the city of Narbonne will be flooded; and that there will be war in Europe."

Here the *Prophecies of Merlin* ends, on this quiet note that still suggests that Merlin will continue to prophesy from within his tomb, that his sayings will be copied down, and that one day they will be published in a book, such as the one we have been reading.

It seems quite extraordinary that this book has lain almost forgotten for so many years. Eighteen copies of the various manuscripts have seldom been explored, and only one other edition exists, in medieval French—that of Lucy Allen Paton. Yet given the hold of the Arthurian legends over our imagination, it seems unlikely that it should have been so ignored. If we have to have a reason, the occasionally confusing and confused text may well be enough, but we hope we have proven that it was worth the effort of decoding it for the sake of the fragments of story hidden amongst the strange prophecies and religious excursions of the text. In the end Merlin himself remains the centre of the focus, and despite the sometimes confusing nature of the narrative, we may see hidden within its turns and twists the presence of a remarkable being whose wisdom and insight underpins so much of the Arthurian legends—touching it at every point, from the moment when Merlin arranges the birth of Arthur, through the quest for the Holy Grail, to the very end in the death and departing of the Knights of the Round Table, and of Arthur's departure to the realm of Avalon—just as Merlin prophesied.

APPENDIX I

EARLY WELSH POEMS CONTAINING PROPHECIES ATTRIBUTED TO MYRDDIN WYLLT

Translated by John and Caitlín Matthews

Apart from the books of prophetic writings such as the ones in the manuscript we present here, the oldest prophecies of Merlin, known as Myrddin Wyllt (Merlin the Wild), are contained chiefly in poetic dialogues either between himself and the bard Taliesin, or Merlin's own sister, Gwenddydd/Ganeida, who was herself recognized as a prophet. They were composed sometime during the sixth century AD but not written down—from oral recital—until the early fourteenth century and found in *The Red Book of Hergest* and *The Black Book of Carmarthen*. All are set during a period (usually the late sixth century) during which Merlin lived the life of a divinely inspired madman in the wilderness and was visited by various people in search of wisdom. Though most were not copied out until the fourteenth or fifteenth centuries they are the nearest we can get to the authentic voice of Merlin. The timing of these first written works curiously shadows that of the *Prophecies* presented here. It is unlikely that the French author of the original manuscript or even Antoine Vérard himself could have seen these, since they were compiled in Wales, but we include a selection of the poems here for the sake of comparison.

The prophecies are for the most part of a general kind, referring to political events, battles, and so on—and to known events and people. These are identifiable as separate from the underlying matter of the poems, which deal with the story of Myrddin's madness, and of the period he spent in the wilderness. Included in the more personal works are prophecies of events that took place long after—anywhere from the eighth to the eleventh centuries, when heroes like Cynan and Cadwaladyr had replaced Arthur as the expected deliverer of the Cymry from Norman overlordship.

At one time these poems may have formed verse interludes of a longer prose account of Myrddin's life—such a one as evidently formed the basis of Geoffrey of Monmouth's Latin poem the *Vita Merlini*, which made use of the poems attributed to Myrddin and included its own selection of prophecies.

Avallanau (Apple Trees) includes a series of general prophecies, mostly added long after Myrddin's time, which refer to events current at the time they were written down, probably in the fourteenth or fifteenth centuries. In *Oianau* (Greetings), Merlin addresses his words to a small pig, which became his companion in the wilderness. In *A Fugitive Poem of Merlin in His Grave*, the seer's life underpins the prophetic content. Much of the imagery is powerful and unforgettable in its stark simplicity. For a complete collection of these early prophetic poems, see *The Book of Merlin* by John Matthews (Amberley Books, 2020).

Affalannau (Apple Trees)

I   Sweet appletree, your branches delight me,
    Luxuriantly budding, my pride and joy!
    I will prophesy before the lord of Macreu,
    That on Wednesday, in the valley of Machawy
    Blood will flow.
    Lloegyr's blades will shine.
    But hear, O little pig! on Thursday
    The Cymry will rejoice
    In their defence of Cyminawd,
    Furiously cutting and thrusting.
    The Saesons will be slaughtered by our ashen spears,
    And their heads used as footballs.
    I prophesy the unvarnished truth—
    The rising of a child in the secluded South.

II Sweet and luxuriant appletree,
    Great its branches, beautiful its form!
    I predict a battle that fills me with fear.
    At Pengwern, men drink mead,
    But around Cyminawd is a deadly hewing
    By a chieftain from Eryri—until only hatred remains.

III Sweet, yellow, appletree,
    Growing in Tal Ardd,
    I predict a battle at Prydyn,
    In defense of frontiers.
    Seven ships will come
    Across a wide lake,
    Seven hundred men come to conquer.
    Of those who come, only seven will return
    According to my prophecy.

IV Sweet appletree of luxuriant growth!
    I used to find food at its foot,

When, because of a maid,
I slept alone in the woods of Celyddon,
Shield on shoulder, sword on thigh.
Hear, O little pig! listen to my words,
As sweet as birds that sing on Monday—
When the sovereigns come across the sea,
Blessed be the Cymry, because of their strength.

V   Sweet appletree in the glade,
Trodden is the earth around its base.
The men of Rhydderch see me not.
Gwendydd no longer loves nor greets me,
I am hated by Rhydderch's strongest scion.
I have despoiled both his son and daughter:
Death visits them all—why not me?
After Gwenddoleu no-one will honour me,
No diversions attend me,
Nor fair women visit me.
Though at Arderydd I wore a golden torque
The swan-white woman despises me now.

VI   Sweet appletree, growing by the river,
Who will thrive on its wondrous fruit?
When my reason was intact
I used to lie at its foot
With a fair wanton maid, of slender form.
Fifty years the plaything of lawless men
I have wandered in gloom among spirits.
After great wealth, and gregarious minstrels,
I have been here so long not even sprites
Can lead me astray.
I never sleep, but tremble at the thought
Of my Lord Gwenddoleu, and my own native people.
Long have I suffered unease and longing—
May I be given freedom in the end.

VII   Sweet appletree, with delicate blossom,
Growing, concealed, in the wood!
At daybreak the tale was told me
That my words had offended the most powerful minister,
Not once, not twice, but thrice in a single day.
Christ! that my end had come
Before the killing of Gwendydd's son
Was upon my hands!

VIII   Sweet appletree with your delicate blossom,
Growing amid the thickets of trees!
The Chwyfleian foretells,
A tale that will come to pass:
A staff of gold, signifying bravery
Will be given by the glorious Dragon Kings.
The graceful one will vanquish the profaner,
Before the child, bright and bold,
The Saesons shall fall, and bards will flourish.

IX   Sweet appletree of crimson colour,
Growing, concealed, in the wood of Celyddon;
Though men seek your fruit, their search is vain,
Until Cadwaladyr comes from Cadfaon's meeting
To Teiwi river and Tywi's lands,
Till anger and anguish come from Aranwynion,
And the long-hairs are tamed.

X   Sweet appletree of crimson colour,
Growing, concealed, in the wood of Celyddon:
Though men seek your fruit, their search is vain,
Till Cadwaladyr comes from Rhyd Rheon's meeting,
And with Cynon advances against the Saesons.
Victorious Cymry, glorious their leaders,
All shall have their rights again,
All Britons rejoice, sounding joyful horns,
Chanting songs of happiness and peace!

Oianau (Greetings)

Listen, little pig,
O happy little pig!
Do not go rooting
On top of the mountain,
But stay here,
Secluded in the wood,
Hidden from the dogs
Of Rhydderch the Faithful.

I will prophesy—
It will be truth!—
From Aber Taradyr
The Cyrmy will be bound
Under one warlike leader
Of the line of Gwynedd.
Usurpers of the Prydein
He will overcome.

Listen, little pig,
We should hide
From the huntsmen of Mordei
Lest we be discovered.
If we escape—
I'll not complain of fatigue!—
I shall predict,
From the back of the ninth wave,
The truth about the White One
Who rode Dyfed to exhaustion,
Who built a church
For those who only half believed.
Until Cynan comes
Nothing will be restored.

Listen, little pig!
I lack sleep,
Such a tumult of grief is within me.
Fifty years of pain I have endured.
Once I saw Gwenddoleu,
With the gift of Princes,
Garnering prey on every side;
Now, he's beneath the sod—
But still restless!
He was the chief of the North,
And the gentlest.

Listen, little pig,
Don't sleep yet!
Rumours reach me
Of perjured chieftains,
And tight-fisted farmers.
Soon, over the sea,
Shall come men in armour
Two-faced men,
On armoured horses,
With destroying spears.
When that happens,
War will come,
Fields will be ploughed
But never reaped.
Women will be cuckolds
To the corpses of their men.
Mourning will come to Caer Sallawg.

Listen, little pig,
O pig of truth!
The Sybil has told me
A wondrous tale.
I predict a Summer full of fury,

Treachery between brothers.
A pledge of peace will be required
From Gwynedd,
Seven hundred ships from Gynt
Blown in by the North wind.
In Aber Dyn they will confer.

Listen, little pig,
O blessed pig!
The Sybil has told me
A frightful thing:
When Llogria encamps
In the lands of Eddlyn,
Making Deganwy a strong fort
Between Llogrian and Cymru,
A child will appear, leaping,
And the Franks will flee.
At Aber Dulas they will fall,
Sweating in bloody garments.

Listen, little pig,
Go to Gwynedd,
Seek a mate when you rest.
While Rhydderch Hael feasts in his hall
He does not know
What sleeplessness I bear
Every night—
Snow to my knees,
Ice in my hair—
Sad my fate!

Listen, little pig!
O blessed pig!
If you had seen
All I have seen

You would not sleep,
Nor root on the hill.
Listen, little pig,
Is not the mountain green?
In my thin cloak
I get no repose!
I grow pale because
Gwendydd comes not.

Listen, little pig,
O bit of brawn!
Don't bury your snout.
Love is neither pledge nor play.
This advice I give to Gwernabwy:
Don't be a wanton youth.
I'll predict now the battle of Machawy,
Where ruddy spears will shine in Rhiw Dymdwy,
—the work of contentious chiefs.
Men will sit, breasts heaving, on their saddles,
And there will be mourning, and woeful mien.
A bear will arise in Deheubarth,
His men will infest Mynwy.
A blessed fate awaits Gwendydd
When Dyfed's prince comes to rule.

Listen, little pig!
Are not the thorn buds green
The mountain fair, the earth beautiful?
I will predict the battle of Argoed Llewifain,
Bloody biers after Owein's assault.
When stewards dispute,
When children are perjured,
When Cadwaladyr conquers Mona—
Then the Saeson will be driven out!

Listen, little pig!
Wonders there will be
In Prydein—but I
Shall not care.
When the people of Mona
Ask questions of the Brython,
That will be a troublesome time!
A superior lord will appear:
Cynan, from the banks of the Teiwi.
Confusion will follow—
But he shall have the music of Bards to follow!

Listen, little pig—
Do you hear the birds at Caerleon?
I wish I stood on Mynydd Maon
Watching the bright ones dance.
Instead I'll prophesy
Battle on battle:
At Machawy, on a river,
At Cors Fochno, at Minron,
At Cyminawd, at Caerleon,
And the battle of Abergwaith,
And the battle of Ieithion . . .
And when this music shall end,
A child will come,
And the Brython will know better days.

Listen, little pig,
O little, spotted friend!
Can you hear the sea-birds crying?
A day will come when even minstrels
Will be sent away, without their portion.
Though they stand at the door,
No gift will come.
A far-flying sea-gull told me

That strangers will come:
Gwyddyl, Brython, Romans.
There will be confusion then!
And the names of the Gods
Will be taken in vain!
Fighting on both banks of the Tywi.

Listen, little pig,
O stout-legged, little one!
Listen to the voices of the sea-birds—
Great their clamour.
Minstrels will get no honour,
No fair portion theirs;
In a time when hospitality's repugnant,
A youth of strong feelings will come.
Then two Idrises will contend for land,
And their contention will be long.

Listen, little pig!
It's no use my hearing,
The scream of the gulls.
My hair is thin,
My covering likewise.
The vales are my barn—
Short on corn.
My summer harvest
Brings little relief.
Once, my passion was boundless;
Now I predict,
Before the world ends,
Shameless women,
Passionless men!

Listen, little pig,
O little trembling one!

Under this thin blanket,
I find no repose.
Since the battle of Arderydd
I no longer care,
If the sky falls
Or the sea overflows.
But I predict that after many kings
With one bridge on the Taw
And another on the Tywi,
There will be an end to war.

A Fugitive Poem of Myrddin in His Grave

He who speaks from the grave
Knows that before seven years
March will die.

I have drunk from a bright cup
With fierce and warlike lords;
My name is Myrddin, son of Morvran.

I have drunk from a goblet
With powerful warlords;
Myrddin is my given name.

When the black wheel of oppression
Comes to destroy exhausted Logres
Defence will be bitter and sustained.
The White Mount will see sorrow
A long regret to the people of the
    Cymry.

Protection won't be found
From the Boar of the Hosts,

Even in the heights of Ardudwy
Or the Cymry's secret ports.

When the red Norman comes
And a castle is built at Aber Hodni
Greatly taxed will be the Logrians—
Even predictions will be costly.

When the Freckled One comes
As far as Ryd Bengarn,
Men will face disgrace,
Their sword-hilts will break,
The new King of Prydain
Will be their judge.

When Henri comes to claim
Mur Castell on Eryri's border
Trouble across the sea will call him.

When the Pale One comes to London
Upon ugly horses
He will call out the lords of Caergain.

Scarce the acorns, thick the corn
When a young king appears
Who will cause men to tremble.

A youth of great renown
Conqueror of a hundred cities—
Tender and frail will be his life.
Strong to the weak will he be
Weak towards the strong of the upland—
One whose coming will bring dark days.

Wantonness will rule,
Women will be easy prey—
Even children will need to confess.

But a time of order will follow
When even churls will do good deeds;
Maidens will be lovely
Youths resolute.

A time will follow, towards the end of the age,
When the young will fail from adversity
And cuckoos die in Maytime.

There will be a time of great hunting dogs,
And buildings in secret places,
When even a shirt will cost a fortune.
There will be a time of great profanity,
When vices are active, and churches empty.
Words and relics will be broken
Truth will vanish, falsehood spread
Faith will grow weak, and disputes abound.

There will be a time when everyone delights in
    clothing
When the lord's counsellors become like vagrants;
Bards will go empty-handed, through priests will be
    happy;
Men will be despised, and frequently refused.

There will be a time of windless days, without rain,
With little ploughing and less food,
One acre of land worth nine.
Men will be weak and unmanly
And corn grown under trees—
Though feasts will still occur.

When trees are held in high estate
There will be a new spring
An evil king—
The cowhouse worse than a single stake.

On Wednesday, a time of violence,
Blades will wear out,
Two will be bloodied at Cynghen.

At Aber Sor there will be a council
Of men following on the battle,
A bright ruler ruling the camp.

In Aber Avon the host of Mona congregate
Angles gather at Hinwedon;
Meryon's valour will be long remembered

In Aber Dwyver the leader will fail
When the actions of Gwidig occur
After the battle of Cyvarllug.
A battle will be on the River Byrri,
Where Britons will have victory;
Gwhyr's men will be heroes.

An Aber Don a battle will occur
And the spears be unequal.
Blood on the brows of Saxons.
Servile you are today, Gwenddydd!

The mountain-spirits come to me
Here in Aber Carav.

APPENDIX 2

SELECTIONS FROM BOOK VII OF GEOFFREY OF MONMOUTH'S *HISTORIA REGUM BRITANNIAE*

Translated from the Latin by J. A. Giles, in *Six Old English Chronicles*

The cleric and churchman named Geoffrey of Monmouth (c. 1095–1155) was almost single-handedly responsible for the outpouring of prophetic literature attributed to Merlin, of which our text is one of the latest within the period of the Middle Ages. His first published work was called *Prophetiæ Merlini* (or sometimes *Libellus Merlini*) and was written in Latin between 1130 and 1135. Later, when he compiled his *Historia Regum Britanniae* (History of the Kings of Britain) in 1135 AD, Geoffrey described an encounter between the youthful Merlin and the usurping King Vortigern. A visionary description followed in which a red and a white dragon fought a duel in the skies in which the red overcame the white. This was described as a symbolic act which predicted the defeat of the Saxon invaders by the British, under the leadership of Arthur. Immediately following this, Geoffrey describes the young Merlin, at the request of the king, bursting into tears and giving vent to a long series of prophecies.

Selections from Book VII of *Historia Regum Britanniae* — 251

We have included the second section of these here, in the edition translated by J. A. Giles in 1896 (revised in 1910), as a point of comparison with the later selections included in our book. The similarities and differences will be clear to all. A full-length interpretation of this material can be found in *Merlin: The Prophetic Vision and the Mystic Life* by R. J. Stewart, the author of the foreword to this book.

Book VII: Concerning the Prophecies of Merlin[164]

Chap. I.–Geoffrey of Monmouth's Preface to Merlin's Prophecies
I had not got thus far in my history, when the subject of public discourse that concerned Merlin arose, I was obliged to publish his prophecies at the request of my acquaintance, but especially of Alexander, bishop of Lincoln, a prelate of the greatest piety and wisdom. There was not any person, either among the clergy or laity, that was attended with such a train of knights and noblemen, whom his settled piety and great munificence engaged in his service. Out of a desire, therefore, to gratify him, I translated these prophecies, and sent them to him with the following letter.

Chap. III.–The Prophecy of Merlin
As Vortigern, King of the Britons, was sitting upon the bank of the drained pond, the two dragons, one of which was white, the other red, came forth, and, approaching one another, began a terrible fight, and cast forth fire with their breath. But the white dragon had the advantage and made the other fly to the end of the lake. And he, for grief at his flight, renewed the assault upon his pursuer, and forced him to retire. After this battle of the dragons, the king commanded Ambrose Merlin to tell him what it portended. Upon which he, bursting into tears, delivered what his prophetical spirit suggested to him, as follows:

"Woe to the red dragon, for his banishment hasteneth on. His lurking holes shall be seized by the white dragon, which signifies

---

[164]. See Giles, *Six Old English Chronicles*, 194–206.

the Saxons whom you invited over; but the red denotes the British nation, which shall be oppressed by the white. Therefore shall its mountains be levelled as the valleys, and the rivers of the valleys shall run with blood. The exercise of religion shall be destroyed, and churches laid open to ruin. At last the oppressed shall prevail and oppose the cruelty of foreigners. For a boar of Cornwall shall give his assistance and trample their necks under his feet. The islands of the ocean shall be subject to his power, and he shall possess the forests of Gaul. The house of Romulus shall dread his courage, and his end shall be doubtful. He shall be celebrated in the mouths of the people; and his exploits shall be food to those that relate them. Six of his posterity shall sway the scepter, but after them shall arise a German worm. He shall be advanced by a sea-wolf, whom the woods of Africa shall accompany. Religion shall again be abolished, and there shall be a translation of the metropolitan sees. The dignity of London shall adorn Dorobernia, and the seventh pastor of York shall be resorted to in the kingdom of Armorica.

Menevia shall put on the pall of the City of Legions, and a preacher of Ireland shall be dumb on account of an infant growing in the womb. It shall rain a shower of blood, and a raging famine shall afflict mankind. When these things happen, the red one shall be grieved; but when his fatigue is over, shall grow strong. Then shall misfortunes hasten upon the white one, and the buildings of his gardens shall be pulled down. Seven that sway the scepter shall be killed, one of whom shall become a saint. The wombs of mothers shall be ripped up, and infants be abortive. There shall be a most grievous punishment of men, that the natives may be restored. He that shall do these things shall put on the brazen man, and upon a brazen horse shall for a long time guard the gates of London. After this, shall the red dragon return to his proper manners, and turn his rage upon himself. Therefore shall the revenge of the Thunderer show itself, for every field shall disappoint the husbandmen. Mortality shall snatch away the people and make a desolation over all countries. The remainder shall quit their native soil and make foreign plantations.

A blessed king shall prepare a fleet and shall be reckoned the twelfth in the court among the saints. There shall be a miserable desolation of the kingdom, and the floors of the harvests shall return to the fruitful forests. The white dragon shall rise again and invite over a daughter of Germany. Our gardens shall be again replenished with foreign seed, and the red one shall pine away at the end of the pond. After that shall the German worm be crowned, and the brazen prince buried. He has his bounds assigned him, which he shall not be able to pass. For a hundred and fifty years he shall continue in trouble and subjection but shall bear sway three hundred. Then shall the north wind rise against him and shall snatch away the flowers which the west wind produced.

There shall be gilding in the temples, nor shall the edge of the sword cease. The German dragon shall hardly get to his holes, because the revenge of his treason shall overtake him. At last he shall flourish for a little time, but the decimation of Neustria shall hurt him. For a people in wood and in iron coats shall come, and revenge upon him his wickedness. They shall restore the ancient inhabitants to their dwellings, and there shall be an open destruction of foreigners. The seed of the white dragon shall be swept out of our gardens, and the remainder of his generation shall be decimated. They shall bear the yoke of slavery and wound their mother with spades and ploughs. After this shall succeed two dragons, whereof one shall be killed with the sting of envy, but the other shall return under the shadow of a name. Then shall succeed a lion of justice, at whose roar the Gallican towers and the island dragons shall tremble. In those days gold shall be squeezed from the lily and the nettle, and silver shall flow from the hoofs of bellowing cattle. The frizzled shall put on various fleeces, and the outward habit denote the inward parts. The feet of barkers shall be cut off; wild beasts shall enjoy peace; mankind shall be grieved at their punishment; the form of commerce shall be divided; the half shall be round. The ravenousness of kites shall be destroyed, and the teeth of wolves blunted. The lion's whelps shall be transformed into sea-fishes; and an eagle shall build her nest upon Mount Aravius.

Venedotia shall grow red with the blood of mothers, and the house of Corineus kill six brethren. The island shall be wet with night tears; so that all shall be provoked to all things. Woe to thee, Neustria, because the lion's brain shall be poured upon thee: and he shall be banished with shattered limbs from his native soil. Posterity shall endeavour to fly above the highest places; but the favour of new comers shall be exalted. Piety shall hurt the possessor of things got by impiety, till he shall have put on his Father; therefore, being armed with the teeth of a boar, he shall ascend above the tops of the mountains, and the shadow of him that wears a helmet. Albania shall be enraged, and, assembling her neighbours, shall be employed in shedding blood. There shall be put into her jaws a bridle that shall be made on the coast of Armorica. The eagle of the broken covenant shall gild it over and rejoice in her third nest. The roaring whelps shall watch, and, leaving the woods, shall hunt within the walls of cities. They shall make no small slaughter of those that oppose them and shall cut off the tongues of bulls. They shall load the necks of roaring lions with chains and restore the times of their ancestors.

Then from the first to the fourth, from the fourth to the third, from the third to the second, the thumb shall roll in oil. The sixth shall overturn the walls of Ireland and change the woods into a plain. He shall reduce several parts to one and be crowned with the head of a lion. His beginning shall lay open to wandering affection, but his end shall carry him up to the blessed, who are above. For he shall restore the seats of saints in their countries and settle pastors in convenient places. Two cities he shall invest with two palls and shall bestow virgin-presents upon virgins. He shall merit by this the favour of the Thunderer and shall be placed among the saints. From him shall proceed a lynx penetrating all things, who shall be bent upon the ruin of his own nation; for, through him, Neustria shall lose

Selections from Book VII of *Historia Regum Britanniae*

both islands, and be deprived of its ancient dignity. Then shall the natives return back to the island; for there shall arise a dissension among foreigners.

Also a hoary old man, sitting upon a snow-white horse, shall turn the course of the river Periron, and shall measure out a mill upon it with a white rod. Cadwallader shall call upon Conan and take Albania into alliance. Then shall there be a slaughter of foreigners; then shall the rivers run with blood. Then shall break forth the fountains of Armorica, and they shall be crowned with the diadem of Brutus. Cambria shall be filled with joy; and the oaks of Cornwall shall flourish. The island shall be called by the name of Brutus: and the name given it by foreigners shall be abolished. From Conan shall proceed a warlike boar, that shall exercise the sharpness of his tusks within the Gallic woods. For he shall cut down all the larger oaks and shall be a defense to the smaller. The Arabians and Africans shall dread him; for he shall pursue his furious course to the farther part of Spain. There shall succeed the goat of the Venereal castle, having golden horns and a silver beard, who shall breathe such a cloud out of his nostrils, as shall darken the whole surface of the island. There shall be peace in his time; and corn shall abound by reason of the fruitfulness of the soil.

Women shall become serpents in their gait, and all their motions shall be full of pride. The camp of Venus shall be restored; nor shall the arrows of Cupid cease to wound. The fountain of a river shall be turned into blood; and two kings shall fight a duel at Stafford for a lioness. Luxury shall overspread the whole ground; and fornication shall not cease to debauch mankind. All these things shall three ages see; till the buried kings shall be exposed to public view in the city of London. Famine shall again return; mortality shall return; and the inhabitants shall grieve for the destruction of their cities. Then shall come the board of commerce, who shall recall the scattered flocks to the pasture they had lost. His breast shall be food to the hungry, and his tongue drink to the thirsty. Out of his mouth shall flow rivers, that shall water the parched jaws of men. After this shall be produced a tree upon the Tower of London, which, having no more than three branches, shall overshadow the surface of the whole island with the breadth of its leaves. Its adversary, the north wind, shall come upon it, and with its noxious blast shall snatch away the third branch; but the two remaining ones shall possess its place, till they shall destroy one another by the multitude of their leaves; and then shall it obtain the place of those two, and shall give sustenance to birds of foreign nations.

It shall be esteemed hurtful to native fowls; for they shall not be able to fly freely for fear of its shadow. There shall succeed the ass of wickedness, swift against the goldsmiths, but slow against the ravenousness of wolves. In those days the oaks of the forests shall burn, and acorns grow upon the branches of teil trees. The Severn sea shall discharge itself through seven mouths, and the river Usk burn seven months. Fishes shall die with the heat thereof; and of them shall be engendered serpents. The baths of Badon shall grow cold, and their salubrious waters engender death. London shall mourn for the death of twenty thousand; and the river Thames shall be turned into blood. The monks in ther cowls shall be forced to marry, and their cry shall be heard upon the mountains of the Alps."

[. . .]

"Three springs shall break forth in the city of Winchester, whose rivulets shall divide the island into three parts, Whoever shall drink of the first, shall enjoy long life, and shall never be afflicted with sickness. He that shall drink of the second, shall die of hunger, and paleness and horror shall sit in his countenance. He that shall drink of the third, shall be surprised with sudden death, neither shall his body be capable of burial. Those that are willing to escape so great a surfeit, will endeavour to hide it with several coverings: but whatever bulk shall be laid upon it, shall receive the form of another body. For earth shall be turned into stones; stones into water; wood into ashes; ashes into water, if cast over it. Also a damsel shall be sent from the city of the forest of Canute to administer a cure, who, after she shall have practised all her arts, shall dry up the noxious fountains only with her breath. Afterwards, as soon as she shall have refreshed herself with the wholesome liquor, she shall bear in her right hand the wood of Caledon, and in her left the forts of the walls of London.

Wherever she shall go, she shall make sulphureous steps, which will smoke with a double flame. That smoke shall rouse up the city of Ruteni and shall make food for the inhabitants of the deep. She shall overflow with rueful tears and shall fill the island with her dreadful cry. She shall be killed by a hart with ten branches, four of which shall bear golden diadems; but the other six shall be turned into buffalo's horns, whose hideous sounds shall astonish the three islands of Britain. The Daneian wood shall be stirred up, and breaking forth into a human voice, shall cry: Come, O Cambria, and join Cornwall to thy side, and say to Winchester, the earth shall swallow thee up. Translate the seat of thy pastor to the place where ships come to harbour, and the rest of the members will follow the head. For the day hasteneth, in which thy citizens shall perish on account of the guilt of perjury. The whiteness of wool has been hurtful to thee, and the variety of its tinctures. Woe to the perjured nation, for whose sake the renowned city shall come to ruin. The ships shall rejoice at so great an augmentation, and one shall be made out of two. It shall be rebuilt by Eric, loaden with apples, to the smell whereof the birds of several woods shall flock together. He shall add to it a vast palace, and wall it round with six hundred towers.

Therefore shall London envy it, and triply increase her walls. The river Thames shall encompass it round, and the fame of the work shall pass beyond the Alps. Eric shall hide his apples within it and shall make subterraneous passages. At that time shall the stones speak, and the sea towards the Gallic coast be contracted into a narrow space. On each bank shall one man hear another, and the soil of the island shall be enlarged. The secrets of the deep shall be revealed, and Gaul shall tremble for fear. After these things shall come forth a heron from the forest of Calaterium, which shall fly round the island for two years together. With her nocturnal cry she shall call together the winged kind and assemble to her all sorts of fowls. They shall invade the tillage of husbandmen and devour all the grain of the harvests. Then shall follow a famine upon the people, and a grievous mortality upon the famine. But when this calamity shall be over, a detestable bird shall go to the valley of Galabes and shall raise it to be a high mountain. Upon the top thereof it shall also plant an oak and build its nest in its branches. Three eggs shall be produced in the nest, from whence shall come forth a fox, a wolf, and a bear. The fox shall devour her mother and bear the head of an ass. In this monstrous form shall she frighten her brothers and make them fly into Neustria. But they shall stir up the tusked boar, and returning in a fleet shall encounter with the fox; who at the beginning of the fight shall feign herself dead and move the boar to compassion. Then shall the boar approach her carcass, and standing over her, shall breathe upon her face and eyes. But she, not forgetting her cunning, shall bite his left foot, and pluck it off from his body. Then shall she leap upon him, and snatch away his right ear and tail, and hide herself in the caverns of the mountains. Therefore shall the deluded boar require the wolf and bear to restore him his members; who, as soon as they shall enter into the cause, shall promise two feet of the fox, together with the ear and tail, and of these they shall make up the members of a hog.

With this he shall be satisfied and expect the promised restitution. In the meantime shall the fox descend from the mountains, and change herself into a wolf, and under pretense of holding a conference with the boar, she shall go to him, and craftily devour him. After that she shall transform herself into a boar, and feigning a loss of some members, shall wait for her brothers; but as soon as they are come, she shall suddenly kill them with her tusks, and shall be crowned with the head of a lion. In her days shall a serpent be brought forth, which shall be a destroyer of mankind. With its length it shall encompass London and devour all that pass by it. The mountain ox shall take the head of a wolf and whiten his teeth in the Severn. He shall gather to him the flocks of Albania and Cambria, which shall drink the river Thames dry. The ass shall call the goat with the long beard and shall borrow his shape. Therefore shall the mountain ox be incensed, and having called the wolf, shall become a horned bull against them. In the exercise of his cruelty he shall devour their flesh and bones but shall be burned upon the top of Urien.

The ashes of his funeral-pile shall be turned into swans, that shall swim on dry ground as on a river. They shall devour fishes in fishes and swallow up men in men. But when old age shall come upon them, they shall become sea-wolves, and practice their frauds in the deep. They shall drown ships and collect no small quantity of silver. The Thames shall again flow, and assembling together the rivers, shall pass beyond the bounds of its channel. It shall cover the adjacent cities and overturn the mountains that oppose its course. Being full of deceit and wickedness, it shall make use of the fountain Galabes. Hence shall arise factions provoking the Venedotians to war. The oaks of the forest shall meet together and encounter the rocks of the Gewisseans. A raven shall attend with the kites and devour the carcasses of the slain. An owl shall build her nest upon the walls of Gloucester, and in her nest shall be brought forth an ass. The serpent of Malvernia shall bring him up and put him upon many fraudulent practices.

Having taken the crown, he shall ascend on high, and frighten the people of the country with his hideous braying. In his days shall the Pachaian mountains tremble, and the provinces be deprived of their woods. For there shall come a worm with a fiery breath, and with the vapour it sends forth shall burn up the trees. Out of it shall proceed seven lions deformed with the heads of goats. With the stench of their nostrils they shall corrupt women, and make wives turn common prostitutes. The father shall not know his own son, because they shall grow wanton like brute beasts.

Then shall come the giant of wickedness and terrify all with the sharpness of his eyes. Against him shall arise the dragon of Worcester and shall endeavour to banish him. But in the engagement the dragon shall be worsted and oppressed by the wickedness of the conqueror. For he shall mount upon the dragon, and putting off his garment shall sit upon him naked. The dragon shall bear him up on high and beat his naked rider with his tail erected. Upon this the giant rousing up his whole strength, shall break his jaws with his sword. At last the dragon shall fold itself up under its tail and die of poison. After him shall succeed the boar of Totness and oppress the people with grievous tyranny. Gloucester shall send forth a lion, and shall disturb him in his cruelty, in several battles. He shall trample him under his feet and terrify him with open jaws. At last the lion shall quarrel with the kingdom and get upon the backs of the nobility.

A bull shall come into the quarrel and strike the lion with his right foot. He shall drive him through all the inns in the kingdom but shall break his horns against the walls of Oxford. The fox of Kaerdubalem shall take revenge on the lion and destroy him entirely with her teeth. She shall be encompassed by the adder of Lincoln, who with a horrible hiss shall give notice of his presence to a multitude of dragons. Then shall the dragons encounter and tear one another to pieces. The winged shall oppress that which wants wings and fasten its claws into the poisonous cheeks. Others shall come into the quarrel and kill one another. A fifth shall succeed those that are slain, and by various stratagems shall destroy the rest. He shall get upon the back of one with his sword and sever his head from his body. Then throwing off his garment, he shall get upon another, and put his right and left hand upon his tail.

Thus being naked shall he overcome him, whom when clothed he was not able to deal with. The rest he shall gall in their flight and drive them round the kingdom. Upon this shall come a roaring lion dreadful for his monstrous cruelty. Fifteen parts shall he reduce to one and shall alone possess the people. The giant of the snow-white colour shall shine and cause the white people to flourish. Pleasures shall effeminate the princes, and they shall suddenly be changed into beasts. Among them shall arise a lion swelled with human gore. Under him shall a reaper be placed in the standing corn, who, while he is reaping, shall be oppressed by him.

A charioteer of York shall appease them, and having banished his lord, shall mount upon the chariot which he shall drive. With his sword unsheathed shall he threaten the East and fill the tracks of his wheels with blood. Afterwards he shall become a sea-fish, who, being roused up with the hissing of a serpent, shall engender with him. From hence shall be produced three thundering bulls, who having eaten up their pastures shall be turned into trees. The first shall carry a whip of vipers and turn his back upon the next. He shall endeavour to snatch away the whip but shall be taken by the last. They shall turn away their faces from one another, till they have thrown away the poisoned cup. To him shall succeed a husbandman of Albania, at whose back shall be a serpent.

He shall be employed in ploughing the ground, that the country may become white with corn. The serpent shall endeavour to diffuse his poison, in order to blast the harvest. A grievous mortality shall sweep away the people, and the walls of cities shall be made desolate. There shall be given for a remedy the city of Claudius, which shall interpose the nurse of the scourger. For she shall bear a dose of medicine, and in a short time the island shall be restored. Then shall two successively sway the scepter, whom a horned dragon shall serve. One shall come in armour and shall ride upon a flying serpent. He shall sit upon his back with his naked body and cast his right hand upon his tail. With his cry shall the seas be moved, and he shall strike terror into the second. The second therefore shall enter into confederacy with the lion; but a quarrel happening, they shall encounter one another. They shall distress one another, but the courage of the beast shall gain the advantage. Then shall come one with a drum and appease the rage of the lion.

Therefore shall the people of the kingdom be at peace and provoke the lion to a dose of physic. In his established seat he shall adjust the weights but shall stretch out his hands into Albania. For which reason the northern provinces shall be grieved and open the gates of the temples. The sign-bearing wolf shall lead his troops, and surround Cornwall with his tail. He shall be opposed by a soldier in a chariot, who shall transform that people into a boar. The boar therefore shall ravage the provinces but shall hide his head in the depth of Severn. A man shall embrace a lion in wine, and the dazzling brightness of gold shall blind the eyes of beholders. Silver shall whiten in the circumference and torment several wine presses. Men shall be drunk with wine, and, regardless of heaven, shall be intent upon the earth. From them shall the stars turn away their faces and confound their usual course.

Corn will wither at their malign aspects; and there shall fall no dew from heaven. The roots and branches will change their places, and the novelty of the thing shall pass for a miracle. The brightness of the sun shall fade at the amber of Mercury, and horror shall seize the beholders. Stilbon of Arcadia shall change his shield; the helmet of Mars shall call Venus. The helmet of Mars shall make a shadow; and the rage of Mercury pass his bounds. Iron Orion shall unsheathe his sword: the marine Phœbus shall torment the clouds; Jupiter shall go out of his lawful paths; and Venus forsake her stated lines. The malignity of the star Saturn shall fall down in rain and slay mankind with a crooked sickle. The twelve houses of the star shall lament the irregular excursions of their guests; and Gemini omit their usual embraces and call the urn to the fountains. The scales of Libra shall hang obliquely, till Aries puts his crooked horns under them. The tail of Scorpio shall produce lightning, and Cancer quarrel with the Sun. Virgo shall mount upon the back of Sagittarius and darken her virgin flowers. The chariot of the Moon shall disorder the zodiac, and the Pleiades break forth into weeping. No offices of Janus shall hereafter return, but his gate being shut shall lie hid in the chinks of Ariadne. The seas shall rise up in the twinkling of an eye, and the dust of the ancients shall be restored. The winds shall fight together with a dreadful blast, and their sound shall reach the stars.

APPENDIX 3

THE TALE OF PRESTER JOHN

From *Il Novellino: The 100 Ancient Tales*

Translated from the Italian by Edward Storer

The author of *Il Novellino* remains unknown. He was probably a medieval minstrel who traveled from castle to castle, entertaining his listeners with moralistic and humorous tales from Arthurian sources and the Bible, as well as of French, Provençal, and Eastern origins. Edward Storer, in his introduction to the following translation, summed this up:

> One day about the end of the thirteenth century or the beginning of the fourteenth, when the Middle Ages still darkly curtained the Renaissance from view, a "man of the Court," or minstrel, of some Italian lord had one of those inventive flashes which go to the making of literatures. This "man of the Court" who was perhaps a minstrel or *giullare* in little more than name—for his talent would be especially literary—knew by heart the little archaic tales which make up the slender corpus of the *Cento Novelle Antiche*, or *Novellino*. Often he told them or heard them told in baronial halls, and in lordly places, in rough huts after days of hunting, and in the encampments of battlefields. Before audiences of seigneurs and

knights, in the company of stately prelates, and in the rollicking gatherings of dashing young *donzelli*, he had narrated or heard narrated by humbler men of his craft these simple stories, some of them redolent of the wisdom of ages, others piquant with the flavour of his own times.

Of the Rich Embassy That Prester John Sent to the Noble Emperor Frederick[165]

Prester John, most noble Indian Lord, sent a rich and honourable embassy to the noble and powerful Emperor Frederick, he who was in truth a mirror to the world in matters of speech and manners, who delighted generally in fair speech and sought ever to return wise answers. The substance and intention of that embassy lay in two things alone, to prove at all hazards, if the Emperor were wise both in word and in act.

So Prester John sent him by his ambassadors three most precious stones, and said to the ambassadors: Question the Emperor and ask him on my behalf to tell you what is the best thing in the world. And take good notice of his answers and speech, and study well his court and its customs, and of what you shall learn bring me word, omitting nothing at all.

And when they came to the Emperor to whom they had been sent by their master, they greeted him in a manner suitable to his majesty, and on behalf of their master, whom we have named, they gave him the precious stones. The Emperor took them, asking nothing of their worth. He ordered them to be taken charge of, and praised their exceeding beauty. The ambassadors asked their questions, and beheld the court and its customs.

Then after a few days, they asked permission to return. The Emperor gave them his answer and said: Tell your master that the best thing in this world is moderation.

The ambassadors went away and related to their master what

---

165. Storer, *Il Novellino*, 37–40.

they had seen and heard, praising mightily the Emperor's court with its fine customs and the manners of its knights.

Prester John, hearing the account of his ambassadors, praised the Emperor and said that he was very wise in speech but not in deed, since he had not asked the value of the precious stones. He sent back his ambassadors with the offer that if it should please the Emperor they should become seneschals of his court. And he made them count his riches and the number and quality of his subjects and the manners of his country.

After some time, Prester John, thinking that the gems he had given the Emperor had lost their value, since the Emperor was ignorant of their worth, called a favourite lapidary of his and sent him in secret to the Emperor's court; saying to him: Seek you in every way to bring me back those stones, whatever it may cost.

The lapidary set out, bearing with him many stones of rare beauty, and began to show them at the court. The barons and the knights came to admire his arts. And the man proved himself very clever. When he saw that one of his visitors had an office at the court, he did not sell, but gave away, and so many rings did he give away that his fame reached the Emperor. The latter sent for him, and showed him his own stones. The lapidary praised them, but temperately. He asked the Emperor if he possessed still more precious stones. Then the Emperor brought forth the three fine gems which the lapidary was anxious to see. Then the lapidary grew exultant, and taking one of the stones, held it in his hand and said: this gem, Sire, is worth the finest city in your land. Then he took up another and said: this gem, Sire, is worth the finest of your provinces. Then he took up the third gem and said: Sire, this stone is worth more than all your empire. He closed his hand on the gems, and the virtue in one of them rendered him invisible, so that none could see him, and down the steps of the palace he went, and returned to his lord, Prester John, and presented him with the stones with great joy.

APPENDIX 4

THE LETTER OF PRESTER JOHN

From *Selections from the Hengwrt MSS Preserved in the Peniarth Library*, Vol. 2

Translated and edited from the Welsh by Robert Williams, 1859

The following edition of the *Letter of Prester John* is from the book entitled *Selections from the Hengwrt MSS Preserved in the Peniarth Library*, which is composed of various early Welsh texts translated by Robert Williams in the nineteenth century from an important collection held by the National Library of Wales. The manuscripts listed in Williams's compilation include *Llyfr Gwyn Rydderch* (Peniarth MS 5) and *Llyfr Coch Hergest* or Red Book of Hergest (now held by the Bodleian Library in Oxford as Jesus MS 111). The first of these includes the *Letter* and the latter contains, among other materials, poems attributed to the Welsh Merlin, Myrddin Wyllt.

This Is the Beginning of the Account of the Land of Blessed John[166]

This is a book that the King of India sent to the Emperor of Constantinople, in which many diverse strange things are understood, and in it there are new things that have never been found in other books and never shall be found. And this is the force of that book.

I.—John the priest, by the might and strength of God, our Lord Jesus Christ, King of earthly kings, and Lord of lords, sends to him that stands in the place of God, namely, the Ruler of Rome, joy and greeting by the grace of poetry, and thereby rising to things that are above. It was told our majesty that thou lovest our excellence and the plenitude of our greatness; and we have learnt through our messenger that thou art fain to send us things that are amusing, and some that are pleasant, and, as I am a man, that is good in my sight. And of the things among us we send by our messengers other things to thee, and we send and desire to know whether thou hast the faith with us, and believest wholly in our Lord Jesus Christ.

II.—When those among us recognise that we are men, thy Greeks think that thou art a God. Yet, since we know that thou art mortal, and that thou art subject to human corruption, if thou dost desire any of the things that belong to joy, do thou notify it through thy messenger, and, by the wonted munificence of our bounty, thou shalt have it. Do thou take this gift, in my name, and make use of it, and we will joyfully use thy gifts, so that we may strengthen ourselves mutually in our power turn by turn, and, as proofs thereof bethink thee and look to it. If thou wouldst fain come to the nation whereof we are sprung, we will place thee over the greatest things in our palace, and so thou canst make use of our abundance, and the many things that are in our midst, and if thou wouldst fain

---

166. See Williams, *Selections from the Hengwrt MSS*, vol. 2, 665–69.

return, thou shalt go back rich. Remember, however, the last thing, that is, thy end, and thou wilt never more sin,

III.—Now, if thou wouldst fain know our majesty, and the excellence of our highness, and in what lands our power holds sway, understand and believe without doubt that I am John the priest, lord of lords, excelling all the kings of the earth in strength, and power, in all kinds of high riches that are under heaven. Seventy-two kings are tributary to me. I have taken a vow that I am a Christian; the greatest power of our righteousness is to defend and support them from our alms. We are likewise under vow to visit the sepulchre of our Lord with a great host, even as it befits the glory of our mightiness to subject and subdue the enemies of the Cross of Christ, and to exalt His Blessed Name. And our land stretches from the extremities of India, where the body of Thomas the apostle rests; and it extends through the wilderness to the setting sun, and reaches back, sloping to deserted Babylon, near the tower of Babylon.

IV.—Seventy-two kingships serve us in bondage, and of those but few are Christians; and each of them has a king, by itself, and these are all tributary to us. In our country are born animals,—elephants, dromedaries, camels, hippopotami, crocodiles, metagalinarii, cametenirii, ownsiritæ, pantheræ, onagri, white and red lions, white bears, white ousels, silent grasshoppers, gryphons, tigers, ogresses, hyenas, wild buffaloes, sagitarii, wild men, men with horns, chorniti, correre, satyrs, and women of the same race, pigmies, cenofali, giants forty cubits in height, one-eyed men, cyclopes, the bird that is called phœnix, and almost all the kinds of animals under heaven. In our country there is abundance of milk and honey; in another quarter in our land no poison hurts, no frog croaks, no snakes hiss in the herbage; no venomous animals can abide there, or do harm to anyone. In the midst of some races called Pagans, through one of our provinces, a river called Idon runs, and this river, after coming from Paradise, runs noiselessly through all that kingdom by various mazes. And here are found natural stones; these are their names, smaragdi, saphiri, carbunculi, topazion, crysoliti, onichini, berilli, amethysti, sardinæ, and many other precious stones.

V.—There springs the herb called Affidos. Whoever bears the root of that plant with him, it will drive the evil spirit from him, and will constrain him to say who he is, and what is his name; and, therefore, the evil spirits dare not corrupt any man there. In another kingdom of ours there grow all kinds of pepper, and they are collected and exchanged for wheat, and skins, and cloth, and men's food; and those regions are wooded, as if thickly planted with willows, and all full of serpents. And when the pepper ripens, all the people come from the nearest kingdoms, and bring with them chaff, and refuse, and dry branches; and they kindle the wood round about; and when a mighty wind blows, they set fire within and without the wood, so that not one of the snakes may escape; and so within the fire, after it has been thoroughly kindled, all the snakes perish, save those that reach caves; and when all the fire has died out, all come, men and women, small and big, with forks in their hands, and fling all the snakes out of the forest, and make high heaps of them sky high. And when they have finished shaking that refuse, the grain that is gathered from among the fagots is dried, and the pepper is boiled, but how it is boiled no one from another country is allowed to know.

VI.—And that forest is situate under Mount Olympy, and from there an excellent spring flows; and the water has every kind of taste, and the taste changes each hour, day and night. And from there, not further than three days' journey from Paradise, from which Adam was driven out. Whoever drinks of the water of that spring during his fast, no disease will come upon him from that day forth, and he will ever be thirty years of age. There, too, there are stones called Midiosi; and eagles bring these towards us, and through these they revive and recover the light, if they lose it. Whoever bears this stone on his hand, light never fails him, and if he would fain hide himself, it will cause that no one may see him. It drives hatred from all, and induces unity, and repels jealousy. This, too, is a strange thing that our country has, among other things:—there is a sea of sand there, and the gravel moves without water, and it surges in waves like another sea, and never rests; and one cannot go on it by vessel or in any other way, nor can it be in any way known what kind of laud there is beyond; but on the side towards us there are found divers kinds of fish, so sweet and so good that man never saw their like.

VII.—There are likewise, three days' journey from that sea, some mountains from which flows a river of stones, and that flowing like water, and it runs through our land to the sea of sand, And when the river reaches the sea, the stones disappear, so that they are not seen thenceforth. Three days in the week the stones move and slide, both small and great, and take with them some trees, as far as the sea of sand, and, so long as they move, no one can ever cross it; on the other four days a passage is obtained. This is another marvel that is there; hard by the desert near the mountains, where no one dwells, there is a river beneath the earth, and no one can find a road to it, except by chance; sometimes the earth trembles, and whoever then happens to be passing by can find a road to the river, and he must travel in haste, lest perchance the earth close upon him; and whatever sand he brings with him will be precious stones and jewels. And this river runs into another river larger than itself, and therein there is none of the gravel or sand, but precious stones; and into this river the men of that country go, and seize and bring with them thence a multitude of precious stones and jewels, and they dare not sell those, until they first inform our excellency. And if we would fain have them in our treasure, we take them, and give them half their value. If we do not want them, they are free to sell them where they will. Children are brought up in that land to seek the stones, so that they can live under the water three or four months.

VIII.—Beyond this stony river there are ten tribes of the Jews. Though they presume they are kings, yet they are subject to us, and are tributaries to our majesty. In another kingdom of ours, beyond the place where the island lies, there are worms, called in our tongue Salamandre, and those worms can live only in fire, and they have around them skins like the skins of worms that make silk. And to spin this is the work of our ladies in our palace, and thereof is made all kinds of apparel for the use of our majesty; and these clothes cannot be washed save in a large and strong fire. In gold, silver, precious stones, in dromedaries and camels, is the abundance of our greatness. No one is poor among us; no adulterer is found there; all men of strange lands, to wit, guests and pilgrims, our gentleness receives. No thieves, no oppressors, no misers are found in our midst; there is no envy in our midst.

IX.—Our men have abundance of all kinds of riches; there are not many horses among us, and they are but sorry. We liken none on the face of the earth to us in riches. When we go to war in force against our enemies, we let carry before us fifteen large, magnificent crosses made of gold and silver, with precious stones therein, one in each car, instead of standards, and behind each one of them twelve thousand men of arms, and a hundred thousand foot soldiers, without counting the five thousand who have to do with bearing food and drink. But when we walk abroad in peace, a wooden cross precedes our majesty, without any legend whatever, either of gold or silver, that the suffering of our Lord Jesus Christ may be brought back to our remembrance constantly; and a vessel full of earth, that we may recognize that our flesh returns to its own source, that is, to earth; and other vessels, full of gold, are borne before us, that all may understand that we are lord of lords.

X.—In all the kinds of riches that are in the world our greatness abounds and excels. No one tells a lie among us, and no one can tell one; and whoever tells a lie willingly, straightway he dies, and no ill will is borne about him. All of us follow after truth, and all love one another mutually; no kind of sin reigns there. Every year we go on a pilgrimage to the place where lies the body of Daniel the Prophet, taking great hosts with us, to deserted Babylon, and those too under arms, because of animals called tyri and some other serpents called devils. In our country some fish are caught, and with the blood of these the most precious purple is coloured.

XI.—We have many places, the bravest nation in the world, and ugly withal. We lord it over the races called Amazons and Bragmans. The palace wherein our majesty dwells was made in the form and likeness of that which the Apostle Thomas ordained for Wyndofforus, King of India; and its wings and structures are exactly like it. The columns of the hall, its pillars, and its fretwork, conic from some tree called cethim. The roofing of the hall is made of some plants called hebenus, the reason being that no one in the world can in any way burn it. On the farthest extremities on the top of that hall there are two apples of gold, and in each of them there is the precious stone called carbunculus, so that the gold may give light during the day, and the stones by night. The largest parts of the hall are made of stones called sardonichi, blended with cerastes, the reason being that no one may secretly bring in poison with him. Other things in the hall are made of the plants called hebenus; the windows were of crystal; the tables to eat on in our palace are, some of them, gold, and others of the precious stone amestic. The pillars that support the tables are of whalebone. Before our palace there is a street, wherein our justice is wont to look on those who fight in duel. The top of the hall and its walls are made of onichinus, the purpose being that energy may arise in our combatants by the virtue of the stones. In that hall light is not kindled at night, save that which the precious oil called balsam feeds.

XII.—The chamber wherein our majesty rests was fitted with wondrous work, and that of gold, and every kind of precious stone in the world, because of the excellence of onichinus instead of light. Around this is made a work, four-square, as large as itself, that the harshness of the onyx may be tempered. Precious ointment is ever burned in this chamber; our bed is made of sapphire, because of the virtue of chastity. We have the fairest wives in the world, and they come in to us only four times in the year, that we may have heirs, and thereafter each one returns to her own place, as healthy as Beersheba from David.

XIII.—In our palace we eat once a day; each day thirty thousand men eat at our board, besides the guests that come and go. And these all receive their charges from our palace, both in horses and other things also. That table is made of precious stone called smaragdus, and it is supported by two pillars of amethyst. The virtue of this stone is that it suffers no one to get drunk so long as he sits thereon. Before the doorposts of our hall, near where the combatants are, there is a watch-tower of great height, and thereto one climbs by one hundred and twenty-five steps; and these steps, some of them are made of porphyry, blended with the blood of serpents, and alabaster ointment. The third part at the bottom of these is made of crystal, and jasper, and sardonyx, and another part, at the top, is of amethyst, and amber, and jasper, and sardonyx, and panthera. This watch-tower is supported by one pillar, and on this there is a base, that is, some stone-work so called, and on this base two columns, that is to say, arms; and on these there is a base, and on this four columns, and again a base, and on this sixteen arms; and so the work proceeds, until the number thirty-four is reached, and then the number of the bases lessens, and the columns, until they come to one, and that by ascending upwards, as they increased before, ascending to thirty-four.

XIV.—Now the columns and bases are of the same kind of precious stone as the steps through which men ascend. On the summit of the highest there is a watch-tower placed by some graceful skill, so that no one in the various kinds of land subject to us can work any fraud, or treachery, or dissensions against us whatever, nor those among us, without it being clearly seen from that watch-tower, and without its being recognised who they are, or what they do. There are three thousand men of arms ever guarding this watch-tower night and day, lest by chance it be broken or overthrown to the ground.

XV.—Each month in the year seven kings serve me, each one of them in his order, and forty-two princes, and three hundred and fifty-six earls. That number is always at our board, without those placed in the various duties in our palace. At our board there eat each day, on the right twelve archbishops, and on my left hand twenty bishops, and the patriarch from the place where is the grave of the Apostle Thomas and he that is in place of a pope.

SOURCES AND FURTHER READING

Bruce, Christopher W. *The Arthurian Name Dictionary*. New York: Garland, 1999.

Bryant, Nigel, ed. and trans. *Perceforest*. Suffolk, UK: Boydell & Brewer, 2011.

Carey, John. "The Kindred of a Boy without a Father: Merlin's British Forebears and Irish Cousins." In *Arthurian Literature*, vol. 38, edited by Megan G. Leitch and K. S. Whetter, 20–47. Cambridge, UK: D. S. Brewer, 2023.

de Boron, Robert. *Merlin and the Grail: Joseph of Arimathea, Merlin, Perceval*. Translated by Nigel Bryant. Suffolk, UK: D. S. Brewer, 2008.

Dobin, Howard. *Merlin's Disciples: Prophecy, Poetry and Power in Renaissance England*. Redwood City, CA: Stanford University Press, 1990.

Gardner, Edmund G. *The Italian Legend in Arthurian Literature*. London: J. M. Dent & Sons, 1930.

Geoffrey of Monmouth. *Vita Merlini*. Edited and translated by John Jay Parry. University of Illinois Press, 1925.

Giles, J. A., ed. and trans. *Six Old English Chronicles*. London: G. Bell & Sons, 1910.

Hoffman, Donald L. "Was Merlin a Ghibelline? Arthurian Propaganda at the Court of Frederick II." In *Culture and the King: The Social Implications of the Arthurian Legend,* edited by Martin B. Shichtman and James P. Carley, 113–28. Albany, NY: State University of New York Press, 1994.

Holder-Egger, Oswald. "Italienische Prophetieen des 13. Jahrhunderts I." *Neues Archiv der Gesellschaft für ältere deutsche Geschichtskunde* 15 (1890): 143–78.

Lacy, Norris J., ed. *Lancelot-Grail: The Old French Arthurian Vulgate and Post-Vulgate in Translation.* 8 vols. Translated by Samuel N. Rosenberg. Suffolk, UK: D. S. Brewer, 2010.

Malcor, Linda A., and John Matthews. *The Sword in the Stone: A 4,000-Year-Old Story Written in the Stars.* Gloucester, UK: Amberley, 2026.

Malory, Thomas. *Le Morte D'Arthur.* Edited by J. Matthews. London: Cassell, 2000.

Manning, Robert of Brunne. *The Story of England.* Vol. 1. Edited by Frederick James Furnivall. Cambridge, UK: Cambridge University Press, 2012. First published 1887.

Markale, Jean. *King Arthur, King of Kings.* New York: Scribner, 1977.

Matthews, Caitlín. *Mabon and the Guardians of Celtic Britain: Hero Myths in the* Mabinogion. Rochester, VT: Inner Traditions, 2002.

Matthews, Caitlín, and John Matthews. *Ladies of the Lake.* New York: Harper Collins, 1992.

———. *The Lost Book of the Grail: The Sevenfold Path of the Grail and the Restoration of the Faery Accord.* Rochester, VT: Inner Traditions, 2004.

Matthews, John. *The Book of Merlin.* Amberley Books, 2021.

McGinn, Bernard. *Visions of the End: Apocalyptic Traditions in the Middle Ages.* New York: Columbia University Press, 1979.

Mills, Ed Maldwyn. *Six Middle English Romances.* London: J. M. Dent & Sons, 1973.

Nicholson, Helen. "Echoes of the Past and Present Crusades in *Les Prophecies de Merlin.*" *Romania* 122, no. 487–88 (2004): 320–40.

———. *Women and the Crusades.* London: Oxford University Press, 2023.

Novati, Francesco. *Storia di Merlino.* Bergamo Instituto Italiano d'Arti Grafiche, 1898.

Paris, Gaston, and J. Ulrich, eds. *Suite du Merlin.* Paris: Didot, 1886.

Paton, Lucy Allen, ed. *Les Prophecies de Merlin; Part One: Introduction and Text.* New York/London: D. C. Heath/Oxford University Press, 1926.

———. *Les Prophecies de Merlin; Part Two: Studies in the Contents.* New York/London: D. C. Heath/Oxford University Press, 1927.

———. "Notes on Manuscripts of the *Prophécies de Merlin.*" *Publications of the Modern Language Association of America* 21, no. 2 (1913): 121–39.

———. *Studies in Fairy Mythology of Arthurian Romance.* New York: Burt Franklin, 1960.

Schofield, William Henry. *Mythical Bards and the Life of William Wallace.* Cambridge, MA: Harvard University Press, 1920.

Skeels, Dell. *The Romance of Percival in Prose: A Translation of the Didot Percival.* Seattle: University of Washington Press, 1966.

Skene, William F., ed. *The Four Ancient Books of Wales.* 2 vols. Edinburgh: Edmonston and Douglas, 1868.

Skuggsjá, Konungs. *The King's Mirror (Speculum Regale).* Translated by Laurence Marcellus Larson. Ulan Press, 2012. First published 1917.

Stewart, R. J. *Merlin: The Prophetic Vision and the Mystic Life.* London: Arkana, 1995.

Storer, Edward, trans. *Il Novellino: The Hundred Old Tales.* London: George Routledge, 1925.

Vollet, E.-H. sv. "Blaise," in *La Grande Encyclopédie,* vol. 6. Paris, 1887.

Wace and Layamon. *Arthurian Chronicles.* Translated by Eugene Mason. J. M. Dent, 1962. First published 1912.

Weston, J. L. *Gawain and the Lady of Lis.* London: David Nutt, 1907.

Wheatley, E. B., ed. *Merlin, or the Early History of King Arthur.* 4 vols. Reprint. New York: Greenwood Press, 1969.

Williams, Robert. *Selections from the Hengwrt MSS. Preserved in the Peniarth Library.* 2 vols. London: Thomas Richards, 1892.

Young, Francis. *Magic in Merlin's Realm.* Cambridge, UK: Cambridge University Press, 2022.

Zumthor, Paul. *Merlin le Prophète ou, Le livre du Graal.* Paris: Stock, 1991.

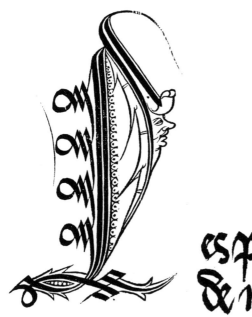

Opening of the text of the *Prophecies of Merlin*, 1498.
Photo by Maarten Haverkamp.

ACKNOWLEDGMENTS

First, to Maarten Haverkamp for inviting me to be involved in this extraordinary work. I have learned more than I thought possible from the reading and editing of the Prophecies. Second to R. J. Stewart for his wonderful foreword. It has been a delight to share this work with him after all that we explored together back in the 1990s. To my wonderful wife, Caitlín, for spending so much time checking every word and making sure she caught the howlers! To my agent Severine Jeauneau for her belief in this curious work. To my faithful readers Dwina Gill and David Elkington, for picking up the pieces, and to my editor Jon Graham at Inner Traditions for taking on its publication with such enthusiasm and wisdom.

JOHN MATTHEWS

To my wife Nicole, for every time over the past five years I have said: "I have to work on my book again." To John Matthews, without whose knowledge of the Arthurian Romances the book would not have been possible.

MAARTEN HAVERKAMP

"Merlin" by Aubrey Beardsley, illustration for Malory's *Le Morte D'Arthur*. From John Matthews's personal collection.

INDEX

Abbé d'Orcanie, 34
Abel, 62–63, 148
Abiron, Lady of, 118–19, 216–17
Abomination of Jerusalem, 194
Accolon of Gaul, 78n77, 170
Adam, 269
Aeneas of Troy, 63n49, 141, 158
Afallach, 179
Aglentine, the Damsel of Avalon, 107–9, 119, 205–8
Agricola, 16
Aí (poetry), 3
Alberecht von Scharfenburg, 21, 198
Alchendic, the Giant. 115–16, 214
Alexandria, 139
Annwn, Cauldron of, 46–47
Antichrist, x, xi, 22, 23, 24, 34, 140, 148, 149, 156, 188, 197
Antioch, 101n108, 198
   Duke of, 101–2, 198–99, 223–25
Argante, 38, 42
Armenia, 63
Aquitaine, Queen Eleanor of, 145

Arimathea, Joseph of, 179
Arthur, King, 7, 11, 40, 41, 42, 49, 80, 86, 90, 101, 113, 140, 147, 156, 172, 194, 234
   death of, 61, 146–47
   wedding of, 208–9
Arthurian
   legends, 16, 29, 36, 186, 204
   literature, xiii, 8
   romance, xi
Atlantis, 156
Aubiron, King of 163, 164
Avallanau (Apple Trees), 236, 237–39
Avalon, 11, 12, 41, 48, 49, 154, 203, 234
   Maiden of, 203–8
Avrences, Forest of, 72–75, 88, 92, 131, 161, 162–63, 187, 224, 229

Babylon
   Dragon of, 63
   Sultan of, 155

Bacon, Roger, 192
Balin, 41
Ban of Benoic, King, 39, 170, 174, 202
Baudac, King, 116–17
Belle Garde, 217–18
Berengier de Gomeret, 123–24 221–23
Bertold of Regensburg, 159
Black Book of Carmarthen, 235
Blaise, Saint, 31–32
Blake, William, 8
Blamor, 211
Bleeding Spear, 148
Blioberis, 113, 211
Boccaccio, Giovani, 20
Book of Blaise, 175
Bors, 170, 200, 211
Boutemont, Robin, 14
Brendan, Saint, 46
Brequehem, Queen of, 60, 145
Breuse Sans Pitie, 121–28, 219–21
Brighid, Goddess, 48
Brittany, 163, 186, 204
Brocéliande, Forest of, 163
Brutus, 148–49
Burma (Berne), 100, 198, 200
  King of, 100, 198, 223

Caesar, Julius, 224
Caiaphas, Lady of, 97, 192–93
Cain, 62–63, 148
Camelot, 9, 40, 90, 101, 173, 185, 198, 210
Camlann, 43

Carmelyde, 114, 117, 212, 215–16
Cathars, 36, 139
Catholic Church, xiii, 24, 27, 58, 158, 210
Celyddon, forest of, 239–40
Cento Novelle Antiche (*100 Ancient Tales*), 20
Cerridwen, 3
Charlemagne, xii
Chrétien de Troyes, 45, 148
Claudas, King, 50, 106, 170, 202, 211, 220
Codex Marciana, 14
Corbenic, 133n150, 230–31
Cornwall, 160, 172
Cri de Merlin, 6–7, 150
Crown of the Emperor of Orbance. *See* Orbance, City of: Crown of
Crusades, 17, 26–27, 142, 158, 201, 210, 211–15
Cymphones, 69

Dante, 20
Der Jüngere Titurel, 21, 198
Diana, Goddess, 173
Didot Percival, 51–52
Diu Crône (*The Crown*), 43
Dragon of Babylon, ix, 103, 140, 149, 152, 188, 200
Dragons, 60–61, 142–43
Dr. Who, 7

Eastland, Queen of, 217
Elucidation, 31
esplumoir (moulting cage), 7
Eric and Enide, 43

Esglantine, Lady (see Aglentine)
Evalac, King, 178
Excalibur, 40–41, 42
   scabbard of, 41

faery, ix, 204, 223
Falone, Lady of, 68–69, 157
Fata Morgana, 44
Fibonacci, 155
Fionn Mac Cumhail, 176
Fisher King, 206
Flor de Lis, 123–24, 222
flood, 140
Four Ancient Books of Wales, 139
Frederic I, Emperor, 25
Frederic II, Emperor, 21, 25, 140, 148, 151, 154, 159, 210, 264–65, 267
Fugitive Poem of Myrddin in His Grave, 246–49

Galahad, 60n41, 200, 213
Galeholt/Galehaut, 86, 113–14, 180, 181, 209
Galgano, Saint, 143–45, 211
Gandalf, 7
Ganieda, 165
Gawain, 6, 114, 141, 208
Gawain and the Green Knight, 43
Gawain and the Lady of Lis, 222
Geoffrey of Monmouth, 4, 13, 38, 47, 141, 149, 157, 165, 250–62
   Prophecies of Merlin, 250–262
Gesta Regum Britanniae, 48
Ghibellines, 36
Giant's Dance, 165

Giraldus Cambrensis (Gerald of Wales), 45
Gloucester, Nine Witches of, 46–47
Good Mariners, the, 69–70, 149, 158, 223
God, 57, 60, 64, 148, 151, 189, 192
Goddess, 24, 45
Gog and Magog, 158
Grail, 7, 12, 21, 62, 147–48, 175, 198, 206, 223
   quest for, 12, 41, 200, 210, 230, 234
Great Dragon, xi, 21–25, 56, 63, 67, 148, 193
Gregory X, Pope, 159
Guinevere, xi, 45, 85, 106, 209
   her strange dream, 85–88, 178–83
Guillaume du Pas Fort, 220–21
Gwenddoleu, 238–39
Gwenddydd, 5

Hamlet's Mill, x
Hector of Troy, 50
Helias/Helyas, the Hermit, 32–33, 130, 226–28
Hell, 57, 89, 183, 192, 197, 199, 217
Hidden Gospel of Childhood, 231
Historia Regum Brittaniae, 4, 13, 43, 141
Huth Merlin, 30
Hugon Sachies, King, 89, 183
Huon de Bordeux, 163, 183

Il Novellino. See *Cento Novelle Antiche*

India, 68, 82, 100, 110, 156, 174, 197, 198, 205, 207, 225, 267
Ireland, King of, 147, 212
Isabella, Queen, 145

Jaffa (Tel Aviv), 213
James, Saint, 146, 207,
Jerusalem, 55, 6, 106, 113, 115, 147, 203, 210, 211, 213
  Abomination of, 97, 193, 200
  Richard of, 115–16
Jesu/Jesus, 23, 56, 65, 89, 101, 113, 142, 148, 199, 200
Joachim de Fiore, 10, 25, 197
Johannites, 36, 139, 146
John the Baptist, 139
John the Evangelist, 15, 139
Jonah, Prophecies of, 10, 189, 194

Kentigern, 4

Lailoken, 4
Lancelot, xi, 40, 42, 101, 170, 203, 217, 229
Lancelot-Grail, 44, 141, 180, 193, 214
L'Atre Périlleux, 206
Lady of the Lake, xi, 7, 12, 37–43, 72–81, 150, 160, 161–71, 189, 203–5, 229
Layamon, 37–38, 42
Leodegrance, King, 215
Letter of Prester John, 197, 266–274
Lile of Avalon, 41
Lionel, 170

Léonois/Lionesse, 71, 160, 189
Livre d'Artus, 32
Logres (Britain), 180, 204
Loholt, 180
Lord of the Rings, 7
Lost Book of the Grail, xiii
Lot of Orcanie, 59, 141
Lucent, Lady, 162
Lucifer, 96, 192, 196

Mabinogion, 208
Macedonian Wolf, 69, 157
Magic in Merlin's Realm, 10
magpies, 102, 200
Maistre Antoine, 29, 33–34, 188
Maistre Blaise, 29, 30–32, 33, 83, 93, 133, 187, 231
Maistre Petroine, 34
Maistre Raymon, 2, 3, 34, 93–94, 135, 172, 174, 188, 233
Maistre Richard of Ireland, xii, 66, 151
Maistre Rubens, 29, 34, 134, 232
Maistre Tholomer, 29, 33, 52–55, 188
  as Bishop of Wales, 65
Malory, Sir Thomas, 40–43, 50, 186
Mandeville, John, 209
Manichaeans, 156
Manning of Brunne, Robert, 30
Maponus, 39
Marc, 103–5, 188, 201
Marduk, 23–24
Marvels of Rigomer, 188
Mary, Blessed Virgin, 58, 100, 134, 197, 209, 225, 231–32

Matrona, 39
Meliadus/Meliodas 37, 49–50, 71, 79–80, 89, 93–94, 97–99, 160, 170, 170, 183, 184–85, 186, 188–89, 194–95, 200, 223
Merlin, ix
  demonic origins, 99–100, 134, 171, 196
  and image of brass, 96, 192
  and Lady of the Lake, 40–41, 72–79
  nature of, 6
  prophecies, 9, 10–12, 18–19, 182, 250–62
  and the judges, 129–30, 227–28
  and three ministers/cardinals, 70–71, 159
  tomb of, 7, 76–78, 88, 94, 97, 168–69, 182, 184, 223
Merlin Continuations, 141
Merlin, or the Early History of King Arthur, 224n163
Merlin, the Prophetic Vision and the Mystic Life, 251
Miaus, Count Thomas of, 220–21
Modron, 39
Mordred, 7, 61n46, 147, 180
Morgain, 38, 42, 43–49, 87, 100, 119–21, 160, 180, 218–19, 220
  and an angel, 91, 185–86
Morgan(a) le Fay, 160–64
Morgause, 146, 180
Morguenete, 223
Morrigan/Muirgen, 45
Morte d'Arthur, 40–41, 48, 50, 170, 213, 217

Moses, 182
Muhammed, 69, 157
Myrddin Wyllt, 4, 5, 235
  Poems of, 235–49

Naymar, 83–84, 177
Nennius, 4
Nestor, 211
Nestorian Christianity, 207
Night of the Long Knives, 141
Nimuë, 40
Noah, 140
Norbellande (Northumberland), 175, 191
Norgales, Queen of, 217–19
Novellino, Il, 154, 263–65

Oberon, 163
Obi-Wan Kenobi, 7
Oianau (Greetings), 236, 240–46
Orbance, City of, 67, 152, 164
  crown of, 67–68, 147, 151–52, 155–56
Orlando Furioso, 44
Orlando Innamorato, 44
Outer Isles, Queen of, 217
Owain Glyndwr, 11

Palamedes, 50
Paradise, 57, 269–74
Paton, Lucy Allen 16, 18, 233
Pellinore, King, 226
Percival, xi, 50–52, 60n41, 101, 105, 124–25, 130–33, 194, 199, 200, 223, 224, 225–32
Perceval: The Story of the Grail, 28

Peter St., Order of, 190
Pierre Ronde. *See* Round Stone, the
Plato, 156
Polo, Marco, 156, 209,
Pope, the, 9, 27, 33, 105, 112–16, 158, 203, 212, 213
Pre-Raphaelite Brotherhood, 14
Prester John, xi, 20, 101, 153–56, 197, 198, 205, 264–65
   Letter of, 266–74
Prophecies de Merlin, xii, 16
prophecy, 10–12
Prose Lancelot, 34
Prose Tristan, 201
Ptolemy, Claudius, 139

Rambarge, Lady, 82–84, 175–77
Red Book of Hergest, 235, 266
Rennes Manuscript, 16, 18, 55, 141
Rhiannon, 45
Rhydderch, 240
Richard I (Lionheart), 36
Richard of Ireland, 35–36, 154, 214
Richard of Jerusalem, 213–14
Rigantona, 45
Robert de Boron, 145, 148
Roman du Graal, 41
Roman le Roi Artus, 156
Romans du Merlin, xii,
Rome, Emperor of, 61, 70, 112, 146, 159, 210–13, 213
Round Stone, 34, 100–2, 195–199, 198
Round Table, 6, 9, 27, 90, 101, 113, 119, 134, 147, 160, 185, 203, 205, 234
Rustichello da Pisa, 156

Sadaine, 187
San Francisco del Deserto, xiii, 14, 149
Saracens, 9, 157, 211
Sarras, 115, 179, 213
Savariz, 117, 215
Saxons, 211
Scott, Michael, 155
Scotland, Queen of, 172, 189
Sebile the Sorceress, 87–88, 123–24, 181–82, 217–19, 221–23
Selections from the Hengwrt MSS, 266, 267–74
Serpents, White and Black, 71, 72, 75, 160, 161, 169, 181, 193
Serpent Stone, 143
Sibyl, 47
Sibylline Oracles, 8
Simon Magus, 130, 139
Sir Gawain and the Green Knight, 43
Sir Gowther, 9
Speculum Ecclesiae, 45
Speculum regale, 4
Stonehenge, 141
stones, magical, 34, 153–55, 164, 182, 183, 229
Storia di Merlino, La, 154
Story of England, 30
Suite du Merlin, 6, 170
Swinburn, Algernon, 14
Sword in the Stone, 42, 61n43, 145

Sybil, the, 242
Synaublans, 91

Taliesin, 3, 4, 5, 139, 176
Tavola Rotunda (Round Table), 44
Tennyson, Alfred, 14
Thomas, Saint. 197, 207, 225, 272, 274
Thomas the Rhymer, 11
Tiamat, 23–24
Triads, Welsh, 180
Tristan, 112, 79, 90, 93, 160, 171, 184–85, 201
  death of, 93, 105–6, 188, 201–2
Troy, 50, 63, 141, 148, 158

Ulfal, 214–15
Urien, 220, 259
Uther Pendragon/Uterpendragon 8, 30, 38, 61, 107–8, 140, 204–5

Valley of No Return, 164, 180, 186, 221
Vengeance that the Descendants of Hector . . . took upon the Greeks, 50
Venice, 149, 158, 190, 194
Verard, Antoine, xii, 14, 15, 16, 236
Virgil, 72, 162
Vita Merlini, 4, 6, 14, 43, 45–46, 157, 165, 236
Vita Sancti Kentigerni, 4
Vitré, 203–4, 207, 210
Vortigern, 30, 60, 143, 145, 187

Waite, A.E., 198
Wales, Bishop of, 151
William of Normandy, 13
Williams, Charles, 198
Williams, Robert, 266
Winchester, 173, 181, 256–57

Yseut/Isolde, 185

"Merlin as a Druid" by Louis Rhead, from a series of illustrations for Tennyson's *Idylls of the King*.
From John Matthews's personal collection.

BOOKS OF RELATED INTEREST

Taliesin
The Last Celtic Shaman
by John Matthews with Caitlín Matthews

This new translation of the poems of sixth-century Celtic bard and shaman Taliesin uncovers for the first time the meanings behind these great works and establishes his work as a precursor to the Arthurian legends.

The Lost Book of the Grail
The Sevenfold Path of the Grail and the Restoration of the Faery Accord
by Caitlín and John Matthews

Unveiling the long-lost prequel to the Grail quest stories, Caitlín and John Matthews show how it offers the key to understanding the sevenfold path of the Grail and to restoring the Faery Accord, an agreement that once existed between humans and the Faery and upon which the spiritual and physical health of the land depends.

The Complete King Arthur
Many Faces, One Hero
by Caitlín and John Matthews

Presenting the culmination of more than 40 years' research, John and Caitlín Matthews examine the historical and mythological evidence for every major theory about the existence of Arthur, piecing together the many fragments that constitute his image.

Scan the QR code and save 25% at InnerTraditions.com. Browse over 2,000 titles on spirituality, the occult, ancient mysteries, new science, holistic health, and natural medicine.

— SINCE 1975 · ROCHESTER, VERMONT —

InnerTraditions.com • (800) 246-8648